Praise for *The Ye*

"*The Yellow Envelope* is an intriguing and riveting tale of Kim's travel adventures. I was especially intrigued by her process of self-discovery, which is tightly woven into her experiences. She talks openly and honestly about earth-shaking moments, marital doubts, and quiet insights, often in the tone of sharing secrets with a best friend. Also, I loved the idea of a physical 'yellow envelope,' a gift to be given away in ways that make you smile and make your heart sing. It's a story with passion, risk, and humor."

—Rita Golden Gelman, author of *Tales of a Female Nomad: Living at Large in the World*

"I often say that once you embark on the road of adventure, you never know where you'll end up. Kim's story is the epitome of this lesson. Read *The Yellow Envelope* for an honest, refreshing account of personal transformation."

—Chris Guillebeau, *New York Times* bestselling author of *The Happiness of Pursuit* and *The $100 Startup*

"An honest and heartfelt memoir about the ways marriage, travel, and personal dreams can sometimes clash up against each other, *The Yellow Envelope* is likely to inspire both wanderlust and random acts of generosity in readers. Set against the changing scenery of a backpacker's life on the road, the story examines important questions about what it means to give and what it means to let go. A captivating read from start to end, it's impossible not to become entangled in Dinan's devoted worldwide search for finding a balance between love, life, and one's dreams."

—Torre DeRoche, author of *Love with a Chance of Drowning*

The

YELLOW

ENVELOPE

The
YELLOW
ENVELOPE

One Gift, Three Rules, and a
Life-Changing Journey Around the World

KIM DINAN

Copyright © 2017 by Kim Dinan
Cover and internal design © 2017 by Sourcebooks, Inc.
Cover design by Connie Gabbert
Cover images © Curioso/Shutterstock, Phonlamai Photo/Shutterstock, Valentin Agapov/Shutterstock, sword_sf/Shutterstock

This book is a memoir. It reflects the author's present recollections of experiences over a period of time. Some names and characteristics have been changed, some events have been compressed, and some dialogue has been re-created.

Published by Sourcebooks, Inc.
P.O. Box 4410, Naperville, Illinois 60567-4410
(630) 961-3900
Fax: (630) 961-2168
www.sourcebooks.com

Library of Congress Cataloging-in-Publication Data

Names: Dinan, Kim, author.
Title: The yellow envelope : one gift, three rules, and a life-changing
  journey around the world / Kim Dinan.
Description: Naperville : Sourcebooks, [2017]
Identifiers: LCCN 2016040631 | (pbk. : alk. paper)
Subjects: LCSH: Dinan, Kim--Travel. | Voyages around the world. | Generosity.
Classification: LCC G226.D56 A3 2017 | DDC 910.4/1--dc23 LC record available at
https://lccn.loc.gov/2016040631

Printed and bound in the United States of America.
VP 10 9 8 7 6 5 4 3 2 1

For Michele and Glenn Crim,
in response to rule number two.

HAMPI, INDIA

Prologue

WENDY AND I STEPPED OUT OF A CREAKY, MULTICOLORED boat onto the dust-packed bank of the Tungabhadra River. The river ran as dark and lazy as a slough. Three women in colorful saris beat their laundry on rocks near the riverbed. A small gang of boys splashed and shrieked in the sleepy current, naked and skinny as baby birds. We started a slow, meandering walk along Hampi's main road. Heat pulsed from the dirt streets and crawled up my legs as we shuffled past coffee shops, tourist hostels and roadside stands that sold miniature Ganesh figurines.

Across the road a teenage boy sat slumped in a black and yellow rickshaw that he'd parked in the shade under an outcropping of boulders. He perked up when he saw us. "Hello!" he waved. "HELLOOO! YOU NEED RICKSHAW?"

I looked up and squinted into the sunlight. "How much?" I yelled, swiping my arm across my sweaty forehead.

"For you," he called back, "eight hundred rupees. GOOD PRICE!"

The price he asked was nothing, really, in the scheme of things, but I knew he charged more than he should. I shot him my best *you've-got-to-be-kidding* look. During my time in India I'd developed a cat-in-the-bathtub response to being ripped off. Plus, haggling was a way of life in India. He'd double the price, I'd halve it, and we'd meet in the middle.

I shook my head no and resumed my slow pace down the road; tiny beads of sweat flew from my hair and plopped onto the dirt street like raindrops. "Too much!" I yelled. Rule one of haggling: you must be willing to walk away.

But the rickshaw driver wasn't giving up so easily, and I didn't expect him to. He called after us, "Ma'am, fair price. It is *fair* price! I will drive you anywhere you want to go! We go to Monkey Temple and Lotus Temple and Old Town. All day we drive. FAIR PRICE!"

He jumped in his rickshaw to follow us. "It's true ma'am, it's true. A very fair price." His rickshaw bumped beside us on the pockmarked road as he leaned his head out trying to woo us.

My eyes fell on Wendy, who shrugged her shoulders, then back on the driver, and I shook my head in disagreement. "No, it is not a fair price. Six hundred rupees is what I will pay." It was true that I wanted a fair price. But I realized with surprise that a part of me just wanted to win this bidding war. I'd come a long way from my first tentative days on the road, nine months ago.

"Ma'am, okay, okay. I will drop the price. Six hundred rupees. If you are happy you pay seven hundred."

Pausing for a second, I calculated the math in my head.

Wendy leaned over. "Kim, you're arguing over two dollars. It's hot as hell. Let's just take the rickshaw. He seems like a nice guy."

I turned to him and smiled, conceding. "Okay, six hundred rupees. If we are happy we will pay seven hundred."

He smiled back, a white, toothy smile, and his hair flopped down into his eyes. Wendy and I climbed into the back of his rickshaw, and together we bumped off down an empty dirt road toward the Monkey Temple.

The craggy ruins of Hampi spread out before us. I stole a glimpse at Wendy, her head cocked toward the window as she watched the rocky geography pass. The terrain looked like nothing I had seen in India, or anywhere for that matter, like an ancient giant had dropped boulders the size of houses haphazardly across the open land.

The bright sun scorched my face, and I closed my eyes. A hot breeze whipped my hair into a cyclone. I folded my hands into my lap and absentmindedly felt at the place on my left ring finger where my wedding band used to be. My thoughts turned toward Brian. What was he doing right now? Did he miss me?

I was imagining him in southern India, stopped at a roadside stall drinking chai, when the windshield of our rickshaw, violently and without warning, exploded into thousands of jagged pieces. Shards of glass blew over our driver and toward Wendy and me in a powerful wave.

My eyes snapped open. Outside of the rickshaw, the world paused—still and silent. Inside, my heart slammed against my chest, and the sudden rush of blood drummed in my ears. Had we been shot? It seemed like a ridiculous notion, yet *something* had shattered the windshield. I looked down at my body. It was covered in glass but intact. "What happened?" I finally uttered. I looked up at our rickshaw driver, who still puttered down the road, wide-eyed and blinking, skinny rivulets of blood streaming down his arms.

"Stop driving," Wendy finally managed. She leaned forward to tap our driver on the shoulder. "You need to pull over."

We steered onto the side of the road and our driver sat silently, unmoving, his hands still gripped tightly to the steering wheel. Tiny pieces of glass were stuck in his eyelashes like snowflakes. His arms were dripping blood.

"What happened?" I said again. "Did a rock hit the windshield? Were we shot?"

Our driver did not answer.

Wendy and I climbed out of the rickshaw. We picked the glass from our clothing and out of the backseat. After a few moments our rickshaw driver stood too and began to dust the glass from his body.

"Are you okay?" he asked us.

We nodded and I pointed to his arms. "You're bleeding."

Our driver looked down and wiped his bloody arms on his jeans and for a second I thought he might cry.

"This is not my rickshaw," he said. "I just rent it." He shook his head in disbelief. "Bad karma," he muttered, more to himself than to us. "Bad karma."

We stood in silence on the side of the road, staring at the

rickshaw like we would a lame animal, and watched as our driver pulled the remaining jagged shards of glass from the windshield. The frantic beating of my heart began to slow. *We are fine*, I told myself. *The windshield just broke because of the potholes.*

Our driver climbed back into the rickshaw, and Wendy and I followed his lead. "What is your name?" I asked him.

He turned to look at me. "Mahaj," he said. "And what is your name?"

"Kim." I smiled.

"Wendy," said Wendy.

Mahaj raised his eyebrows in surprise. "Windy? So *you* are responsible for this." His eyes held the spark of a smile, and Wendy and I chuckled.

Mahaj revved the engine to life and steered the rickshaw back onto the road. "These things happen," he said, catching my eye in the rearview mirror. "What to do? Many things happen in life. Still, we must be happy."

⌒

Many hours later I folded seven hundred rupees up in my hand, the day's fee for Mahaj's rickshaw services. Then I dug through my purse until my fingers found the yellow envelope I had tucked into an interior pocket. Discreetly, I pulled some bills out of the envelope, and I folded them up too. It would be enough to fix Mahaj's windshield and a little extra to turn his luck around.

When I handed the money to Mahaj, he smiled and thanked

me, putting it into his pocket without counting. Then he offered to drive us back to the boat dock. But evening had finally arrived, and the sun was retreating below the horizon. The small village cooled in its afterglow.

"It's a nice night," I told him. "I think we'll walk. But thank you for the wonderful tour of Hampi."

Wendy and I walked through the calm flush of evening, our feet crunching over the gravel in the streets. I thought of Mahaj and his life in India, of my life back in Oregon and how it had led me out into the world. Earlier in the day I told Mahaj that I was a writer. He'd told me that he dreamed of becoming a filmmaker, and I'd heard in his voice the same conviction I had in mine when I spoke of my own life of writing. "Mahaj, you must do everything you can," I'd told him. He'd smiled his wide smile at me and said, "I am."

The river had just come into view when Wendy broke the silence. "How would you describe the yellow envelope money to Mahaj, if you had to?" she asked.

I paused for a minute, thinking. It wasn't the first time I'd pondered the question. In the beginning, I considered typing out a small note to accompany the money when I gave it away. But what would I say? And how could I even ensure that I would have a note prepared in the recipient's own language?

"I would tell Mahaj that the money I am giving him is not mine but a gift from someone else. I would tell him that it is my job to pass it on to him, that he is supposed to have it." Wendy nodded, understanding.

Behind us, I heard a shout and turned to see Mahaj running toward us, his right hand waving above his head, money clenched in his fist.

He caught up to us, breathless. "Wait, wait," he said between gulps of air. "You've paid too much."

When I looked down at the rupees in Mahaj's hand I felt a flush of embarrassment. *I should have explained the extra money*, I thought. But I remembered the words I'd just spoken to Wendy. It wasn't my money; I was just the conduit. And I remembered too the first rule of the yellow envelope: don't overthink it.

"No Mahaj, the extra money is for you." I told him. "Please, fix your rickshaw."

"Oh," he said, taken aback. "But are you sure?"

Wendy and I both nodded. We were as awkward as two dashboard bobbleheads. For the second time that day Mahaj looked stunned. And then he smiled his big toothy smile and said those universal words, *thank you*.

CHAPTER 1

ON MAY 11, 2012, I WALKED OUT OF MY JOB AND INTO A warm and beautiful spring day.

A few weeks earlier I'd sat in my cubicle nervously typing up my resignation letter. My hands were trembling as I took a seat in my boss's office and told her what Brian and I intended to do.

Maybe I should have known that my plans to sell everything, quit my job, and travel wouldn't come as such a shock to her. Six months before, during my annual review, she asked me what kind of future I envisioned for myself at work. Never a good liar, especially when caught off guard, I'd blurted, "Brian and I want to travel!" She'd cocked her head slightly, processing my confession, and then said, "Well, if that's the case, it's best to do it while you're young." More recently, she knew that Brian and I had sold our home and moved into a temporary apartment. She must have anticipated that changes were in store for me.

Still, I worried she'd be upset that I planned to leave or mad about the extra work she'd be responsible for while she looked for someone to replace me. But my boss had taken the news well. She'd been encouraging and supportive, excited for me, even. Exiting her office afterward I'd felt light and free. The secret I'd been keeping from my coworkers was no longer a secret.

That evening, Brian and I and our friends piled into a pleather booth in our favorite bar and clinked our beers together to toast new beginnings. I no longer had a job. Brian had one week of work remaining. And then we would embark on a cross-country drive back to Ohio to visit with family before our international travels began. Soon, every day would be Saturday. We would have *time*, a commodity more precious to me than money, and we were going to spend every minute of it.

Three years earlier I'd first uttered out loud a truth that had changed the trajectory of my life. I'd been on a solo trail run, crunching over leaves in the winter stillness of Portland's Forest Park, when a raw admission had bubbled up from the center of my chest and out of my mouth in a burst of winter air. I was not happy with my life. I did not want my desk job, my mortgage, or my car. I wanted to write, and I wanted to travel the world. I *needed* to.

It had been an overcast morning, as most November mornings are in the Pacific Northwest. Weak sunlight filtered down through the leafless trees as my feet crunched over the ground in rhythm with the inhale and exhale of my breath. The steady sound calmed me somewhat, the familiar escape of my morning run.

As I usually did on my runs, I mulled over my life, thinking back over the last seven years and wondering how I'd veered offtrack. To the outside world I knew I didn't look offtrack at all. I'd married my college sweetheart, we had good jobs, and we owned a home. My type A personality kept everything in order: the house stayed clean; the Roth IRAs were funded. I ran four to eight miles after work each day. You could set your watch to the militant rigidity of my daily routines. Externally I appeared to be thriving. But internally I felt off-kilter. Somewhere along the way I'd lost the feeling of potential and excitement I'd once felt for my life.

And in the past few months I'd developed a crippling, ever-present anxiety. It had begun as a small thing, a feeling of unease, but had manifested over time into shortness of breath, heaviness in my chest, and squeezing in my throat. What had started out as an annoying but manageable discomfort quickly grew into an overwhelming feeling of intense panic.

This panic would sideline me seemingly out of nowhere. While working or running or driving, or while my mind was wandering through mundane to-do lists or upcoming weekend plans, I'd be struck with anxiety so strong it nearly brought me to my knees.

Running was my time to think, and the topic that most captured my thoughts in those dwindling days of 2009 was the root of my unease. On my run that quiet November morning,

I considered the state of my chronic anxiety. For some time, I'd known that the anxiety correlated with the twinges of dissatisfaction I'd been feeling about my life. I was unhappy, and I knew it, but the thought of admitting it filled me with a suffocating dread.

In 2008, I'd left a job that I liked pretty well and taken a new job, jumping ship for a shorter commute and a lot more money. Yet I'd known from the first moment I walked into the office that the job was a bad fit. Immediately, I felt out of place, like a clown bumbling into a formal dinner party. But they'd offered me a position with two weeks of vacation and a salary almost 50 percent more than I'd been making, so I shushed my inner voice as it screamed *No! No! No!* and said yes. Yes, I'll take it. When would you like me to start?

They assigned me a desk in a windowless cubicle; my closest—and loudest—neighbor was the color copy machine. My job was isolating and lonely, but I felt trapped there, roped in by the money. I had a mortgage and a car payment, after all.

And more important than the car and mortgage, I had a husband. And he had only the faintest idea of the vast emptiness that had begun to consume me.

The hours and hours I'd logged running had helped me uncover the crux of my anxiety: I'd spent the past seven years building a life I no longer wanted. I didn't want the career, the house, or the car. For nearly a decade, I'd chased a life that I thought I was supposed to chase, following one path because I hadn't known that there were others that branched off it.

In college, I'd majored in English and dreamed of writing. My entire life I'd been a writer. In some of my earliest memories I am lying in the grass, five years old, writing poems about the sunset. But now, even my bedside journals lay unfilled. For years I'd had an intense desire to see the world, but here I was, stuck in a job that afforded me only two weeks of vacation. I was twenty-eight years old, and in the seven years since I'd graduated from college, I'd let go of everything I'd always dreamed of doing. I wasn't writing. I wasn't traveling. I wasn't happy.

I wasn't happy. Somewhere along the line, I'd traded in the person I wanted to be, the person who I really was inside, for the traditional model of success. Deep in my bones, I knew that there was more to life, but I was desperately fearful of finding out what.

That morning, once again, the uncomfortable reality of my unhappiness scrolled past the screen of my mind. The harder my anxiety squeezed, the faster I ran. Darting among the ancient pines, I jumped tree roots and loose rocks.

The truth kept rising to the surface: *You don't want what you have.* And then, quickly, my brain would form a rebuttal and come back swinging: *You have everything. Why aren't you happy?* My arms pumped like wings as I ran. The truth: *You can't continue on like this.* The rebuttal: *It's too late to want something else.*

Anxiety squeezed at my throat, building and building until I couldn't breathe. Unable to keep running, I stood in the middle of the muddy trail, gasping, the silence of the forest all around me. My hands found my knees, and I doubled over, trying to take a breath. It was suddenly clear that I had two choices. I could either say the truth out loud and admit my desire for a different kind of life, or I could keep the truth inside of me forever.

If I said the truth out loud, I knew there would be no unsaying it, no unknowing it. I'd have to accept the consequences. I had a whole life! It was pretty inconvenient not to want any of it anymore. But I also knew that if I kept the truth inside, I would have to tuck it into the soft belly of my soul and starve it of oxygen, and, as it withered and died, a part of me would too.

It was impossible to go on like this, barely breathing in the Purgatory between knowing and not knowing, between telling the truth or denying it. I had to make a choice.

And then I did the bravest thing that I have ever done. I let the truth slide into the center of me and take over. My heart pounded like a war drum.

My eyes surveyed the landscape of my body. Over the past year I'd molded it into the thin and strong form of a runner. The black spandex of my pants sat tight over the outline of muscles in my legs. Beneath my shirt my taut stomach rose and fell with my breath. As a marathoner, I was often asked, "What are you running from?" The question always annoyed me. But wasn't it true? I *was* running from something.

My legs straightened, and I looked around me. The trees stood solid and patient. Quietly, into the empty forest, I whispered: "Kim, you do not want this kind of life."

It was shocking to hear my own voice out loud in the silence of the trees. Little puffs of breath clouded against the cold air when I spoke. I said it again, slightly louder. "Kim, you don't want this kind of life. You're not happy." And then, because it felt safe to say it out there, "You want to write. You want to see the world."

It existed now, out in the open. And as I stood there in the silence of the morning, my anxiety receded like it had been grabbed by the tide and sucked out to sea.

⌒

That day I did not go home, sit my husband down, and tell him what I needed to do. No, that day I simply finished my run and continued on with my morning. My revelation remained a secret. But inside of me a door cracked opened and the truth stuck its head into the world. I could not go on pretending that it did not know the fresh air of possibility.

Speaking the truth out loud during my morning run brought me some peace, because now I knew what I had to do. And the truth bought me time, a few anxiety-free months, to gain the courage to actually do it.

A plan began to form in my mind. Because I wanted to travel the world—and not just for a week or a month at a time, but for as long as I possibly could—I'd have to quit my job. The burden of debt was intimidating, so even though I loved our house, we'd have to sell it. The same went for the car.

But the biggest hurdle of all was that I'd have to persuade

Brian, who would be receiving this news out of the blue, to give up his own life—to step away from a job that he liked and in which he had been recently promoted, to follow me to the ends of the earth to chase something I couldn't even properly explain.

Three months after my run in the park, Brian and I went for a hike. The Pacific Northwest reveled in a burst of sun and warm temperatures, the first we'd seen in many weeks. The winter had been long and dark. We'd been slogging through the days for months, just waiting for the rains to stop.

But on that February day, the sun shone and the sky beamed a birds-egg blue. We packed a backpack and drove to Oregon's Opal Creek Wilderness area to go hiking.

It was a Sunday, and as we climbed the empty trail, the smell of tree bark and moisture thick in the air and the moss green and plump with months of rainfall, we talked our normal Sunday talk about the dread of Monday.

We walked past turquoise pools at the headwaters of Battle Ax and Opal Creek, climbing in elevation among the earthy pines. At an overlook we stopped to catch our breath. I sat down on a rock and dug through the backpack for my water bottle, then looked up at Brian. My heart pounded, not from exertion, but from the truth I so badly needed to speak. I took a deep breath, then said, "I just keep wondering why we're doing this if we aren't happy. We don't have to, you know. We could quit our jobs tomorrow."

Brian looked at me, surprised. "Who says we're not happy?"

I drew the water bottle to my lips and took a long swig.

"What I mean is that there are other ways to live. Sometimes when I'm sitting in my cube, I look thirty years down the road and see a bigger house, a nicer car, a management position, and one of those terrible clocks people set that count down the days to retirement. It's depressing." I did not tell him about my run or the truth I already knew. "I guess I keep wondering what the point is. Don't you ever want something more?"

Brian looked skeptical. "Sure, sometimes I want something different. But I don't think that things are as bad as you're making them out to be."

I shrugged. "I know they're not bad, but they're not great either. Are they? Is that all we want, a *not bad* life?"

Brian leaned back on his heels and knocked the mud from his boot. "Listen, I know we aren't tripping over ourselves to get to work every morning, but we have more than a not bad life, Kim. We have a good life."

The rich, brown dirt at my feet smelled of earth and rain, and I swirled my finger through it. He was right; we did have a good life. And that was what made my desire so hard to accept. It was one thing to give up a bad life, or even a *not bad* life, but who in their right mind wanted to throw away a good life?

"All right," Brian continued, "say we do quit our jobs tomorrow. Then what? We move under the Fremont Bridge?"

"We could travel. I could take a shot at writing. You know I've always wanted to write." I paused, unsure of how to continue. "You could take time off to figure out what you really want to do. I've been thinking about it a lot, actually."

Brian looked out over the treetops toward the eastern sky. He enjoyed his job, I knew, but it didn't fulfill him. "In a perfect world that sounds nice. In the real world that sounds implausible."

"People do it, Brian. I've read blogs and researched it. We could sell everything and just explore for a little while."

He shook his head. "Do you know how much that would cost? And what about our house? What about health insurance? Retirement? There are too many factors."

I knew about those things and had considered them all. I didn't know what we would do about our house, about health insurance, about the complicated details of deconstructing our life. I didn't know anything except for that I wanted to go.

Brian screwed the lid on to his water bottle and stuffed it in the backpack. "Ready?"

When I stood to follow him I said, "Just hypothetically, where would you go if you could go anywhere?"

He turned to look at me and rolled his eyes.

"Come on," I said. "Indulge me!"

"All right, anywhere?" He walked in silence for a moment. "I'd go to Nepal and hike the Himalayas and to France to walk the Alps. I'd spend all of my time in the mountains." This did not surprise me; we were both happiest in the mountains. Brian turned to look at me. "What about you?"

"Iceland. Thailand. I want to ride the train from Russia, through Mongolia, to China."

Brian only nodded.

"Do me a favor and just think about it, okay? I'm serious."

He turned to look at me. "All right, I'll think about it."

And I left it at that, for awhile.

But telling Brian about my idea had only strengthened my resolve. The more I spoke of it, the more I thought about it, the more certain I became that what I'd experienced during my run in Forest Park was real and that my desire for more could not be ignored. I'd presented it to Brian as a question: *What if?* But I already knew what I needed to do.

Soon I was bringing up the sell-it-all-quit-our-jobs-and-travel topic regularly. And each time I did, Brian shot it down. To be fair, he did not object to the idea of traveling. He liked the idea of a road trip around the United States and Canada, or hiking the Appalachian Trail. But he wasn't sold on the big, bold plan I'd drawn up in my head. Quitting our lives to take an open-ended trip around the world was, in his very rational mind, the equivalent of playing hopscotch for a living. Of course, I knew there were plenty of good reasons to stay. But I'd spent my entire life staying. I wanted to be the kind of woman bold enough to go.

One night, after a marathon nag-fest, Brian collapsed on the couch. He set his beer on the table and rubbed his hands over his face. He looked worn down, and I felt a flicker of pride in that. I would outlast him. "How do I know that this isn't just one of the big, ambitious ideas that you get crazy passionate about and then dump three weeks later when the luster wears off?"

"I don't do that."

"What about vegan baking? You went out and spent one

hundred dollars on supplies, and then you got bored of it in two weeks."

"That's not fair. That's one thing." It was true that I'd adopted my fair share of passion projects over the years. Rather than owning up to what I truly longed to do and the fear I felt that I might fail at it, I'd filled the empty space inside of me with safe alternatives that I burned through like matches. I didn't care about failing at vegan baking because I didn't care about vegan baking. So I threw myself into it to distract me from my true desires. How could I convince Brian that *this time* I was serious? *This time* it was real? My game plan had been to hope that, eventually, he'd just see that this was different. But looking at it from his perspective I understood how the plan I presented just seemed like another one of my meanderings.

"Roller Derby? Triathlons? Yoga? The thing is Kim, when you first brought up this trip I thought it was in the, *Oh, if I had a million dollars* kind of way. Now you say you're serious, that you *have* to do it. How do I know? And where does that leave me?"

It was the question I'd been dreading, because I didn't know where it left him. Would I be willing to do it all without him? Brian was content with the life we had.

I was the one who had come unmoored.

Three months later, something surprising happened: Brian said he'd go.

Through a series of negotiations, a plan began to take shape. At first, Brian agreed to travel for six months if we requested leaves of absence from our jobs. I wanted my freedom, but I feared it too, and Brian's plan felt safe, so I agreed to a six-month sabbatical. But when we sat down to sketch out all of the places we wanted to go we realized that six months wasn't nearly enough time to see the world. Even Brian agreed that if we were going to do it, we might as well do it right. So we decided to go for a year, quit our jobs, and rent the house out.

Ultimately, though, that idea also left us dissatisfied. We'd have a mortgage but no paycheck, and we weren't sure if the going rate for rent would cover our mortgage payments. Plus, what if the roof leaked or the water heater died? There were so many unpredictable variables, and they scared us. Eventually we worked our way around to the plan I'd come up with in the first place. We'd sell it all and travel indefinitely. I'd take a shot at writing. We'd both use the time to figure out what we really wanted out of life.

When I asked Brian what had changed, he told me a story from his past. Brian is fascinated and amazed by the natural world and knew that he wanted to spend his life outdoors as a naturalist. So when it came time to choose a career, he packed up and left for an out-of-state college where he could study to become a park ranger. But after only one year he quit the program and transferred to the school where I'd met him. I'd heard that version of the story a dozen times and didn't know there was more to it.

"Here's the truth," Brian confessed one night over dinner. "It was the first time I'd left my comfort zone, and it terrified me so much that I transferred colleges to live near my best friend. The story I told myself was that I'd never be able to make a living as a naturalist, but actually I was just too scared. My dream slipped through my fingers because I couldn't overcome my own fear. I'm not going to let the same thing stop your dream too."

I'd cried because I knew what he said was true, and I was touched by his willingness to be brave. But I also felt sadness for him and happiness for me and guilt for my steadfast refusal to give up what I wanted.

With Brian on board, I renamed our savings account the "World Travel Fund." We paid off our debts bill by bill. Our cable and gym memberships and magazine subscriptions were all canceled. We sold the car we owed money on and kept the seventeen-year-old clunker I'd had since college. I squirreled away every extra dime we had in a change jar. Every three months I'd count it, wrap it up in coin paper, and deposit it into our World Travel Fund.

In July 2011, almost two years after I first spoke my truth out loud, we put our house up for sale. The country was in the middle of the housing bubble collapse, and the real estate market was in shambles. A house just down the street, very similar to ours, had been sitting on the market for months, and we expected ours to do the same. We were shocked when it sold in one day, *furnished*, and the buyer wanted to move in by the end of the following month.

We had to scramble to find a temporary rental and scramble some more to sell the rest of our nonessential possessions. We held a garage sale one weekend under the yellow August sun, and by Sunday afternoon, 98 percent of every material thing we owned in this world was no longer ours. It felt both liberating and heartbreaking to watch it all go. I had to imagine each thing we owned as a solitary weight that, collectively, kept me tied to the ground when I wanted to fly. Thinking like that helped me, but I knew getting rid of our stuff was harder on Brian because his heart was not in this journey in the same way mine was.

Turning the house over was a different story; it nearly ripped both of our hearts out. Brian and I had moved into our house as renters a year after relocating to Portland. We loved it, our neighbors, and the neighborhood, so when the chance came to buy it, we jumped. Then we spent the next three years replacing floors, knocking down walls, painting, and landscaping. Every piece of our tiny house had been restored with love. It was *ours*. And I always felt myself opening up a little at the sight of the front door.

Our house held so many good memories of holidays and cookouts and evenings with friends. Brian proposed to me in the living room. At the end of bad days that house had been a refuge for us. It was the first place that had ever truly felt like home to me.

On the day that we handed the keys over to the new owners, I walked through the empty rooms and wailed like a baby, running my hands along the walls and replaying favorite memories in my head. I thought of our first Christmas there together, alone in our still-new city, the tree bright and twinkling in front of the picture window. As I moved from room to room, I remembered dinner parties and movie nights and the way I loved to sit by the window in the family room and watch the first rains of the season pour from the sky.

My mind recalled the dreams we had for our lives when we bought the house, of the babies that we imagined might one day crawl on the floor and all of the other things that would never come to pass, not there anyway, because we were choosing a different direction. Letting go of all that the house represented was extremely hard, but it was what I wanted and what Brian had ultimately agreed to.

When I voiced that truth in the forest I wasn't sure if Brian or I had the courage to turn our lives upside down and shake them until all of the loose pieces fell away. But against the odds we'd done it. We no longer owned a house or had nine-to-five jobs. What we had instead were three boxes of personal artifacts stored in my best friend Wendy's basement and a few more that we'd shortly store in Brian's parent's basement in Ohio. And we had freedom. And time.

We *also* had two 65-liter backpacks and two one-way tickets to Ecuador, our first stop, selected solely because the fares were the cheapest we could find. We wanted to go everywhere, we reasoned, so it didn't much matter where we started.

Even with our departure date looming I *still* didn't really know exactly why traveling was the thing that I needed to do more than any other. I only knew that the truth welled up from deep inside of me that day in Forest Park. It was a truth that the most essential part of me had always known. I needed to see the world. I needed to write. I didn't have to know why. Wanting it was enough.

CHAPTER 2

ONE THING THAT BRIAN AND I NEVER QUITE GOT USED TO
was that we'd ended up in Portland, Oregon, in the first place.
We'd met in college in the Appalachian foothills at Ohio
University. We'd fallen in love, and when I managed to land my
first job all the way across the country in Oregon, Brian came
with me.

I was 23 and had barely left the state of Ohio. But somehow
I'd managed to get hired by a woman named Michele to run the
recycling program at an Oregon university. It was the luckiest
break I'd ever had.

Much from those early days eludes me. If I felt scared or
apprehensive about moving across the country with a boyfriend
I'd known for less than two years, those memories have been lost.
I can only recall the thrill of the adventure and the shock I felt
that someone had actually hired me for my first real job.

Over email I told my new boss about our plans, outlining the
date we'd leave Ohio, the date we expected to arrive in Oregon,

and the day I anticipated I'd be able to start my new job. *Oh*, I added, *and we're going to camp until we can find an apartment.* Brian and I were broker than broke. We had both just completed a postcollegiate year of volunteering in AmeriCorps where we earned a stipend that kept us well below the poverty line. We had a sum total of seven hundred dollars with which to drive across the country and put a deposit down on an apartment. We had to camp. We couldn't afford a hotel.

Michele must have thought we were crazy. There were no legal campsites within the city limits of Portland. Yet instead of telling me that I'd lost my mind, she simply extended an offer: *Why don't you stay with my husband and me until you find a place to live?*

We couldn't accept their offer. I'd be arriving in Portland with my boyfriend and my two dogs and my friend Jenny who decided to tag along for the road trip. Had I been coming alone I might have said yes, but I'd be showing up in Portland with a posse.

Over the phone a few days later I explained the situation to Michele. "Stay anyway," she'd said. Her voice sounded kind and encouraging through the receiver. And because Brian and I were ridiculously broke *and* ridiculously naïve, and because we clearly had no idea how much we were putting Michele and her husband out, I said okay.

We all arrived at Michele's door on a rainy August evening in 2004, tired and wide-eyed and so far away from everything we'd ever known. "You brought the rain with you," Michele said by way of greeting. "This is the first time it's rained in months, I promise." It'd struck me as odd, her sensitivity about the weather.

Such was my lack of knowledge about my new home—I hadn't even known about the rain.

In the days that followed, Michele and her husband, Glenn, showed us around the city. They took us to the movies and to dinner and refused to let us pay for a thing. And when we found an apartment a week or two later they gave us their old furniture and dishware and sent us on our way. Brian and I were flying by the seat of our pants. Michele and Glenn were pure goodness and kindness.

Over the years, Brian and I had reminisced about the sequence of events that brought us to Portland, and we were always awed that we had the good fortune to show up at the door of two of the kindest humans in America.

For two years I worked for Michele, and then I moved on to another job. A year after that, I took the job that I'd just quit—the one that left my bank account full but my spirit incredibly empty.

~

Since Michele had brought us to Portland, and Portland had changed our lives, we wanted to make sure that we thanked Michele and Glenn for taking us in and showing us such kindness in those early days. We set up a final dinner with them at a local pizza shop.

The evening unfolded easily as we fell into the familiar conversation of catching up. Brian and I talked about where we planned to travel and what we hoped to see and do on our big trip. Michele and Glenn told us about their jobs, dogs, and families.

As the evening wound down, Michele folded her napkin into her lap and leaned down to dig into her handbag. "Glenn and I have a small gift for you," she said.

My eyes followed her hand into her purse. "Michele, you shouldn't have done anything. We brought *you* here to thank *you*."

"I know, I know, but we wanted to," she said. Then she reached across the table and handed me a beautiful yellow envelope tied with an elaborate silk bow.

I looked over at Brian who eyed the envelope perplexedly. "Should I open it?" I asked Michele.

"Yes. But let me explain first. There's a letter inside that I'd like to read to you so that you understand the gift."

The silky bow unraveled easily as I pulled it. Inside of the envelope my fingers found a letter. I pulled it out, and as I did, a check for one thousand dollars fluttered to the table. I gasped and looked up at Michele, "Michele, we can't accept this."

"Wait," she said. "Let me read the letter to you." I handed it across the table to her.

The cramped restaurant bustled around us. Michele unfolded the letter and began to read.

Kim and Brian,
We can't believe that the date of your departure is almost here. We are so inspired by what you are doing and proud of you for having the courage to do it.

As is often the case when someone is about to experience a major life event: moving into a new home, getting married, having a child, celebrating a big anniversary—quitting their jobs and traveling the world!—we (society) feel the need to commemorate the occasion with a gift.

So, as we were pondering over this grand adventure you are about to embark upon, we kept bumping into this compulsion to get you a gift of some sort. In part, this is probably because we sincerely want to acknowledge the enormity of what you are about to do.

But we also think it is because we have the distinct and unique honor of being the first people to welcome you to Portland. It seems like only yesterday you both rolled up to our house after having driven halfway across the country, with everything you owned in your car, including your friend and your two crazy pups. You were both so excited to be off on this new adventure called "Portland" and had such determination and complete faith that it was all going to work out.

It's been fun to watch your life in Portland take shape—getting and changing jobs, making friends, buying a house, getting married. We have been so thrilled to be a small part of it. While we are sad to see you go (setting out with even less stuff than when you showed up!) we are so excited for you.

Which brings us back to this gift-giving dilemma. We thought about this long and hard. After all, what can you get people that are about to strap all of their belongings on their backs? And then the answer struck us like a bolt of lightning.

While you are out experiencing a myriad of countries and all of their wonders and adventures, we want you, at the same time, to make the world a better place.

Enclosed you will find the money to create what we are affectionately calling the "Kim and Brian Yellow Envelope Fund."

During your travels, we want you to give all of this money away in whatever way you want. You can give it here in the United States or in some foreign land. You can be serious in your giving or be totally crazy, funny, or harebrained. You can give it away visibly or anonymously. You can plan how you are going to do it, or just give it spontaneously. You can give it to adults, to children, to animals, or to the environment. You can give it all away at once, or you can spread it out and give a little bit here, a little bit there. You can give it away in any combination above. We don't care.

We do, however, have three simple rules:

Rule #1: Don't over think it

Don't stress about doing the "best thing" with the money. Don't dwell on all of the world's ills and feel pressure to try to fix them. We want you, instead, to listen to your soul. Give the money away in any way that makes you come alive.

It can be as simple as handing out some candy to the local village children or buying admission for the family behind you in line at the museum. Give it to some group you discover doing environmental work that moves you. Give it to a local women's co-op. Pay the dinner bill of the family sitting next to you. Buy someone a new pair of shoes or a bike. Give the funny waiter or helpful cab driver a fifty-dollar tip. Whatever you want.

Rule # 2: Share your experiences *(...if you want to)*

We encourage you to share your experiences with friends and family. But only share what you want—keep the rest in your heart. You are not accountable to us or anybody else for how you choose to give the money away.

Rule # 3: Don't feel pressured to give it all away

We want you to tuck this money away in your back pocket (somewhat figuratively of course) and give it away as the mood strikes. We imagine it might be hard at first...but once you get used to doing it we hope it becomes fun and adds richness to your travels. While we encourage you to find ways to give it all away, at the end of the day we don't want you to feel pressured or stressed about doing so. You can come back with all, some, or none of the money.

You are both two of the most inspiring, fun-loving and compassionate people we know. It seems you have always wanted to make a difference with your lives, and when you found you weren't quite living up to that dream, you had the courage to hit the "reset" button in a grand way. We can think of no one else we would rather live vicariously through. In many ways this will make it feel like we are traveling right along with you. And for us, this promises to be much more rewarding than writing that annual check to our favorite nonprofits (don't worry, we'll keep doing that too).

At the end of the day, the money itself is just paper. What gives the whole experience meaning are the thoughts, emotions, and feelings that come with giving the money away in ways that make you smile and make your hearts sing. While doing this bit of creative philanthropy isn't going to cure cancer or save the rain forest, we hope it can bring a bit of happiness and joy to folks you meet along your adventure—and that it will give you even more fond memories to look back on.

Good luck, have fun and be safe!
Two of your biggest fans,
Michele and Glenn

By the time Michele finished reading the letter I was crying right there in the restaurant. When I tried to say thank you, I fumbled over my words, feeling dumbstruck and awed. Michele and Glenn were asking us to be a conduit for their goodness, and I felt blessed by the amazing opportunity and humbled that they trusted us with their money.

Steering off of the well-worn path had been hard and scary. Oftentimes the dream felt so far out of reach that it would paralyze me, and I'd be unsure of what to do next. But one truth kept revealing itself to me: the next step would appear when I needed it to. That wasn't something that I'd ever believed before, but so many things had fallen into place to make this dream possible that I couldn't chalk it all up to chance anymore. The gift from Michele and Glenn felt like the next step.

The gesture inspired me so much that I told everyone I knew about the gift. I felt certain it would lend more weight and meaning to our travels. Secretly I dreamed up how far it could go, my mind somersaulting with the possibilities. Nothing seemed too big or out of reach.

———

As our remaining days in Portland ticked down, my anxiety level reached gargantuan proportions. Brian and I spent hours packing up the remaining boxes in our apartment, making endless trips to Goodwill and tracing and retracing the walk out to our car to load it full of the things we'd decided to keep: Christmas ornaments, my wedding dress, and old journals— the things that served no useful purpose but that I couldn't bear to get rid of.

I cried constantly, overwhelmed by the sadness I felt over leaving our life in Portland. My heart ached like it'd been beaten with a hammer and I couldn't say for sure whether I even wanted to go anymore. My life felt like it dangled from a pendulum, swinging through every emotion: joy, trepidation, back to happiness, and then on to pure terror.

Two days before we were scheduled to leave, we threw a going away party in Laurelhurst Park, a beautiful expanse of green grass and ancient trees in one of Portland's oldest neighborhoods.

Our friends gathered around us, arriving with dishes of food and cards inscribed with wishes. We filled the cooler with beer and rented a bingo set, and Brian called out letters and numbers into the sweet, warm air of spring. The lucky winners took home stuff that otherwise would have ended up in our Goodwill pile: a slotted spoon, an out-of-style sweater-vest, a framed picture of Brian and me in our Halloween costumes circa 2006.

I looked around at the faces of the people who had become our family in Portland—Michele and Glenn, Wendy, our old neighbors, our soccer teammates—and I felt a tidal wave of blessings wash over me. The life we'd built in the eight years since we'd moved to Oregon was rich and full. But then I thought, *We're leaving it all. We had so much here. Why couldn't it have been enough?*

The sun set and the park closed, and Brian and I and our closest friends headed to a bar where we squeezed into a photo booth and made faces as the camera snapped, freezing us in time. Back at our table I caught Brian's eye and realized that he was as exhausted as me. Our bed beckoned, but we both fought the urge to leave. We'd squeeze every drop out of this life while we still had it.

~

On Monday morning, May 21, 2012, Brian and I locked our door for the final time and walked out of our apartment building. We pointed our wheels east, heading back in the direction we came from eight years before.

The day dawned damp and gray. Rain puddled on the

roadway, and the windshield wipers swayed back and forth in a rhythmic dance. I couldn't believe we were leaving.

Brian steered the car onto I-84 East, and I watched out the window as Portland disappeared behind me.

My phone buzzed and I looked down to find a text from Wendy. *I know the real reason that Portland cries today,* it said. *Good luck. I love you.* Up until that point I'd been feeling solid, strong even, but her message reduced me to tears. Brian looked over at me and patted my leg. A whole chapter of my life was ending right there on that highway. "Hey," he said. "It'll be okay. I'm sad too."

But it wasn't just sadness I felt. I couldn't find the words to explain that I was both heartbroken and breaking open with possibility.

A few days later we arrived safely in Ohio. We visited with our family and friends and tucked our few remaining possessions onto my in-laws' basement shelves.

On the morning we left for Ecuador neither Brian nor I could choke down breakfast. We sat at the kitchen table wordlessly drinking coffee, wrapped up in our own thoughts. I'd imagined our departure day a thousand times over the nearly three years I'd been absorbed by this trip. And in every daydream, I was overjoyed—triumphant—at finally achieving the thing I'd set out to do. But as I sat at that table on the morning of our departure, I felt only terror. I wondered if we weren't making the biggest mistake of our lives. Digging through my purse for the tenth time to check to make sure our passports and credit cards were still inside, I spotted the yellow envelope. I'd hidden it in an interior pocket and pulled it out to reread Michele's letter once again. Even if we were doing some irrevocable damage to our futures by taking this trip, at least the yellow envelope guaranteed that something good would come out of it. We gathered our bags and boarded the plane to Ecuador, and the whole wide future stretched out before us.

ECUADOR

CHAPTER 3

OUR PLAN WAS TO HAVE NO PLAN. AFTER YEARS OF knowing exactly where I would be Monday through Friday from 7:00 a.m. until 4:00 p.m., I wanted the freedom to go where my heart desired. For months leading up to the trip I'd imagine Brian and me sitting cross-legged in hostel common rooms, swapping stories with other travelers and learning of secret locations deep in the Amazon or high on mountaintops that no guidebook could name, places only *real* travelers visited.

It went against everything that my reservation-making, type A personality felt compelled to do, but we'd managed to arrive in Ecuador with just two nights booked in a guesthouse and one-way tickets from Buenos Aires, Argentina, to Delhi, India, purchased for three months down the road. How we got to Buenos Aires and where we went in between was completely up to us.

We arrived in Quito, Ecuador's capital city, on a cool morning. The city was sprawling and half-built and notoriously riddled with crime. I didn't know if it was inexperience or genuine threat that made me feel uneasy, but something felt just a little off about Quito.

A ten-foot wall rimmed with barbed wire and broken glass bottles surrounded our guesthouse. Downtown, armed guards stood on Quito's street corners swaying shotguns like appendages. It scared the shit out of me. I was sure that Brian and I looked like easy and obvious targets, that our ignorance must be plastered all over our faces. And yet at the same time I felt untouchable—high from that magical mix of jet lag and the miraculous shock of boarding an airplane in familiar territory and deboarding it in a wholly foreign world.

A 150-foot stone monument called the Virgin of Quito stood perched above the city on a hill called El Panecillo, and on our second day in Ecuador Brian and I decided to visit. We wandered through Quito's Old Town district, lost on the meandering streets, winding our way to the base of the hill. But as we drew closer we lost sight of the statue, buried as we were in the narrow, cobbled alleys.

"I think we're officially lost," I said to Brian and stepped into the middle of the road to gain a clearer view. "I don't even know if we're headed in the right direction anymore."

Up ahead of us on the street corner stood a policewoman armed with an intimidating rifle. I nodded in her direction. "Why don't you ask that police officer for directions?" Brian looked skeptical. We'd been in Ecuador for less than 48-hours and the entirety of our Spanish vocabulary could be summed up in two words: *hola* and *gracias*.

"Why don't *you* ask her for directions? You're the one who took Spanish for two years in college."

"All right, fine," I said, irritated at having to take control. As I approached the policewoman I tried to conjure up a sentence in my head that would express my basic question: Which way to the statue? Was it safe to walk there?

"*Hola,*" I said when I reached her. "*¿Hablas inglés?*"

She shook her head no.

"Err… Statue? *¿Arriba?*" I pointed toward the direction of the hill. "Is it safe? To walk there?" I made little walking motions with my fingers and shrugged my shoulders.

She cocked her head at me. "Walk? Safe?" I said again.

It dawned on me that I was doing that annoying thing that tourists do when they're trying to speak to someone in a foreign country. I talked slowly and emphatically, though not, unfortunately, in the native language.

The policewoman smiled and fired off a quick sentence. My very limited comprehension of the language caught the words yes, walk, and statue.

Smiling back at the woman I nodded my head like the words she'd just uttered made perfect sense. "*Gracias,*" I said. I felt confident so I added, "*Muchas gracias.*"

"Well," asked Brian when I returned. "What did she say?"

"I have no idea. But I think she may have said that it is safe to walk to the statue and that we're headed the right way."

"You sure?"

"Fairly sure."

So we walked in the direction of the statue, waving at the policewoman as we passed her by.

A few blocks later I turned to see her running after us, pumping her arms frantically above her head. When she caught up to us, her gigantic gun knocking haphazardly against her leg, she spoke in basic English that turned out to be much better than my broken Spanish. "Don't walk. Very dangerous." Then she pulled out her radio, said something into it, and asked us to wait with her. She looked concerned so Brian and I did as we were told.

I glanced around me. Just minutes earlier the streets had been bustling with tourists and locals alike. Now, Brian and I and this cop were the only souls around. Suddenly, a police car shot around the corner and jolted to a stop in front of us. The policewoman opened the back door and gestured for us to get inside. I shot Brian a look. Before leaving on our trip I'd read online about corrupt cops robbing and kidnapping foreigners. "I don't know if this is a good idea," I hissed to Brian.

"What? We're being coerced into an unknown vehicle in a foreign country by a woman with a semiautomatic rifle. What could go wrong?"

"That's not funny."

"I'm sure it will be *fine*," he said, and nudged me into the back of the car.

There were two other men, cops presumably, in the front seat, so the officer wedged herself into the back with us.

The driver issued us a bellowing hello and began peppering

us with questions. Where were we from? How long would we be in Ecuador? Did we like their country? Wasn't their country beautiful? *"Amigos,"* he said, wagging his finger at us in the rearview mirror. "El Panecillo is very dangerous. Many robberies. We will drive you instead."

"Gracias," I said, using my word. The cop nodded and turned up the music, a fast-paced Latin beat, and I suddenly felt like I was cruising around town with a bunch of friends on a carefree Saturday afternoon. Sitting back in the seat, I let myself relax.

My purse, a black, antitheft, cross shoulder bag that I'd paid a fortune for, sat tucked between my knees. I looked down at it and thought about the yellow envelope money. Before we'd left the states, Brian and I had discussed a system for distributing the money. We'd decided to keep the envelope stocked with the currency of the country we were visiting. When we found an opportunity that felt right, we'd give the money away. We'd restock the envelope as often as needed until the money ran out. I'd even set up an Excel spreadsheet to track the money as we gave it away. Although Michele and Glenn had said in the letter that we weren't accountable to them, I wanted to be able to tell them exactly where their money had gone.

I was hyperaware of the presence of the yellow envelope in my purse. During the few days we'd been on the road I felt almost manic about finding an opportunity to give the money away. But my vigilance sucked some fun out of our first few days of travel. Instead of relaxing into the trip, I'd been overthinking every interaction even though rule number one of the yellow envelope specifically instructed me not to. *Was this an opportunity to give?* I'd wonder. And while living in that state of mind sort of made me feel like a magical fairy sent to bestow kindness on the unsuspecting masses, it also put me in my head too much and pulled me out of the moment.

I leaned into Brian. "Assuming we make it up to the statue alive, should we give some yellow envelope money to the cops?"

Brian looked at me like I'd lost my mind. "They're cops," he said. "We can't give money to cops. What if they think it's some kind of bribe?"

"But they're being so nice to us."

"That's their job. We can't just hand them a wad of money without explaining why."

He had a point. I looked out the window while the car climbed in zigzags up the hill and watched as colorful, colonial, Old Town passed by.

When we reached the statue Brian and I climbed out of the car and thanked the cops for the lift. They made us promise to take a taxi back down the hill. "And make sure to tell all of your friends to come visit us in Ecuador," said the driver.

"We will," I promised.

I slung my knife-proof, lockable, ridiculous purse across my shoulder and waved as the cops pulled away. Our inaugural yellow envelope gift would have to wait.

Ecuador was a beautiful country, mountainous and green. Outside of the city, women in brightly embroidered clothes sat in doorways like decorations, their dark, braided hair roping down their backs. Tropical plants grew alongside the highway in luminous pinks and yellows. The people were wonderfully kind, unrushed, and quick to smile.

It was shocking how fast life could change. Just a few weeks earlier I'd been hunched over my cubicle like a troll protecting a bridge—toiling away at a job I'd been unhappy at for years—and suddenly I was *in Ecuador*—dirty and wandering and covered in bug bites—eating *almuerzo* from roadside stands. It felt like my soul had swapped bodies with the most exciting stranger.

Brian and I spent three weeks traveling through the north of the country and then headed to Baños de Agua Santa, a tiny town tucked high into the Andes. Its claim to fame was an active volcano, Tungurahua, which loomed over the city and blew up on an unnervingly regular basis.

Travelers we'd met in Quito had told us about a nonprofit in Baños called Arte del Mundo (Art of the World). Arte del Mundo, nicknamed La Bib (the library) promoted literacy and the arts to the children of Baños. Volunteers came from all over the world to live and work at La Bib. Brian and I signed up to volunteer. We were already looking forward to unpacking our backpacks and calling someplace home for more than two days at a time.

Our bus dropped us at the station, and we slung our backpacks on and walked toward the center of town. We tracked down

La Bib without a problem—it was hard to get lost in Baños—
and were greeted at the gate by Jane, a relaxed and refreshingly
unbothered twenty-six-year-old British girl with a round face
and a splash of freckles across her nose. She smiled, shook our
hands, and said, "Nice to meet you," then introduced us to Blake,
a gruff Scotsman with a scraggly beard who appeared to be in
his forties. Blake practically levitated with pent-up energy and
reminded me of my childhood dog, Taffy, who used to convulse
uncontrollably when presented with her leash.

Blake showed us to a sparse but adequate room. A double
bed stood in the corner, and two grimy windows looked out
over the gravel yard of La Bib. On the back of the bedroom door
someone had taped hand-drawn instructions of an evacuation
route through town in the event of a volcanic explosion.

"Come on down once you've unpacked," said Blake, "and I'll
give you a tour of the place."

The walls in our bedroom were peeling and water stained,
and the floor in the hallway creaked. Still, it was nice to have a
place to call home for a few weeks. We unpacked our bags and
hung our clothes from a wooden rod propped against the wall,
our makeshift closet.

"Not too shabby," said Brian, plopping down on the bed and
patting the space next to him. "What do you think?"

I sat down. "I like it."

Lying back in bed, I ran my hand over the worn quilt and
looked at Brian. "Do you miss our house when we're staying in
rooms like this?" It was hard to admit it, but I felt incredibly

homesick. I missed Wendy and my coworkers. I missed my sisters and my parents. Even though I didn't talk to them every day back in Portland, I'd never realized how comforting it had been to know they were just a phone call away.

Before now, it had never occurred to me how proud I'd been of our little house and our good careers, of the life we'd built for ourselves from scratch in Oregon. Without all of the material things that had once surrounded me, I felt suddenly disoriented. I'd never thought of myself as someone attached to my stuff, but it'd been harder than expected to let go of it all, and now that I no longer owned any of it, I felt like a piece of my identity had been stripped away. Without realizing it, I'd allowed my stuff to speak for me. My marathon bibs said *I'm a runner.* My outdoor gear said *I'm a nature lover.* Even living in Portland had become a huge piece of my identity. But now all of that was gone.

Brian leaned back in bed beside me and grabbed my hand. "I miss our house," he said. "I miss a lot of things."

I squeezed his hand. "Me too." When we left Portland we'd given up a whole way of life. And I realized, quite to my astonishment, that I mourned the loss of that life.

"Why didn't you tell me you were missing home?" I asked, trying to remember the last meaningful conversation that Brian and I had. Nothing came to mind. Adjusting to our new reality took up so much mental space that we spoke of nothing else. It wasn't just friends and family that I missed, I realized. I missed him too.

"I just did."

Standing, I walked to the window and looked out at the dark-green slope of mountains. During all of the time I'd spent planning and daydreaming for our trip I'd never really considered that traveling might be hard. That seemed so foolish now. "It's weird that we can't go back, huh?"

Brian raised his eyebrows at me and ran a hand through his red beard.

"I mean, I don't want to," I said, backpedaling. "But it's strange to think we don't have a life in Portland anymore."

Brian sat up on the bed. "Are you wishing we hadn't done this? It's what you wanted, Kim."

"I know, I know." I turned toward the bed and looked Brian in the eye. He stared hard at me, anger furrowed in the arch of his brow. I lowered my eyes. "I'm happy we're here."

It wasn't completely true, but it was the part of the truth I felt comfortable telling.

Later we found Blake in his office scribbling into a notebook.

"Come, follow me," he said when he saw us, darting out into the yard and up an exterior staircase.

"Bedrooms are here, but you know that. The classroom is here, the bookshelf is there," Blake said, pointing from room to room as we tromped down the hall.

"You can read the books, but do *not* take them." He looked at us accusingly like we'd just tried to stuff them down our pants.

"The bathroom's here." He nudged open a hollow wooden door with his foot.

"The water is hot, but you need to pull this lever to turn it on." He leaned down and cranked a nozzle in an exposed pipe to demonstrate. He flicked off the light. "*Always* turn off the light!"

He turned to leave but thought better of it, thumbed the light back on again and pointed toward a space at the left of the sink. "This rag here is what we call the floor towel." My eyes wandered over to a pink towel hanging limply on a hook. "You have to put it over the drain to keep the cockroaches out."

I shot a look at Brian and Blake saw it.

"Oh, don't worry," he said, and the tone of his voice gave me the distinct impression that he thought I was being a baby. "The big ones only come out at night."

We were living at La Bib with four other volunteers. There was Stephanie, a smart and serious young teacher from Philadelphia who left her job at a prep school to teach in South America. Louisa, a mature-for-her-age recent college grad taking eight months off to perfect her already-proficient Spanish before heading to medical school, and Alice and Carver, a couple from South Africa who met in Australia and had traveled around South America for the past seven months. They were in their mid and late thirties and, like us, left careers and stable lives behind in order to see the world.

Later in the day we were called to an orientation meeting. We sat around a large, rectangular table in an airy classroom, the walls covered in peeling blue paint, and introduced ourselves.

When my turn came I explained, nervously, that Brian and I had quit our jobs and sold everything, that we were now on an open-ended trip around the world, and Ecuador was our first stop. I was embarrassed because I felt like the declaration sounded braggy or flaky or both. So it surprised me when the group erupted in applause. Blake even let out a "*woot!*"

"Amazing choice," said Carver. He leaned over and clapped Brian on the back. "You won't regret it."

Alice said, "I've come home from traveling and then left again so many times that my family thinks I'm truly mental."

Back home, our decision to travel had seemed so counterculture, so extreme. And on a few occasions, we'd had to defend our decision to acquaintances and colleagues—even family—who accused us of being irresponsible and selfish. But here we were sitting around a table with a whole group of people who were doing the same thing. Outside of our daily bubble, long-term travel seemed like the most normal thing in the world.

Jane gave us the lowdown on what our day-to-day experiences would be like at La Bib. The children arrived at three thirty each afternoon, and we would read with them for half an hour. Afterward, we'd conduct an activity focused on creativity and art.

Blake told us about volunteer expectations. He rattled them off like a shopping list. We were expected to keep our living space clean, to treat each other with respect, and to participate in all meetings and activities. We were expected to represent ourselves well while we were out in public in Baños. It was a small town, and people talked.

"*No* drugs! *No* going home with the locals! *No* bringing the locals home with you! *No* getting drunk and making a scene in the streets!" Blake practically lost his mind at the thought of it.

"You won't imagine what some people do here," he continued. "We had a lady, a *mother*, if you can believe it, giving blow jobs to guys in the bathroom of a bar."

I looked around to see if anyone else was as shocked as I was that Blake was telling us this.

"We had to kick her out. What other choice did we have?" He scanned the room like we had just accused him of being an asshole for doing it. I saw Alice in the corner shaking her head as if to say, "No, you had no choice."

"You wouldn't believe what we've had to put up with." He paused, took a breath, and slapped the table with this hand. His lips curled into a smile and the red tint of rage drained slightly from his face. "But this looks like a good group. I don't think we'll have any trouble with you."

He kept doing that, telling us how bad he'd had it but then assuring us that we surely wouldn't disappoint and embarrass him the way the others had.

Each day at exactly 3:30 p.m. we rolled up the door to La Bib and the kids came bounding in and bowled me over with their energy. They talked in hurried Spanish, but even though Brian and I were taking Spanish language courses each morning, I couldn't understand a word they said. Oftentimes I felt overwhelmed and, ridiculously, like I could cry. It was so frustrating not knowing the language.

I developed a coping mechanism for dealing with reading time. I'd choose an illustrated book with the name of the pictured item listed in both English and Spanish, and I'd sit down on a beanbag chair and practice my elementary-level vocabulary.

During orientation, Blake had filled us in on some of the kids. One little girl named Agatha hung back during reading time. She preferred to sit alone in the corner with a pile of books instead of teaming up to read with a volunteer. Blake said that her father had died the year before and that his loss had been hard on the family and especially hard on Agatha. Her reading comprehension had stalled, and she skipped many afternoons at La Bib because she had to stay home to help her mother with the housework and care for her younger siblings.

Her story touched me, and while pretending to read, I'd peek at Agatha over my board books and cook up elaborate ways to give yellow envelope money to her family, then talk myself out of each one. First I decided that I would find out where she lived and anonymously drop money in her mailbox. But that wouldn't work, because no one even had mailboxes. Next I decided to start a college fund for Agatha and her siblings, but then determined that my measly contribution wouldn't make any difference.

Agatha's sad brown eyes scanned the page before her, her body slumped away from the rest of the room. I knew that even if I figured out how to pull off some kind of Oprah-like give-away, no amount of money would bring back the one thing she needed most.

One evening after our volunteer duties were up I trapped

Louisa in the communal kitchen and asked her to repeat some phrases I wanted to memorize, while I scribbled them down in my notebook.

The next afternoon I approached Agatha during reading hour. Brian had quizzed me on my phrases before bed and again when we woke up that morning.

"*Hola*, Agatha," I said.

She glanced up at me with wide eyes. "*¿Quiere leer conmigo?*" Do you want to read with me?

She nodded her answer wordlessly. I patted a beanbag chair. "*Aquí.*"

We settled in beside one another. The weight of her small body warmed mine. I picked up a book of tongue twisters and began to read, thumping comically over the words. Beside me, Agatha giggled.

"*No está bien,*" she said.

I slapped my palm to my forehead. "*¿Puedes enseñarme?*" Can you teach me?

She grabbed a new book, cracked its spine, and read the first sentence, pausing so I could repeat it. "*Bueno,*" she gave a serious little nod. From that moment on, Agatha and I were reading buddies.

Each day after reading time we launched into arts and crafts hour. The kids would crowd around a long table and we'd set markers and paper down in front of them, then Stephanie would lead the group in her teacher Spanish.

I usually sat on a child-sized stool and made whatever the

kids were making. They often asked me for things. Markers? Scissors? Finally, Louisa would lean over and whisper something like, "Kim, they're asking for the tape." It should have been obvious since the Spanish word they said translated to "masking."

By the time the kids left and we put the crafts away and mopped up the floors, I was completely exhausted. I'd take a warm shower, making sure to carefully place the floor towel over the cockroach drain *just in case*, and collapse into bed before 9:00 p.m. The days were so full that I barely had time to think. I still missed home, and I still missed having meaningful conversations with Brian, but those feelings would have to wait. In the back of my mind the larger issues drummed their fingers, waiting for my attention.

CHAPTER 4

BAÑOS WAS A BEAUTIFUL LITTLE TOWN WITH TWO MAIN squares, one grocery store, a few restaurants run by expat hippies and a few more run by locals. It had two thermal hot springs, a sprinkling of Internet cafes, and plenty of adventure companies offering a chance to jump off a bridge, raft down a river, rappel over a waterfall, or rent a bike and speed down a winding Andean highway. I loved it there.

About a week into our volunteering gig, Brian and I went to dinner with the other volunteers. We scrunched around a big table at our favorite restaurant called The Meeting Place.

"What are everybody's plans after Ecuador?" asked Stephanie.

Brian said, "We will probably go to Peru." We'd been discussing where to go next and had decided to make our way south. Since Peru was Ecuador's southern neighbor, it became our next destination.

"Law school starts for me next fall," said Louisa. "But I'm going to travel around South America for a while first." A bolt of envy shot through my chest. Lately, I'd been daydreaming of traveling alone.

"I don't know where I'll go next," responded Carver. He paused and fiddled with his fork, lost for a moment deep in thought. "Maybe back to Australia. Maybe back to South Africa." I noticed that he said "I" and not "we." I knew he and Alice were having problems. They had the bedroom next to ours, and I'd heard them arguing, more than once, late into the night.

I understood their discontent. Traveling as a couple was proving to be difficult. Brian and I had been bickering on a daily basis over dozens of small annoyances. I found myself getting mad at him over things I'd never given a second thought to back in Portland, like how he'd ask me repeatedly how much to tip instead of just making the decision himself, or how his stubbornness prevented him from asking for directions even though we spent at least half of our time lost. When we deboarded the plane in Ecuador, everything we'd ever known had disappeared, including the roles we'd carefully carved out for ourselves over time. I'd been the grocery shopper, Brian the lawn mower. I managed the money; Brian maintained our cars and our house. Now the roles were up for grabs again. I didn't want to be the direction asker and the tip calculator. It was hard to tell if we were just exhausted and adjusting to our new life or if traveling had exposed some kind of unavoidable flaw in our relationship.

"What I'll miss, though," continued Carver, "is how life just spills onto the streets here. Everything happens outside for everyone to see. Life back home will seem so bland and ordinary in comparison."

It was true. A few days ago Brian and I had been walking to the fruit and vegetable market when we ran into a funeral procession headed down the main street toward the graveyard at the edge of town. A group of men carried a casket on their shoulders. At least a hundred people walked behind it, crying, bouquets of flowers clutched in their hands.

The next day I'd asked our Spanish teacher about the procession. A woman had died of cancer, he'd told me. She was beloved in the community. He had loved her too. I touched his arm and told him I was sorry. "I know. It's okay," he said. "When we lose someone we lose them together. It makes losing easier." Agatha came to mind, and I nodded solemnly.

On our walk back to La Bib after dinner it started pouring big, dramatic raindrops like I remembered from Midwestern summers as a kid. We'd been walking slowly, chatting, and were totally caught off guard by the sudden downpour. We ducked under awnings and sidestepped puddles, trying to stay dry.

But it was useless. So Carver veered onto the rainy street, stretched his arms out like an airplane, and started cackling like the joker. Before I had a chance to think I'd swerved into the street too. The rain pounded and the gutters flooded, water sloshed everywhere. I started laughing, first quietly and then uncontrollably, dripping wet and doubled over, laughing in a way I hadn't laughed in years.

Behind me, Alice, Louisa, Stephanie, and Brian were laughing too, running down the middle of the street like maniacs. I hoped it wasn't the sort of scene that might get us kicked out of La Bib. But even if it was, I just couldn't help myself, because I was overcome with an incredible sense of freedom. Standing there in the middle of a little Ecuadorian town, sopping wet and laughing, I wasn't sure that I'd ever felt so alive.

By the time we got back to La Bib, we were all soaked to the bone. I rang my clothes out and hung them on a hook at the back of our bedroom door. After changing into dry clothes and warm socks I padded out into the common area and dropped into a beanbag chair.

I hadn't felt that young since…when? As the oldest child I was perpetually responsible, constantly concerned about doing the right thing. I always felt old for my age. But since leaving to travel I felt myself growing younger. It was a Tuesday night, and in the life I left behind I would be slouched on the couch in my sweatpants, computer unfolded on my lap and *American Idol* blaring away on the television screen, unwinding from another exhausting and unfulfilling day. But I didn't feel exhausted in that moment. Life had cracked me open.

"Where's Brian?" Carver asked as he plopped down into the chair beside me.

Shrugging my shoulders, I said, "He's reading, I guess."

I had the urge to yell "*Why are you asking me?!*" though I knew why he asked, of course. Carver saw me as half of a whole: *Kim and Brian.* Everyone we met on the road knew us only as a package deal. Back home I'd had my own identity; out here I was defined only in relation to Brian. But I didn't want to be Kim and *anyone.* The label made me feel like I was suffocating, or like my clothes were too tight. Carver raised his eyebrows and looked at me strangely, then popped a movie into the DVD player.

"What?" I said. "I don't have him microchipped."

"Okaaaay."

Waving him off, I unfurled a blanket and wiggled until the chair molded to my body. Above me, Louisa's compact body was stretched out on the couch. Unexpectedly, I felt a sinking in my gut that I was *Kim and Brian*, and she was happily, enviably, alone.

～

It was someone's bad idea—probably mine—to host mock Olympics in a park on the outskirts of Baños one afternoon.

The *real* Olympics had taken place over the summer, but fall was upon us, and the games had already faded into history. Besides, the Olympics weren't exactly a big deal in Ecuador. The kids barely knew what they were, save from one former Olympian named Jefferson Pérez, the only Ecuadorian to ever bring home a medal. In 1996 he won the gold in racewalking, but that was years before these kids were even born.

Nonetheless, the Olympic planning committee dove into the details like the good volunteers that we were. We had the kids construct medals out of foil and cardboard and instructed them to use their imagination to design their own country flag and uniform bib.

Over the next few days we spent our meetings planning offi-cially sanctioned Olympic events like tug-of-war and the egg toss. We hyped it up at La Bib all week. "Friday we're holding the Olympics. It's going to be epic. You don't want to miss out!" Except, I couldn't say any of those things in Spanish so I'd just say, repeatedly, "*¡Viernes! ¡Muy bien!*" and hope my enthusiasm drove my point home.

On Olympic Day the kids and volunteers gathered as a group at La Bib before marching through town to the park. We carried an Olympic torch made from construction paper and tromped past corner shops selling empanadas and Coke. The locals giggled at our unwieldy group and snapped photos with their cell phones.

As soon as we reached our destination it began to rain, and the kids huddled under a gazebo, sitting on a picnic table, while the volunteers stood in the drizzle attempting to explain the Olympic virtues of peace and brotherhood. The kids wiggled impatiently and waited for us to get on with it.

Our first event was racewalking, an homage to the great Jefferson Pérez. Louisa explained the event to the kids in Spanish while Alice walked in looping circles, arms pumping, to demonstrate.

"Do you understand?" Louisa asked the kids.

Of course they understood. Racewalking is what seven-year-olds also refer to as *running*. Brian counted down: "*...tres, dos, uno... ¡Vamos!*" and the kids took off in a heated sprint toward the finish line. The only kid who got the concept and maintained control all the way across the finish line came in last place.

The egg-and-spoon race was a bit more successful until Sam, a whiny, blond-haired gringo boy, dropped his egg. It smashed into a yolky mess, and Sam started wailing. We ended the event and handed out medals, and everyone wanted gold. When we ran out of gold and passed out silver, the kids began to argue. Sam was still crying about his broken egg. A few boys wandered to the edge of the park and peed.

"So much for peace and brotherhood," Brian whispered to me.

We'd lost control of the situation, so we did what any desperate babysitters would do. We started a game of tug-of-war.

The fierce warrior hidden inside each of the La Bib kids emerged as they yelled and grunted and pulled with all of their might on the tug-of-war rope.

Suddenly, kids from all over Baños were running toward us like stray dogs to meat. A small child who looked about three years old with dreads down his back grabbed on to the rope, then a shoeless girl, then a young teenage boy.

The mania couldn't last, and eventually we all tumbled down, one side falling backward and the other side falling forward from the momentum. We were piled into the mud, volunteers and children alike, and the rain poured down. We were laughing, laughing, laughing.

What was it with the rain and all this laughing?

~

On a Tuesday night after the Olympics, the mud finally removed from under my fingernails and inside of my ears, we went out on the town with the other volunteers to a family-run karaoke bar. We ordered rounds of beers and put in our song requests. I threw back my pilsner and tried to find the courage for my solo rendition of "Eternal Flame," relieved each time the DJ called out a name other than my own.

The music blared much too loud for conversation, so I sat back in my chair and watched a young Ecuadorian guy belt out a Bob Marley song. My mind wandered. I'd been so caught up helping out at La Bib, in making friends with the other volunteers and thinking through the weird issues with Brian, that I'd all but forgotten about the yellow envelope money. An internal ping of guilt pulsed in my gut. I couldn't believe we hadn't given away any of the money yet, especially because the rules gave us the freedom to be as creative as possible with our giving. Brian and I could walk through the town square and throw dollar bills into the air if we wanted. I had hoped that our gifts would be more meaningful than that, but I began to feel that we just needed to give something, *anything*, to get the ball rolling.

An urgent drive to put a plan of action into place suddenly consumed me. I leaned across the table and yelled over the music to Brian, "We need to talk about the yellow envelope!"

Brian's eyes were fixed on the stage where Carver was scream-singing at the crowd. I banged my hand down on the table in front of him and half a dozen beer bottles bounced from the force. He looked over at me and cupped his ear with his hand. "WHAT?"

"WE NEED A PLAN! FOR THE YELLOW ENVE-LOPE!"

Brian shrugged and mouthed the words *I can't hear you.*

Frustrated, I wagged my wrist at him. Yellow envelope rule number three was *Don't feel pressured to give it all away,* but right now I was afraid that we'd never give *anything* away.

The night wore on, and as it did, Alice, Carver, and a new volunteer Anna, began to spill drinks and climb on top of chairs to dance. One of them dropped the karaoke microphone and it broke into pieces. Their behavior embarrassed me, and I stood to leave, but as we filed out of the door we were stopped and told we owed an additional three dollars. This set off a round of drunken complaining from Carver, so I quickly paid the fee and headed back to La Bib, ashamed to be lumped in with a group that fit the mold of the argumentative and self-centered Westerner.

The next morning while the other volunteers were sleeping off their hangovers, Brian and I set off on a hike high in the hills above Baños. The path led us almost vertically up, past tiny shacks and farmland built onto severe slopes. Baños sat at six thousand feet elevation, and I sucked wind as we trudged upward into the ever-thinning air. I had hoped that a bit of time outside alone might calm the tension I sensed between Brian and me. But I could not talk through my panting.

Twenty minutes up the trail we passed a leathery old woman standing behind a barbed wire fence. She waved us down and yelled to us in quick-fire Spanish. Only a few words stood out: *man, down, cow.* I looked at Brian. "Do you have any idea what she's saying?" He shook his head. I turned to her and spoke one of the only phrases I'd learned since landing in Ecuador. "*Lo siento, no entiendo.*" I'm sorry, I don't understand.

I silently beat myself up for being such a lousy Spanish student during my years of mandatory study in college. Even now, during our self-inflicted Spanish classes, Brian had to convince me almost daily not to skip. "We're paying good money for these classes, and you're going," he'd say as he stood over the bed in the morning. "Get up and grow up. You're not sixteen."

We continued our hike in silence, and I thought of the previous night. I was ashamed of the scene our group had made, yet I also felt envious of Alice, Anna, and Carver's ability to just let go. I'd never danced on a table or broken a microphone, and I didn't want to, but I knew that somewhere in between drunken asshole and responsible schoolmarm was a middle ground. I wanted to learn to let go too.

Once, not long before leaving Portland, I'd been out to lunch with my old coworkers, a group of women a bit older than me. They were talking about mistakes they'd made in their lives: relationships that ended in divorce, wrong career moves, regrets. During the conversation I'd sat in silence until one of them asked me about my biggest mistake. Caught off guard I'd gaped at them, scanning my brain for an answer. Finally, one of them said, with a bit of conde-scension, "Kim's never made a mistake in her life." At the time I'd shrugged off the comment, but I couldn't let it go. It haunted me as I lay in bed at night dreaming of changing my life. My coworker had been wrong about me. I'd made the biggest mistake of all: I'd spent my entire life playing it safe.

Ahead of us in the distance an old man walked slowly toward us hobbling with a makeshift bamboo cane. As we passed him, Brian nodded solemnly and offered up an *"hola."* The old man looked up and grimaced and then directed his attention back at the ground. Following his gaze, my eyes dropped to his feet. He was wearing beat-up navy Crocs, a few sizes too big, and his feet were sliding around inside of them. If he fell out here he'd be in trouble. I wanted to offer help but I didn't know how.

I looked out over the lush green peaks and crevices of the Andes Mountains. From up here, Baños looked like a toy town, a colorful splattering of churches and houses and buildings plopped into a never-ending sea of green. As I took in the beautiful landscape, my heart pinged for the towering pines and ancient ferns of home. A deep piece of me felt sad, but I could barely admit it to myself and definitely not to Brian. I'd pressured him into giving up everything to come out into the world with me. I couldn't admit that it wasn't yet living up to my expectations.

In front of me, Brian stopped abruptly and jolted me from my thoughts. I glanced up to see a rustling in the bushes. *A bear?* Brian walked slowly up the trail toward the commotion and turned to me, looking relieved. "God, that scared me!"

"What is it?"

He laughed. "It's a black-and-white dairy cow."

The cow stood to the side of the trail, leisurely chewing grass. She was tied to a heavy rope that had come untethered. We put the pieces together. The couple we'd passed had lost their cow. The old man must have been trying to track her down. But there was no way he could catch up to the cow and then drag her back home; he struggled to walk himself.

I set off down the slippery trail to let the man know that

we'd found his cow. When I caught sight of him, I yelled, "*¡Tengo tu vaca!*" I was surprised I'd been able to pull those words from some dusty chamber of my brain. The man looked up at me and, having taken his eyes off the trail momentarily, tripped and fell. If he walked any further he would break a leg. He stood only about five feet tall, a good nine inches shorter than me, and couldn't have weighed more than one hundred pounds. I resisted the urge to just pick him up, throw him over my shoulder, and carry him down the mountain.

Back up the trail, Brian was unsuccessfully trying to wrangle the cow toward home. Together we worked out a system. I stood behind the cow clapping my hands while Brian walked in front of her, guiding her back down the trail.

"Come on Bessie," I yelled. "Move your butt."

"Bessie?"

"Yeah, that's what my mom used to say to our car when it wouldn't start."

"Come on Bessie," shouted Brian. "Come on girl."

In stages, we inched the cow toward home, Brian tugging at the rope, me lightly patting the cow's behind and clapping.

"This is something that would never happen at home," I yelled to Brian.

He laughed. "No kidding!"

The old lady remained where we'd last seen her but now she was trapped in the fence, her bare foot caught on the barbed wire. It occurred to me how desperate the old couple must be to get their cow back. A cow was not always just a cow, I reasoned. A cow could be food and income. An entire livelihood could be tied up in a cow.

Brian handed the tether to me and set about freeing the woman from the fence. She didn't say a word, didn't cry out in pain, just stood there with a steely look on her face until her foot was released.

When she'd been freed, Brian and I stood like stumps and waited for instruction. Soon it came: we were to take the cow further down the trail to their *casa*, a one-room wooden shack with a dirt floor and a corrugated metal roof that we'd passed on the way up. In front of their door was a wooden post. Brian wrapped the tether around it tightly.

We looked at each other and grinned. It felt like redemption from last night's bad behavior. Somewhere in the universe a metaphysical scoreboard clicked over. Visitors: 1. Home Team: 1. Order had been restored.

The old man clapped Brian on the back and shook his hand. The old woman removed her hat, closed her eyes and prayed. Her lips moved soundlessly as she recited the words. Then she reached out with her gnarled hands and blessed us both.

We said our clunky good-byes to the couple, patted Bessie on the rear one last time and then left the way we came; clambering over sharp rocks and navigating sections of the trail so steep we had to slide down on our butts. It was impossible to imagine how the old couple ever made it into town, especially because they didn't have proper shoes or, as far as I could tell in the case of the woman, any footwear at all.

"See, we *can* work well together," said Brian, an admission that he, too, recognized the space between us. He poked me in the ribs lightheartedly, and I slapped his hand away. We walked in silence, and the weight of everything I wanted to talk about pressed into my chest. After a while, Brian spoke again. "The gash in that old woman's foot was nasty. I've been thinking, what if we used the yellow envelope money to buy that couple two pairs of shoes?"

My disappointment over our unspoken conversation momentarily vanished. I was pleased that Brian was taking the initiative. "I love it." At one point during our cow rescue I'd thought of giving yellow envelope money to the couple, but we hadn't packed more than a few dollars on our hike.

"We could just leave the shoes by the door. They don't even have to see us."

I really did love the idea. But inside of my head chirped all of the reasons why we shouldn't do it: We didn't know their shoe size. What if the gift offended them? Maybe they had a room full of shoes and our assumptions about them were wrong. Who were we to make assumptions anyway? *Don't overthink it*, I reminded myself.

There were a handful of shoe stores in town and we passed them all on the way back to La Bib, but we didn't go inside. The next day we didn't go either, or the day after that. As the days ticked by, neither Brian or I mentioned the old couple again. I kept hoping that Brian would take the initiative—it was his idea after all—and I waited for him to insist that we go buy the shoes and haul them up the mountain.

Though I wanted to give the old couple shoes, I'd convinced myself that the gift would be patronizing, much like I'd done with Agatha. I wanted Brian to have conviction, to convince me to get over my hesitations and do it anyway, but Brian didn't bring it up.

Every time we walked past a shoe store in Baños I felt a pit of disappointment in my chest. The yellow envelope wasn't changing me like I'd hoped it would. After all this time, I was still playing it safe.

⁓

It didn't take long for me to learn that the kids at La Bib didn't need me at all. In fact, they gave more to me than I gave them. They helped me learn Spanish. They showed me how to laugh and play more. They taught me to draw self-portraits with Banana Mania and Purple Pizzazz crayons and then, when my artwork turned out even worse than I imagined, they encouraged me to hang it on the wall and be proud of it anyway.

Plus, they'd gotten me to dance. Not on tables, but that was probably for the best.

On music-themed day at La Bib we were instructed to teach the children some popular Western dances. "You know, like the crap you'd dance to at weddings," explained Blake.

We chose the Hokey Pokey, the Macarena, the Electric Slide and some kind of dance where you put one hand behind your head, grasped the other around your ankle and jerked back and forth like you're performing the Heimlich maneuver on yourself.

I wasn't sure which dance I dreaded the most, probably the Macarena or the Electric Slide, for the jumping.

We sat the kids down on the bleachers in the theater. It was my job to teach the Electric Slide. I'd danced the Electric Slide at a few weddings, but never sober. Was it two steps to the left, two steps to the right, and shimmy?

Stephanie taught the Cotton-Eyed Joe and Louisa the Macarena. Alice opted for the Hokie Pokie, and I was envious of her choice. Brian and Carver secluded themselves in the media box and assigned themselves the task of playing the music. I tried to give Brian the evil eye but he wouldn't meet my gaze.

We started with the Macarena. Louisa demonstrated the moves. Right arm out, left arm out, right hand to left shoulder, left hand to right shoulder, right hand behind head, left hand behind head, shake your hips, hop! The children looked on skeptically. I could almost hear Carver and Brian laughing from the sound booth.

The children crowded the dance floor and Louisa stood in front to lead us. The music started and we all attempted to follow. Limbs were flying everywhere; some kids were jumping to the left and some to the right and others were just standing in place dumbfounded. We stopped the music and started again, slower this time, and the kids seemed to pick it up a bit. In fact, they were more proficient than me.

In turn, Alice, Stephanie, and I demonstrated our dances and then had the children repeat them. It was around the time that Stephanie led us all in a frenzied rendition of Cotton-Eyed Joe that the kids started to trickle toward the bleachers. Dancing did not hold their interest. I glanced at my watch. We'd only been dancing for a half hour, and the kids were already bored. We had to entertain them for another hour. Shit.

Since the kids weren't responding to our dance lessons we decided to lose the structure and have a dance *party* instead. We coaxed Brian and Carver out of the sound booth, and we put the iPod on shuffle and danced around on the theater floor. We looked like a pack of drunken monkeys. The kids eyed us wearily. We pulled them from the bleachers one by one and swung them around in spontaneous circles. We formed a conga line and then a tunnel with our arms and the kids danced through it, giggling and smiling.

When the conga line broke up everyone freestyled on the dance floor, and I snuck off to the side to watch. Carver crouched low, moved his hips side to side, and flapped his arms—bent at the elbows—in the most ridiculous chicken dance. Brian stiffly but enthusiastically shook his hips like a dashboard hula dancer. Louisa hopped backward and forward across an invisible line on the floor. They looked like they were all participating in a drug-addled rave, not completely sober adults trying to maintain the enthusiasm of a handful of Ecuadorian schoolchildren.

The whole scene was hilarious. As I stood there on the side of the dance floor watching it all unfold, a wave of unmatched joy washed over me. My friend Kelly once called that flash of jubilance a "*Laverne and Shirley* Moment," when you're suddenly overcome with the feeling of being where you always intended to go. I'd made my way to a tiny Andean town, and an even tinier nonprofit, to dance around with twenty children I could barely speak a word to. I never would have expected I'd wind up here. But I felt so very grateful that I had.

Later, over a beer at the local brewery with the other volunteers, I realized what the children were doing to me. They were disassembling all of the stones I'd stacked atop myself. They were removing the stone of my career, the stone of my hard-packed ideas of success, the stones of the path I followed obediently though it led me in the wrong direction. My relationship with Brain felt more precarious than it had ever been, but I could not deny that other parts of my life were blooming. The children were teaching me to let go.

⁓

Our backpacks were packed and stacked by the door waiting for Brian and me to heave them onto our shoulders. We were headed to the bus station where we'd hop a bus to Cuenca, an old colonial town in southern Ecuador.

But before we went we had one last thing to do. La Bib had just recently built and opened their theater, the one we'd so recently danced in, paid for by a number of donations from former volunteers and even directly out of the pockets of Jane and Blake. They were selling memorial bricks to offset the cost of construction and to improve the theater in the years to come.

My daydreams for Agatha had never materialized, and Brian

and I had been too shy and embarrassed to buy shoes for the old couple with the cow. We'd let our awkwardness impact the intention of Michele and Glenn's gift. But giving to La Bib was a no-brainer, no matter how uncomfortable it felt.

As we prepared to leave, I explained the yellow envelope gift to Blake and told him that I wanted the inscription of the brick we purchased to read *Michele and Glenn Crim, Portland, Oregon, USA.*

We hugged Alice and Carver, Louisa and Stephanie, and Jane and Blake.

"Thanks for your hard work," said Blake. "It meant a lot to us and the kids."

"It meant more to us," I responded. "Thanks for welcoming us here."

"And hey," Brian said, "we didn't even give blow jobs in the bar bathroom."

"Well aren't you a comedian?" said Blake, slapping Brian's backpack. "You two travel safe."

We said we would. I picked up my backpack and walked excitedly out to the street. The unknown held an appeal that the known no longer claimed. To the south, Peru beckoned.

PERU

CHAPTER 5

WE KEPT IN TOUCH WITH ALICE AND CARVER UPON leaving Baños, hopscotching south along the same general path, a well-worn backpacker's trail that knocked us around southern Ecuador.

Alice and Carver emailed to tell us about a great little oasis they'd stumbled upon in the popular surfing town of Mancora, in northern Peru. Normally a tourist hot spot, the beach was all but deserted in shoulder season. They'd rented a thatched-roof bungalow for twenty-three dollars a night. Would we like to join them? I wrote back and told them we'd meet them there.

But in order to reach them we'd need to tackle our first border crossing, and in the middle of the night no less, because we'd booked tickets on an overnight bus.

At the station I'd latched on to another traveling couple, identified right away by their long and unkempt hair, harem pants and backpacks with flag patches sewn onto the front. If the flags they displayed were representative of their travels, they'd visited almost every country in Central and South America. When I asked if they were taking the overnight bus into Peru they answered that they were. Their unbothered attitude calmed my fears a little bit. All morning I'd read online forums about crossing the border before determining that reading on the Internet about South American bus travel was as scary as trying to diagnose the source of a headache on WebMD, where a sinus cold could suddenly morph into an undiagnosed brain tumor. During my research, our little border crossing had degraded into a surefire way to get abducted by drug runners and held ransom until family back home were extorted out of their life savings. According to the Internet this happened *all the time*.

When I tried to express my fears to Brian, he'd blown them off with a flippant, "We'll be fine." So I clammed up and continued to scour the Internet, doubly stressed because I had to worry for us *both*.

Our travels around Ecuador had taught me that even on the higher-priced tourists buses there was never any guarantee of a working bathroom and, as we boarded our bus to Peru, I saw that it was no exception. A *sin servicio* sign was taped to the plastic door. I pointed at it. "We should donate all of the yellow envelope money to the bus company's bathroom maintenance fund," I said soberly.

Brian laughed. "Seriously though. You better be ready to hold it. It's a six-hour ride to the border."

I sighed in frustration and hoped that the three large beers I'd consumed the night before to dehydrate myself in preparation for the ride would do the trick. But despite my best efforts, by the time our bus stopped at the Peruvian border at 2:00 a.m., I was near tears with the urge to pee.

In the pitch-black humidity of a moonless night we deboarded the bus, picked up our backpacks, and formed a line in the immigration office. My fingers fidgeted with my passport, and I fought the feeling that I'd done something wrong, my knee-jerk reaction to any sort of attention from authority. The border guard unceremoniously stamped me out of Ecuador. I resisted the urge to scream "I've got drugs in my backpack!" to the Peruvian border official on the other side—though, of course, I didn't. He flipped through my mostly empty passport, scowled at me, and then slammed his stamp down on the page. The thrill of being allowed admittance into a new country made me momentarily forget about my need to pee.

When Brian had crossed over too, I told him I was going to find a toilet.

He nodded toward the glass doors at another busload of passengers filing in. "You don't have time," he said. "Half of the people on that bus are waiting for the bathroom." Outside, a long line had formed that wrapped around the building.

A bubble of panic rose inside of me. "There is *no way* I can go another four hours without peeing." The pitch of my voice climbed high with desperation, and a few of our fellow bus riders glanced up to see what was wrong.

"You don't have a choice. Our bus is leaving." He gestured outside where a single street lamp illuminated our waiting bus.

The last of the passengers were filing on. We were transferring buses, and Brian assured me there would be a bathroom on the new one. "And if there's not," he said, "you can always pee in your Nalgene bottle."

I flashed my ticket at the driver and stepped aboard. My eyes immediately shot to the back of the bus and I saw, with a great deal of relief, that there was a bathroom. Based on the people lined up in the aisle to use it and the pungent smell inside of the bus, this one worked.

We settled into our seats. Brian drifted off to sleep. While waiting for the line to dwindle I tried to fix my mind on anything other than my urge to go.

When the bathroom was finally free I held my breath and locked myself inside the stinking stall. The light didn't work, and in the dark I hovered above the toilet, trying desperately to maintain my balance as the bus jerked down the road. The release was otherworldly and a low moan of pleasure escaped my lips. But as my marathon-length pee came to an end the bus suddenly slammed to a halt. I toppled backward onto the toilet rim just as the overflowing septic pit splashed its contents down my legs, sopping the jeans bunched around my knees and running over my feet onto the floor. I froze and cursed myself for wearing flip-flops. "No, no, no, no, no," I cried. "Oh God, oh God, oh God." Frantic, my hand flailed around in the dark for the toilet paper but when I finally found it, the empty cardboard roll spun listlessly against my fingers. There was nothing I could do. I pulled my wet jeans up over my wet legs and slinked back to my seat.

I nudged Brian awake. "What happened to you?" he asked when he saw my face.

"I fell in the toilet," I said. "I'm soaked in other people's pee."

"God, that's disgusting. I'm sorry, baby." A delighted little smirk flashed across his face. Then he added, "Please don't touch me," and fell back asleep.

When we arrived at our bungalow three endless hours later my first stop was the shower. But when I turned the nozzle it was broken. Up until that point I'd surprised myself by handling the situation with what I thought of as phoenix-like resiliency. But the broken shower did me in. I lay down on the bathroom floor and cried. I didn't care about traveling anymore, or writing, or the yellow envelope. It was stupid to think that there was some grand purpose for my life. All I wanted was to close my eyes and wake up in my own bed, take a shower in my own bathroom and have an easy life again.

A few minutes later Brian stood above me. "Get up," he said. "I found a hose." Out on the barren lawn I stripped down to my underwear and twirled slowly like a dervish in the predawn twilight as Brian sprayed me down. He started laughing. "Spin!" he yelled. "Faster!" It *was* funny. I bent over at the waist and laughed the maniacal laugh of the sleep deprived.

We finally crawled into bed as the sun began to rise. A rosy light fell across our room. A swelling of love rose in my chest for him. We had our issues, but I felt grateful that he always seemed to pull me back from the ledge. He knew almost instinctually what I needed.

"The last twelve hours have been *terrible*," I whispered. "Right now I just want to go home."

"Oh, baby, I know you're *pissed*," he said, emphasizing *piss* with a playful grin, "but you'll feel better when you wake up."

⌐

I did feel better when I woke up, alone, in bed. By the bright light outside I guessed it early afternoon. When I stumbled out of our bungalow I found Brian, and Alice and Carver, leisurely swinging from hammocks. A salty breeze blew off of the ocean. "Hungry?" asked Carver. I nodded and rubbed the sleep out of my eyes.

The four of us walked into downtown Mancora, a dusty, gritty little street lined with bars and restaurants and thatched-roof stalls selling beach towels and sun hats. My stomach grumbled, and I counted the hours since my last meal—twenty—and realized that I was, in fact, starving. We walked past a burrito stand that smelled delicious. "What about here?" I suggested.

Carver looked at the menu. "Ten *soles* for a burrito? Are they *mad?*"

Eating meals with Carver was terrible. Back in Baños we'd walk and walk, circling the entire town, checking menu after menu while Carver declared each place too expensive. When we'd finally find a place with a cheap "*almuerzo*," an inexpensive set-lunch menu, I'd be unable to eat it because I was a vegetarian, and the *almuerzos* were always all meat. So we'd trudge on, endlessly, and by the time we finally agreed on a place I'd be grumpy and hungry and momentarily over life in general.

Things were pretty good when my biggest complaint in life was the annoying task of tracking down a meal, but I felt like I spent half my days trying to figure out where and what to eat. I desperately missed my refrigerator and the predictable peanut butter sandwiches I used to take to work each day for lunch.

Alice, Carver, and Brian were ahead of me when I stopped abruptly on the sidewalk. "You know what?" I called toward them. "I'm going to have a burrito. Why don't you guys find a cheap *almuerzo*, and I'll meet you back at the bungalow."

Carver nodded. "Brilliant idea!"

Alice mouthed the words *thank you*.

At the burrito stand I sat down alone in a plastic chair and ate my meal, staring out at the dark blue ocean. A gray layer of clouds hung low over the water, and a few beachcombers walked slowly along the shore. In the shop next door a TV blared the news in Spanish. As frustrating as it could be to not know the language, there were times that I appreciated my obliviousness. The chatter from the TV faded into the background, and I sat alone with my thoughts. The last time I'd spent more than fifteen minutes without Brian an arm's distance away was back at La Bib. My lungs expanded as I took a deep breath and closed my eyes. The sound of the waves rolling toward the shore and the beating of my own heart filled my ears. A tension that I hadn't known I'd carried loosened in my neck. It felt great to be alone.

During our time in Mancora I spent hours lounging in the hammocks that were strung between the bungalows, writing in my journal. For the first time in a decade I filled an entire notebook with my thoughts. Most of it was mundane scribbling, simple day-to-day recording of events, but I also reflected on my growing desire to be alone, scary as it was to see it there on paper. It felt so wonderful to make writing a daily part of my life again. Regardless of the problems that nagged, a cup had tipped over inside of me, and a steady feeling of rightness spread like water.

Our schedule was entirely open. Each morning when we woke I'd ask Brian if he wanted to stay in Mancora another night. Then I'd track down the owner of our bungalow and extend our reservation. Back in Portland, I'd once turned down the offer to join a book club because gatherings were held on unpredictable days of the week and I disliked not knowing in advance what day the next meeting would fall on. It wasn't just a type-A thing; I'd been a world-class control freak. Now, it shocked me to see how flexible I was becoming. As I watched my own actions from afar, I felt like a silent observer of a woman that, some days, barely resembled me.

One other couple stayed at the bungalows, and I tried on a few occasions to meet their eye, to find an opportunity to invite them to join us for dinner or to sit with us in the hammocks as we passed around quarts of beer. But they kept to themselves and seemed uninterested in socializing.

They appeared very much in love. Occasionally I'd spot them as they made their way to the beach or out to dinner in the evenings and they were always laughing and holding hands. And because their thin-walled, thatched roof bungalow stood spitting distance from our own, I knew that they had very loud and frequent sex at all hours of the day and night and always in the evenings as Brian and I lay side by side in bed trying to ignore the sounds wafting through the air.

This alone was the gray cloud that hung over me during our time in Mancora. Things between Brian and me were not right, and I knew it, but it had been easy to ignore with the everyday distraction of travel. Plus, the tension between Alice and Carver had grown so intense that I felt like Brian and I were a great couple in comparison. Their relationship was disintegrating right in front of us. Carver was a complainer who hid his complaints in jokes, a one-man comedy routine that I particularly enjoyed. I considered him funny. But Alice's tolerance had obviously withered. At the first sign of any topic that might degrade into a rant (politics, working in advertising, English Premier League soccer, or how you can't get anywhere in Australia unless you're a rugby fan) Alice would preemptively snap, "Oh, shut up about it Carver; no one wants to hear it."

Alice and Carver bickered over everything, while Brian and I grew apart in a quieter way. The truth was, things had not been right with us since before we left Portland. Deep inside I'd known it, but the not-rightness of my relationship was a small, nagging matter when compared to the pulsing, blaring truth of my desire to travel. So I'd thrown all of my energy at our trip.

The thing about telling one truth, though, is that it opens up space for the next truth to slide in. Now that my biggest truth had been born, the next one began chirping in my ear.

Maybe if we'd never left home I could have stayed busy with the everyday distractions of life and convinced myself that the troubles in our relationship were normal. But our twenty-four-hour together time illuminated the problems between us.

We'd been together since I was twenty-one years old and Brian twenty-two. We'd spent a decade growing up together. But how much could I grow with someone who still saw me as a twenty-one-year-old girl? Likewise, Brian often accused me of holding over his head dumb decisions he'd made when he was twenty-two or twenty-three. Neither of us gave the other room to change.

And there were other problems too, deep-seated cracks that'd been growing wider since we'd landed in Quito. Brian was loving and kind but reserved. He rarely shared his deepest emotions, never without prompting, and because he was so closed off, I didn't feel comfortable sharing mine. When we fought back in Portland this was what we fought about: his silence, and my desire for a deeper connection.

Another problem: since we'd left home we weren't having sex, at least not much of it, and that had become a contentious point in our relationship. The trouble was, I could feel the gaping distance between us and could not bring myself to have sex until we closed it. A good, long conversation would have done the trick, but that wasn't happening. Brian, on the other hand, pulled away emotionally because he could not express himself physically. And the more he pulled away the wider the chasm between us grew. We'd entered into a stalemate. The lovers fornicating in the bungalow next to us reminded me that, though we may have been doing better than Alice and Carver, we weren't anywhere near whole.

~

On our last night in Mancora, Alice, Carver, Brian, and I bought rum and Coke and pizza, and we sat under the thatched roof veranda outside of our bungalows. A full Peruvian moon hung in the sky.

Alice dropped a piece of pizza onto a paper plate and turned to me. "Hey, have you given any more yellow envelope donations since La Bib?" Back in Ecuador I'd explained the yellow envelope gift to Alice when she asked why we put Michele and Glenn's name on the donated brick. "Wow," she'd exclaimed, and looked genuinely touched by the story. "Those are some incredible friends you have."

My eyes fell on Alice, and I shook my head. My mouth was full of pizza and I let out a garbled "no."

Brian spoke up. "Not yet… It's actually harder than we thought it would be." He took a sip from his cup. "And to be honest, we kind of forget about it sometimes."

I swallowed my pizza. "Well, we don't really forget..." It was a white lie, and my cheeks flushed pink from the embarrassment of telling it.

Brian shook his head. "Yes we do. We forget."

I felt ashamed about forgetting. When Michele and Glenn had given us the yellow envelope I assumed it would be the light that guided our travels, elevating our experiences and helping us forge meaningful relationships with people we met along the way. But so far the yellow envelope was less like a beacon and more like a beautiful plant that I kept forgetting to water. Each time I saw it drooping in the corner a stab of guilt consumed me.

As the hours rolled by I got more than sufficiently dehydrated for our long bus ride the following day. We emptied our first bottle of rum and opened another one, and Carver began his slide from funnyman to belligerent rambler. The topic turned to religion. Carver ranted about God. In his opinion, God was a wacky figment that depressed and small-minded people turned to for solace from their meaningless lives. Personally, I was unsure of where I stood on the existence of God but thought Carver sounded ignorant in his complete certainty that it was all garbage.

Normally I lacked the confidence to debate big topics like religion. But our time on the road had given me courage, because stepping away from home had shown me that I could travel the world for the rest of my life and still not know it all. The rum gave me courage too. I didn't need to be an expert in order to speak up. My opinion was as valid as anyone else's.

"I hear what you're saying," I said to Carver. "But if it's all bullshit, and there's no God, no higher power, no ethereal energy or whatever you want to call it, then where does that leave the soul?"

"The soul," scoffed Carver, "is bullshit, just like the rest of it."

"I think you're wrong about that."

"Prove it," he demanded.

"Prove that the soul exists?"

"Yes."

I thought about the voice that rose up from inside of me during my run in Forest Park. I thought about the prodding I felt, day after day, to keep going in the direction that I was headed: to travel, to write, to be vulnerable enough to give the yellow envelope money, to find the truth with Brian. My soul had led me to that thatched veranda, to that full moon in Peru, to these new friends, to this very conversation, I was sure of it.

"I can't prove it," I said. "But I know it's real."

⁓

Flying would have been the reasonable option, but we had more time than money, so we settled in for a thirty-six-hour bus journey from Mancora to Puno, a dirt-colored town on the edge of Lake Titicaca. It was a lot of ass-in-seat time, but as long as there was a bathroom, long bus journeys were becoming enjoyable. I looked forward to the hours I'd spend staring idly out the window, pockets of time where the real world felt out of reach. On the bus, there were no museums to visit, hostels to find, or restaurants to track down—just open hours for my mind to wander.

The first leg of our journey would take us as far as Lima, eighteen hours down the road. Once there, we planned to stay for a few days and complete the final leg to Puno when we grew bored of the city. We treated ourselves to *cama* seats, which folded almost completely into a bed, on a posh two-story bus. We'd stayed in hostels that were not as nice. "Traveling in the lap of luxury," Brian declared as we settled into our seats.

The ride was so comfortable that I felt almost sad when our bus arrived in Lima the next morning. I pulled the velvet curtain from the window and looked out onto the city streets. Lima was a massive urban center, and I did not feel up for dealing with it. All I wanted was to pull a blanket up to my chin and stay in my little bus oasis.

"Brian look," I said, as our bus drove by a crowded street corner where a man crouched, a black briefcase unfolded in front of him. Inside it, a selection of brass knuckles and handguns were on display.

Brian gave a low whistle. "That is crazy."

The curtain on the window fell closed. I just did not have the energy to face a gigantic city, especially one where men sold weapons openly on the street.

"Do you really want to stay in Lima?" I asked Brian.

He shrugged. "I don't care. It's up to you."

A pulse of anger throbbed from my center. "Can't you make a decision for once?" I just wanted someone to tell me what to do.

"Well if we don't stay here, what will we do?"

I sighed. "I don't know? Catch the next bus to Puno?"

"Okay," said Brian, "let's do that."

Our bus pulled into the station, and we disembarked and fetched our bags, then piled them in the bus station food court. I plopped down on top of them while Brian wandered off to find out about booking tickets to Puno.

"Good news," he said when he returned. "Our bus leaves in half an hour."

"Half an hour? Shit."

"That's what you wanted, right?"

"Yes, but, aren't you hungry?" I gestured toward the food stalls. "And I want to stretch my legs for a while."

Brian groaned. "Jesus, I can't do anything right."

"Oh, don't act like a victim," I hissed. "You should have used common sense."

Brian only did what I'd asked of him. I was acting irrationally and being mean. But my fuse felt like it'd been halved, and the prospect of immediately boarding a bus for another eighteen hours sent me over the edge.

As I stood, I slung my backpack on and marched out to our bus terminal, expecting to see a rig similar to what we'd just disembarked from. But the bus parked in front of me was no high-end tourist bus. This bus looked like someone had plucked it from a junkyard, slapped some bright blue paint on it, and towed it to its current location. I glared at Brian, shoved my backpack in the storage compartment near the wheel well, and climbed aboard.

Inside, the seats were stained and the fabric ripped, exposing their battered plastic frames. Large TV consoles dropped from the ceiling above every third seat, a loud car-chase movie already blaring. We were the only tourists. I squinted down at our tickets for our assigned seat numbers and then at the rows as we passed them. My heart sank as I realized that our seats were in the very last row, on a long plastic bench right next to the toilet.

Brian looked at me guiltily. "I got the last tickets." He paused before adding, "At least the bathroom works."

A lump rose in my throat as I wedged myself into a space that even a three-year-old would feel uncomfortable in. A short Peruvian man sat next to me knee-to-knee. He had a colorful alpaca wool hat on his head. "*¡Hola!*" he said. "Where you from?"

"*¡Hola!*" called Brian. "The USA."

Over the next four hours we cobbled together our stories. The man played the flute in a traditional Peruvian band. We told him about our lives as best we could, practicing our Spanish and miming the rest. My frustration at having the worst seats on the bus dimmed in the presence of our new good-natured friend. When our bus slammed into a pothole or whipped around a blind curve he would grin, his brown eyes bopping around in their sockets, and yell, *¡Aventuras!* During our time in Peru and Ecuador I'd been impressed by the general grittiness of the people we encountered. If my neighbor could grin and bear this long bus ride, I could too. I felt a sudden kinship with everyone onboard. We were all trapped for a maddening amount of hours on a dilapidated, overcrowded bus. And that was okay, because we were getting where we needed to go.

The yellow envelope money crossed my mind again. It'd be fun to treat the entire bus to lunch, assuming we ever stopped to take a break. Back in Mancora, Brian and I had stocked the envelope with *soles*, the Peruvian currency, and it lay at the bottom of the silly lockable purse I kept at my feet along with my computer, passport and a few other valuables. For a moment I ruminated on the idea but then dismissed it completely. If we were traveling in the United States, I'd do it, I told myself, but it was too weird to make a big, unexpected gesture like that in a foreign country. We didn't speak the language, and, more importantly, we didn't understand the cultural norms around giving. In the United States, people would probably be open and accepting to a free surprise lunch by a random do-gooder. It might even make the news or go viral on social media. But in Peru? I had no idea. What if the people on the bus misunderstood the gesture? What if I offended someone? My hesitation was a complete and utter failure of rule number one, but how could I not overthink it?

When we did finally stop to refuel, there was no place to eat lunch anyway. Instead, everyone on the bus disembarked, pulled toothbrushes from their pockets, and brushed their teeth communally in a gigantic outdoor trough. Between spits, our bus neighbor looked up and waved at us. I elbowed Brian in the ribs and pointed out the toothbrush trough. "I wish we would have known; I'd have kept my toothbrush in my purse."

With clean teeth and bags of snacks everyone boarded the bus once again. Brian reached into the plastic bag he'd placed on the floor between his ankles and pulled out a plastic soda bottle, its contents the ungodly yellow-green color of antifreeze.

"What *is* that?"

"It's called Inca Kola." He turned the label toward me. "Everyone bought it so it must be good!" He screwed off the lid, sniffed, and took a sip. "Oh, God." He pushed the bottle my way. "Try it."

"I don't know…"

"Try it. Tell me what you think."

I put the bottle to my lips, took a small swig and choked on the sweetness. "Bubble gum." I handed it back to him and drank water from my Nalgene to wash away the taste. "Wow, that's…intense."

As I scanned the bus I noticed half of everyone on board drank Inca Kola. A man four rows ahead of me tipped his bottle skyward and drained it. Then he lowered his window and chucked the empty bottle out. An audible gasp escaped my lips. My flute-playing neighbor turned to me and smiled. "*¿Todo bien?*" he asked.

In the front of the bus, others were finishing their drinks and snacks, balling the packaging up, and throwing it all out the windows. A moan escaped my lips. Brian glanced at me. "It's not our culture."

"I know, but… Oh, God." A woman released the entire contents of a plastic shopping bag and it bounced onto the side of the highway. I buried my forehead into my arm, shielding my eyes. "I can't watch." Then I glanced at my bus neighbor to see what he thought of the littering. He stared out the window with a blank face and did not react at all as another bag of garbage went soaring.

The sun set, and our bus shot down curvy mountain roads in the darkness. Our driver did not enjoy braking, and I gripped Brian's hand as our bus careened around hairpin turns at full speed. The moon, nearly full, illuminated the drop-off just inches beyond the edge of the road. Certainly we would die. Brian put in his headphones and tried to ignore it. Our flute-playing friend, unconcerned with our mortality, slept on my shoulder.

Eventually I must have fallen asleep too because my eyes opened again as we pulled into Puno, miraculously still alive. I stood and stretched my legs, waiting impatiently as the passengers at the front of the bus slowly unloaded. Next to me, Brian looked out of place holding his plastic bag of garbage. Our neighbor looked toward us and said good-bye, then dug around in his knapsack and handed Brian a copy of his CD.

"*Gracias*," said Brian, pulling some *soles* from his back pocket and offering them to the man.

"No!" he proclaimed. "To you, from me!" He gave the smallest of bows and a wide smile stretched across his face to reveal his tiny white teeth.

Brian began to protest, but I put my hand on his arm to stop him. We needed to accept the flute player's gift the way I hoped others would accept our yellow envelope gifts, without posturing, with an open heart. "*Gracias*," I said.

Brian shoved the money back into his pocket and smiled. "*Gracias, amigo.*"

We stepped from the bus into the unknown streets of Puno.

CHAPTER 6

PUNO, PERU, WAS A HONKING, POLLUTED CITY PACKED INTO a cramped valley. The rebar of half-constructed buildings reached like bony fingers toward the hazy sky, and houses the color of mud sat pancaked between the mountains and Lake Titicaca, the highest navigable lake in the world.

Through our hostel we booked a tour that included an overnight homestay on Amantani Island, one of the remote islands that dotted the famous lake. We were picked up by a young woman wearing kitten heels and cherry-red lipstick and driven to a boat dock. It was a clear morning and cool. The boats knocked together in the harbor. "Wait here," she said.

She stepped off the dock and into a boat tethered to land with a frayed rope. She disappeared inside the cabin, then emerged a few minutes later and stepped onto the next boat, repeating the process. She climbed from boat to boat like they were slats on a suspension bridge.

"Do you think she's looking for a place for us on one of the boats?" I asked Brian. "I thought we booked a real tour."

Brian shrugged his shoulders. "What I want to know is, how is she doing that in *heels?*"

Finally, the woman waved her arms from the deck of a rickety old houseboat. We scrambled over the other boats to reach it and climbed aboard. Inside, a group of fifteen tourists were sitting in awkward silence. Brian and I squished between them.

A man that looked like a fox, all squinty eyed with a pinched nose and chin, boarded the boat and introduced himself as our guide. He told us that we could call him Herman. He wore a faded leather jacket and one hell of a scowl.

"There are life jackets under your seats," he said. "And you may sit on top of the boat, but, please, no more than ten at a time." Then Herman's short lecture ended and we pulled out of the harbor toward the great blue horizon.

From atop the boat I watched tall torta reeds blow in unison with the wind like hairs on the head of an underwater creature. As we puttered away from Puno, I looked back at the dry brown mountains rising up from behind the city. Away from the chaos of the littered streets, Puno looked picturesque. It was a beauty that took space to see.

We endured a choppy, four-hour ride to Amantani Island. Brian and I sunned ourselves on the deck like sea lions and took in the beauty and isolation of the lake. At 12,500 feet elevation, it felt like we were floating in the sky. Jagged silhouettes of the surrounding mountains ringed the lake, and clouds were projected on the water in perfect reflection.

Amantani Island came into view, a small six-mile-wide blip of land in the great span of lake. Terraced hillsides rose up from the shore, and fluffy white alpacas dotted the slopes above the water. Beyond the boat dock a splattering of bright-roofed houses greeted us.

We stepped onto shore, and a group of Amantani Island women crowded around us like day traders. Herman doled us out, pointing grim-faced at each of us and then snapping his wrist at our assigned hostess like he was shooing away flies. Brian and I were assigned to Veronica, a ruddy middle-aged woman with a streak of dark hair and pensive brown eyes. Clearly she did not want us, larger groups were more profitable, but Herman had dealt the cards. So she turned and gave us a broad grin anyway and pushed aside whatever disappointment she felt from our too-small party of two.

We introduced ourselves in broken Spanish, and Veronica smiled and waved us forward. Then she turned on her heel and marched up the hill toward her home.

She ducked through a tangerine door, and we followed her into a courtyard. Behind her stood a small adobe house with a patched tin roof framed by flowering pink trees.

"Welcome," Veronica said to us, gesturing toward her home.

A man emerged from an arched doorway. Two little girls were giggling behind his legs. "*Soy Diego*," he said, introducing himself. He squatted down and pulled the girls in front of him.

They kicked at each other playfully but would not meet my eye. Diego nudged them and they both raised their heads, their dark eyes dancing, and whispered their names. Then they screeched in glee and bolted back into the house.

Veronica rolled her eyes in mock exasperation—*kids these days*—and then showed us to our room. Inside it, two twin beds were pushed against opposite corners, each stacked high with woolen blankets. Veronica hugged herself and mimed a shiver. Between the beds stood a single wooden table and two candles. Veronica pointed to the candles and then toward the ceiling. "*No luz*," she said.

We dropped our backpacks on the beds and followed Veronica into the kitchen where she ordered us to sit and eat. She served a simple meal of quinoa soup, potatoes, and an unidentifiable but tasty root vegetable with cheese that she cooked over a rudimentary stove. Brian and I ate around the table with Diego and the girls.

We'd been traveling through South America for two months, and our Spanish was better than it had once been, but we still labored through our lunchtime conversation. Spanish was not Diego's first language either, as the native language on Amantani Island was Quecha, so we conducted the majority of our communication with hand gestures. Diego told us that eight hundred families lived on the island and that the men grew food by hand and the women cooked it. His girls kicked in their chairs next to him and eyed us mischievously. What did they think of us, strange foreigners that showed up in their lives for two days and then disappeared forever? Did our presence make them curious about the world beyond their island?

When we were done with our meals Diego walked us to the town square to meet Herman and the rest of our group. There were two mountains on Amantani Island, Pachatata and Pachamama, Mother and Father Earth. And there were ancient Incan ruins on top of both. Diego pointed at the trail that led to the peak of Pachatata and then waved his arm toward Herman to indicate that we would climb the mountain with him.

We wound our way toward the sky. The vertical trail, combined with the altitude, had me panting. A man rode by on his horse and shouted, "Taxi," then laughed and galloped away. Alongside the trail, women sold handicrafts, and weathered old men offered soda, snacks, and single cigarettes for purchase. Children, too young to have such a job, hocked colorful bracelets made of thread.

The people of Amantani Island subsisted almost exclusively on the food and materials they reaped from the island. It was a system of community collectivism, and they shared the burdens and bounty. Yet tourism had quickly become an important part of life for families in the village. If the children of Amantani hoped to receive more than a grade school education, their parents had to send them away to the mainland. The school, board, food, and supplies were more than most of the families could afford. But tourism brought the *soles*, and the *soles* paid for school. So the people of Amantani sold what they could to the tourists.

The view from atop the mountain was spectacular, and the

sky glowed a crushing shade of blue. Over the water, a full moon rose in the evening sky.

On the climb up I'd grabbed four small stones and stuffed them in my pockets. Now I pulled them out and bounced them in my hand. Island tradition stated that if you circled the ruins atop Pachatata four times and left four stones as an offering, Father Earth would grant you what you wished for.

As I walked around the top of the mountain, I laid the stones down and whispered the same wish I'd prayed for in bed at night, wide-eyed and terrified before we left Portland: to discover what it was that I was out here looking for.

From a bench of loose rocks, I watched the moon rise over the water. In the foreground my eyes followed Brian as he made his own circumnavigation of the mountain peak, each time squatting down to leave a stone. What did he wish for as he placed his stones on the ground? Lately I'd been so short with him, so cold, wrapped up in my own internal ping-pong match, grappling with a gut-level prodding that questioned our relationship. But from this distance my heart ached for him. He was mine, the one thing that rooted me on this circuitous trip around the world.

The sun had set when we arrived back at the town square. Veronica's girls were waiting for us on the church stairs. They stood when they saw us and guided us back to the house as the last wisps of twilight drained from the horizon. As we wound through the narrow streets toward their home the littlest one slipped her hand in mine. Charmed, I glanced over at Brian but his eyes were fixed on the bleeding sky.

I turned my attention back to the island. Silence had wrapped her arms around the evening. Had the cards been different it could have been me to grow up on an isolated island protected from the rest of the world by miles and miles of water. Who would I have become if that had been my fate? And who was I now because it wasn't?

Over dinner we talked in choppy Spanish with Diego. A candle flickered on the table between us. The light from the candle cast shadows on Diego's face and carved deep caverns of darkness beneath his eyes. He could not have been much older than Brian or me. I wondered what Diego wished for when he lay down stones for Pachatata, and I wanted to ask him if he was happy, but I knew that the weight of the question would be lost in translation. Maybe it was a luxury to worry about being happy. I looked around at the dark kitchen, the low fire burning in the hearth, and the food in my bowl grown by Diego himself. Maybe Diego never questioned the purpose of his life because he was too busy going about living it.

⌒

The residents of the island were throwing a party for the visitors. After dinner, Veronica brought us traditional clothes to wear to the event. We dressed in the outfits—a big red skirt and white top with hand-stitched flowers for me and a gray poncho trimmed in rainbow colors for Brian—and set off to the party. We navigated through the village by moonlight, the girls silently leading the way on a dirt path beaten into the earth between stone fences.

We entered a large room with harsh florescent lighting. At the back of the room some locals hocked beer and Coca-Cola at exorbitant prices while a band with a big drum and flutes played with enthusiasm. As Diego twirled me across the concrete floor of the only building on the island with lights burning, I could not keep the grin off of my face.

On our walk back to Veronica's house a few hours later we followed the girls as they led the way once again. By the light of the moon we hiked through a field, over a rock wall, and past the occasional stray horse. The moon hung full and brilliant, and our footsteps barely rustled the grass. Exhaustion overcame me, heavy as a winter coat, and for a moment I envied the girls and the solid comfort they must have felt at returning home to crawl into a familiar bed.

Back in our room, I burrowed into my single bed and pulled the heavy blankets up around me. Outside, the world was silent and still. A slit of moonlight fell through the window and illuminated a patch of concrete floor. When I closed my eyes I thought about how beautiful the birth of the evening had been up on Pachatata Mountain. In the darkness, I remembered Brian walking contemplatively around the mountaintop, laying stones, wishing for whatever it was he wished for.

My heart suddenly ached to bridge the gap between us. I longed to crawl into bed beside him and run the warmth of my body against the warmth of his. I wanted everything to be like it had been back before we'd closed some door between us. "Brian?" I whispered, "Brian, are you awake?"

The darkness was so sure of itself, so uncompromising. The moon so steady in its glowing. I waited for his voice to fill the space between us. But in the bed across the room I heard him gently snoring.

⌣

In the softness of morning, we sat in Veronica's small kitchen. She served us a single pancake with jam and a hot mug of coffee. Then Brian and I returned to our room and packed our bags.

From my place on the bed I turned to Brian. "I think we should give Veronica and her family some yellow envelope money."

Brian finished folding his clothes into his bag and nodded. "I've been thinking the same thing."

"How much should we give her?" I asked.

Brian said, "Everything in the envelope. We'll refill it when we get back to Puno."

From inside of my backpack I pulled out the yellow envelope and removed all of the bills. Then I found my wallet and did the same. There were no ATMs on Amantani Island, so we were carrying a larger sum than usual. I counted out what I thought we'd need for our ride back to the mainland and put the rest in a pile for Veronica.

My uneasiness over giving money kicked in again. Veronica had already been paid for hosting us through our tour company, so she wasn't expecting us to give her money. I hated that I didn't have the ability to communicate the gift. If I'd been able to explain about Michele and Glenn, the yellow envelope and the three rules, then I would have been excited to give the money to Veronica. But as it stood I worried that, taken out of context, the money might offend her. I did not want Veronica to interpret the gift as a handout or as some kind of judgment on her life.

"Will you give it to Veronica?" I nudged the pile of money toward Brian. "I just feel so weird about it."

Brian picked up the money and shoved it into his pocket. "Let's try not to worry about what Veronica will think. We're supposed to do what feels good. This feels right, doesn't it?"

"Yeah, it does."

Out in the courtyard we thanked Veronica and Diego profusely. Their two sweet girls emerged sleepy-eyed from the house, and we got down on our knees to say our good-byes. Then Brian shyly passed Veronica the yellow envelope money. We did not know how much it cost to send the girls to school on the mainland, but we hoped that the money we were giving covered a good portion of a year.

Veronica glanced at the money, surprised, and then grabbed Brian in an enormous hug. "We're rich!" she yelled, or she may have said, "You're rich!" Her words were hard to interpret amidst the excitement. I glanced at Veronica's family and then at Brian who stood still buried in Veronica's burly hug and figured she was right either way.

I embarrassed myself by bursting into tears at the scene, though I wasn't sure why I cried. Perhaps it was the pride I felt in giving Veronica the money or my frustration at the language gap that left me unable to properly explain who it was truly from. It could have been the inequity of it all, how a relatively small amount of money could mean so much to Veronica and her family, yet Brian and I used to regularly blow that kind of money on a night out in Portland.

Or maybe I cried because, as I watched Brian give the money to Veronica, I saw a flash of vulnerability that I hadn't seen from him in a long while. We were learning to bear ourselves for the sake of the yellow envelope, but we were not allowing ourselves to open to each other in the same way.

Veronica walked us down to the dock. We took a seat on a stone wall and waited for our departure back to the mainland.

Down by the water a crowd of men had gathered and Herman, as grim-faced as ever, stood in the middle of the commotion. We wandered over to a couple also waiting for the boat. "What's going on?" I asked.

The woman shook her head, disgusted. "Herman has not paid the families our boarding fees. He's been arguing with that group of men for the past half hour."

"You mean the families haven't been paid? At all?"

The woman shook her head.

Amantani Island had no crime and, therefore, no police, but a group of the island's respected men were called upon when needed to oversee conflicts. When prodded by these men, Herman had refused to pay the families or produce his tourism card. Calls to Herman's company on the mainland had gone unanswered.

One hour turned to two as we waited for the corrupt company

to pay up. The women of the homestays had been sitting nearby since the beginning, and I got the sense that it wasn't the first time they had to fight for what they were owed. Some of the people on our boat approached and paid them directly, but others were not so lucky. My eyes locked with Veronica's and she smiled at me. At least we knew that the yellow envelope money had not left her empty-handed.

Eventually the island police agreed they could not hold us forever, so they sent us on our way with the boat captain. But though we were permitted to go back to Puno, Herman was not. They would keep him on the island until the families were compensated. We cheered as our boat pulled away from the dock without him. As far as I know he could still be there today.

CHAPTER 7

A WEEK LATER BRIAN AND I WERE STUCK IN AREQUIPA, AN
old colonial city in southern Peru. I hated Arequipa for its
nonexistent sidewalks and aggressive drivers, for the trash in its
gutters and the sternness of the people we encountered. Plus, I
still felt angry about how Herman's company had swindled us
and Veronica and the other families. The experience had tainted
my feelings, perhaps unfairly, about the entirety of Peru.

Normally if we disliked a place we'd just pack up and move
on, but we'd booked flights out of Arequipa, and it did not make
sense to leave. There were things to do in the surrounding area,
but I just could not rally the enthusiasm.

My mental health shifted 180 degrees from our days in
Mancora. I was miserable and homesick and lonely and tired,
but I couldn't communicate my internal struggle to Brian because
I couldn't make sense of it. From the comfort of our home in
Portland, this trip had felt like a higher calling. Then, when
Michele and Glenn gave us the yellow envelope, I'd been certain

of it. But I didn't feel guided by the hand of destiny now. Instead, I felt lost and guilty for dragging Brian out into the world and then being so unhappy once we'd arrived. We were doing exactly what I wanted to do, and I had no idea why I was so miserable doing it. What the hell was wrong with me?

I was desperate for time alone. We'd booked the cheapest room in the cheapest hostel we could find, a windowless space crammed into the awkward area beneath the stairs, and I dreamed of lying by myself in that sunless room listening to the footfalls of the other guests as they climbed up and down the staircase.

One morning I awoke to Brian, already fully dressed, stuffing his things into a day pack.

"What are you doing?" I asked him.

"I'm going out so you can enjoy the day to yourself. Read a book. Get some writing done. Do whatever you want. I'll be back by dinnertime."

The afternoon before I'd asked for that exact thing when I'd accused him of suffocating me. "I know you can spend every minute together," I'd yelled at him. "But I need time apart! What is wrong with you that you don't ever want to be alone?"

But now *I* didn't want to be alone. I sat up in bed. "Don't go," I whimpered. "Stay here."

A look of exasperation spread on his face, but he didn't have the energy to argue with me. He grabbed his bag and walked toward the door. "I'm going out. I'll be back later."

With the day to myself I decided to go up to the rooftop where hostel staff served a breakfast of bread and butter every morning. In the distance, the tin roofs of other houses glinted sunlight and a conical snowcapped volcano poked the sky.

I sat down alone at a table for two. Beside me a large group of backpackers were eating breakfast together. As I poured coffee I eavesdropped on their conversation, a recap of the night they'd just spent at a bar drinking pisco sours and dancing.

One of them looked at me, a giant man-boy with smooth, tanned skin the color of gold. He had a black T-shirt on that revealed the contours of his long, defined arms. His hands were huge, his fingernails the size of postage stamps. He caught me watching him and smiled a devious half-grin.

I smiled back. It was a thrill to think that he assumed I was alone. He probably thought me mysterious. A woman, alone, in Peru. Without thinking, I dropped my left hand into my lap so that he could not see my wedding ring and then felt instantaneously guilty for the betrayal.

My eyes fell on the group of backpackers again and a feeling of longing swept through me. I'd missed out on the experience of traveling solo. In another life, maybe I'd be at the table with them, discussing last night's vagary and flirting with the boy with the catcher's mitt hands.

But it wasn't another life. I was married. Guilt punched the pit of my stomach for even thinking like that. Slowly, I forced myself to place my left hand back up on the table in clear view. Then I pried my eyes from their table and opened my journal to start a list of everything I missed about home: pizza delivery, napkins, regular exercise, good coffee, baking in my own kitchen, Mexican food and margaritas, reliable Wi-Fi, tap water, and craft beer. I tapped my pen on the page and stared up at the cloudless sky.

It was more than just missing the conveniences of home that contributed to my foul mood in Arequipa. Turning back to my journal, I sketched it out.

The first thing was obvious. I needed time alone, even if I fought it when Brian offered. In the half hour I'd spent by myself, writing on the rooftop, the dark cloud of despair was already blowing over. Why did I fight the things that I knew deep down I needed?

Secondly, exercise had to be a priority, even though it was no longer just as simple as walking out of the front door and going for a run anymore. Since arriving in Arequipa I'd tried once to go running but had received so many hoots and hollers from passing cars that I'd given up and slinked back to our hostel. But my mental health depended on exercise so I had to find a way to get it daily.

Also, I was lonely. It was important to try to make friends with other travelers so that I wouldn't rely on Brian for all of my social needs and then resent him when he couldn't meet them. I desperately missed my friends and family, so I'd need to start doing a better job of connecting with them, of sending emails and setting up times to Skype. Since I'd been keeping a blog, everyone back home knew what we were up to, but I didn't know a thing about their lives. Our communication was an isolated and lonely one-way street.

And, finally, this other thing loomed six weeks in the future, a thing that was causing me all kinds of stress. I'd been trying to ignore it, but that only made the stress worse. Back before we'd even left Oregon I'd agreed, against my better judgment, to participate in an event called the Rickshaw Run with two other women I'd never met before. They were both newly nomadic, as Brian and I were, and we'd connected online months before while we were individually building up the courage to leave our old lives behind. During that time one of them, an Irish woman named Lesley, proposed the Rickshaw Run, emailing me, and another woman, Sarah, a brochure that explained the event:

> The Rickshaw Run is pretty simple. With no preparation and even less luggage, you fly to the Indian subcontinent and do your darnedest to force 150 cc of glorified lawn-mower over thousands of miles of questionable terrain. All this in around two weeks with no support at all. Fools gather from all the corners of the earth to partake in one of three Rickshaw Runs that thunder through India each year.
>
> The un-route is a wonderful concept which ensures you are free to get into trouble anywhere on the subcontinent. We give you a beginning and an end roughly 5,000 km apart but whatever goes on in the middle is entirely up to you. The Himalayas, dirt tracks, tropical jungle, monsoons, massive deserts and many other wondrous things await. Each Rickshaw Run is kicked off and finished with a massive party and ceremony.

It sounded crazy, and it terrified me, yet for reasons that still eluded me I'd been unable to turn down the adventure. Lesley and Sarah were seasoned travelers; they'd both been to India many times before, so I reasoned that if they thought we could drive a motorized rickshaw three thousand miles without getting killed, we probably could, even though the event website displayed a dire warning:

These are genuinely dangerous things to do. You cannot overestimate the risks involved in taking part in these adventures. Your chances of being seriously injured or dying as a result of taking part are high. Individuals who have taken part in the past have been permanently disfigured, seriously disabled, or lost their life. You really are putting both your health and life at risk.

On one of our many bus trips around Ecuador, we'd met a man named Bob. Bob came from India but had lived in Detroit for forty years. When I told him about the Rickshaw Run, a look of genuine terror had flashed in his eyes. "You can't understand what it is like over there. I don't even drive when I visit. It's crazy! You are risking your life!" He'd called his wife over and told her the story. She reached out and grabbed my hand. "Please," she'd pleaded. "Don't do it. You will die." At the time I'd laughed light-heartedly and said, "I'll be careful." But my subconscious kept shouting her warning: *You'll die. You'll die. You'll die.*

Shutting my journal, I glanced over at the cute backpacker, but his attention was back with his friends. Standing, I tucked my chair beneath the table and returned to our dark little room, feeling lighter after completing my list. For the rest of the day I'd pamper myself, I decided, by painting my toenails, shaping my eyebrows and trimming my hair. My eyes fell on a small mosaic mirror that hung above our bed. I removed it from the wall and sat down cross-legged on the floor with my tweezers.

Holding the mirror in front of me, I started to tackle my eyebrows but became distracted by the sight of my double chin. Recently in the shower I'd noticed the translucent pink scars of new stretch marks on my hips, the result of my downtick in running and uptick in French fry consumption. With a mix of concern and fascination, I stripped naked and propped the mirror up on the floor. It'd been months since I'd seen the reflection of my own body. In the mirror my stomach bulged, newly pudgy, and the muscles in my legs looked less defined. Twisting my body, I pinched my butt and stared at the cellulite on the back of my thighs. Free from mirrors, I hadn't noticed the changes in my body. As I climbed back into my clothes and returned the mirror to the wall, I vowed not to do that ever again.

In late afternoon Brian found me in the common area of the hostel cleaning out my backpack, purging myself of all of the things I brought on the trip but didn't need: malaria medicine, extra clothes, and my stupid pickpocket-proof purse. We'd spent a lot of money and bought a lot of stuff without realizing that we could buy whatever we needed wherever we were. It hadn't occurred to me beforehand that the entire world had shopping centers.

Over dinner we discussed the hours we'd spent apart, though I left out my solo fantasies and my time with the tweezers and the mirror. It was nice to have something to talk about. Back before we quit our jobs, recapping our days over after-work drinks was something I always looked forward to. I missed the ritual of sharing those stories. It dawned on me that I never had a chance to miss Brian anymore. But today I'd missed him. The hours apart had been good for us.

"Did you give away any yellow envelope money?" I asked.

"Um, I don't know. I tipped a street performer a lot more than I usually would. Does that count?"

"It only counts if you *intended* for it to count. Did you?"

"No, not really. I just liked his shtick."

"Then no."

We fell into silence, and I looked out through the restaurant window. The moon, just a sliver, rose on the horizon.

The moon on Amantani Island came back to me, and I realized that I'd never asked Brian about the wish he'd made. "Hey," I said, reaching my hand toward his. "What did you wish for on top of the mountain when we were on Amantani? From Pachatata?"

Brian smiled but his eyes looked far away in thought. "Do you really want to know?" he asked, cocking his head toward me.

I squeezed his palm. "Of course I want to know."

He pulled his hand away and set it in his lap. Then he fixed his gaze on me. It felt like the first time I'd seen him in many days. "I wished for happiness," he said. "I wished for us to always be happy together."

It was an odd thing to wish for, out of all the wishes in the world. I gave him a smile but felt a pit of guilt in my stomach thinking of the way I'd hidden my hand earlier to conceal my wedding ring. Perhaps he already had an idea of what would happen next.

GERMANY

CHAPTER 8

As our train glided toward the airport, I stared out the window at the charcoal gray of a sunless afternoon. Young couples walked on the sidewalk holding gloved hands, and parents strolled shoulder to shoulder in winter coats, their children running ahead of them. I looked around the compartment of our train at the other travelers. Many were carrying shopping bags filled with gifts, off to the warmth of their own holiday celebrations.

Brian sat across from me, his head tilted against the window. His breath made hazy puffs of fog on the cold pane of glass. He'd been distant all day, claiming jet lag, but I knew the truth was that we weren't quite sure how we should be acting toward each other anymore.

That morning in the soft hue of dawn I'd burrowed under our pile of blankets and curled my arm around the warmth of his waist, timing the rise and fall of my breath with his. "Merry Christmas," I'd whispered into the solid space between his shoulder blades. He'd entwined his fingers in mine and squeezed my hand. He didn't chide me for finally offering up the one thing he'd been asking for. He just whispered back, "Merry Christmas."

Two weeks earlier, Brian and I had been in Buenos Aires to catch our flight to India via this three-day layover in Germany. It was December; summertime in the southern hemisphere, and Christmas decorations lined the sidewalks in festive seasonal displays. The holiday decor contrasted the intense summer heat in a way that made me feel like I couldn't get a grip on my own existence. It was Christmas. It was summer. My connection to life back home felt more drifting and unreliable than it had ever been.

One evening we left our rented apartment to take a walk. Buenos Aires crackled with energy. The sidewalk cafes were packed with groups of friends sipping after-work drinks and young families eating dinner around candlelit tables. Brian grabbed my hand and squeezed it, and we walked with the weight of his warm palm in mine. The last few months I'd been silently battling a growing desire to be on my own, but in that moment I just wanted to be happy with Brian.

We strolled slowly down the sidewalk. Hand in hand, but with an unbridgeable distance between us. My head screamed: *You are not happy! This is not working!* But my heart couldn't bring me to say it. I knew Brian wouldn't say it because he never did.

Dropping his hand, I turned to him, and the words tumbled out of me in a landslide, one word triggering the next. "Brian, I can't have a nice evening with you and just pretend that every-thing is okay when we both know it's not. Are you really okay with this? Are you really okay walking down the street holding hands pretending like we are just a normal, happy couple?"

Since leaving Peru six weeks earlier, our crumbling had been rapid and painful. We were both homesick and lonely and needy, but we were also frequently moved by our experiences together, and that made us patch over the holes in our relationship. But I could no longer pretend that the holes weren't there.

The internal deliberation over what I wanted was exhausting. I couldn't keep ignoring the question that had begun to beat louder and louder in my chest. *What if I were alone? Who would I be on my own?* Traveling and writing were not enough. I needed to know the answer to this too.

Brian let out a deep sigh and stopped walking. He looked drained of emotion and color. "What makes you think that I'm okay with this?" he asked. "Of course I'm not okay. But can't we just have one night where we aren't walking the goddamned tightrope in our relationship? We're in Buenos Aires, and it is a beautiful evening. Can't we just enjoy ourselves?"

He so rarely raised his voice at me, and I stared at him, shocked. Sometimes when I felt lonely or upset I'd push him until he did finally yell, feeling satisfied to get a reaction out of him. But I hated being yelled at. I looked down at my hands and started to cry.

I knew how utterly un-understandable I was. My unhappiness made me feel like a monster, and I hated myself for that. But I also hated Brian for his silence, for allowing me to treat him in a way that I hated myself for. Each time he allowed me to steamroll on without even a peep about how dysfunctional we'd become I'd add another slash to the tally of my resentments. I wanted him to blow the whistle on the whole mess even though I didn't have the courage to do it myself.

"Don't yell at me," I said.

"I wasn't yelling."

"*Yes, you were!*" I was yelling now.

Brian looked backed into a corner. He put his hands up like I'd pulled a gun. "Listen, I'm sorry. If I yelled at you, I'm sorry."

It was another thing I resented him for: overapologizing.

"You're not sorry," I snarled. "You're just saying that to shut me up. You're taking the easy way out."

Over the past few months I'd thrown that accusation at him dozens of times as I lashed out in my unhappiness. *Here we go again*, I thought, and I readied myself for another fight.

Brian put his hands up to his head. He looked as though he wanted to disappear. He took a deep breath. When I was upset it elevated to crying and screaming. When Brian was upset he grew quieter and calmer, his anger simmering into a vicious boil.

"I can't do this anymore," he said calmly.

"What?"

"I can't. I can't do it anymore. I'm tired of having the same argument over and over again, Kim. We had these problems in Portland. We had them in Ecuador, in Peru, in every goddamned country we've been in. We can't get away from them. Nothing ever changes. I'm miserable. You're miserable." He took a deep breath and raised his head to meet my eye. "You make impossible demands on me without acknowledging how far I've come. I've done everything you've asked me to do. I quit my job and left my entire life behind to come traveling with you. I'm not perfect, but I'm improving. I'm *trying* Kim. I've tried so damn hard."

The anger drained from my chest as I stared hard at him. What he said was true. He had tried hard. Upon my request back in Portland, Brian had begun to see a therapist to address some of the issues that had kept him so inaccessible. For a while we'd done better. And yet, he wasn't the only one in our relationship that needed guidance. I was no perfect partner. But I was too stubborn to admit it, and Brian, for whatever reason, did not mention it either. His indifference hurt me.

Whatever progress we'd made back in Portland had been erased on the road. Adjusting to the tilt-a-whirl reality of constant togetherness had caused us to retreat into the confines of our own heads again. Brian once again enveloped himself in silence, and I felt lonelier than I had ever been.

"I love you, Kim, but I'm not sure I can be the person you want me to be. I'm not sure *anyone* can be the person you want me to be."

Brian gestured to a park across the street sprinkled with wrought iron benches and began walking toward one. The muscles in the back of his neck tensed as he walked. I loved his neck, his back, his shoulders. Was I about to lose him? A sudden rush of affection flooded me as it always did when I thought about life without him.

Crumpling onto the park bench, I folded my knees up to my

chest. The evening had turned dark, but I slid the sunglasses over my eyes, hopeful that they'd hide my tears.

"Kim, I've done everything you've asked of me. I've opened up to you and supported you through this gigantic change in our lives that you initiated. When you've asked for alone time I've given it to you, and I've tried to take control by starting conversations and asking directions and buying bus tickets and booking rooms in hostels for us. I gave Veronica the yellow envelope money because you didn't want to. Do you know how uncomfortable that made me? It's not easy for me, but I do those things because I know it's important to you that I do them. And yet at the same time you can't give me the one thing I ask for. You won't even try. Do you know how it feels to me, how much it hurts, that you won't even cave to my one request? Trust me, I know it's hard because it's hard for me too. But you make me feel like the smallest person on the planet when you ignore the one thing I ask you to work on."

He was right. Throughout the ups and downs of the past few months he'd had only one request, and I hadn't even attempted to meet it. Brian communicated physically, with hugs and kisses and snuggling and sex. Even back home, he'd only ever asked that I give of myself in the same way. He wanted me to kiss him in the kitchen and snuggle with him on the couch, to reach for his hand sometimes when we walked down the street. But I hadn't even tried. And since we'd left home I'd grown even colder, shrugging off his advances. I sat on my high horse issuing demands while building a fence around my vulnerability.

There was a reason, but it wasn't one that I could tell Brian because I could barely admit it to myself. *I was not sure that I wanted to be married anymore.* And in some warped corner of my mind I'd convinced myself that if I gave Brian what he needed without first being certain that I'd stay in the relationship that I would be leading him on. How could I make him happy and then leave? I told myself that if I kept him miserable, my departure—if it came— would be met with some relief. I didn't want to admit it to myself or to him, but that's what I had been doing the entire trip.

The harder he tried to love me, the more terrified I felt. He was in a situation that he could not win. Yet I still pushed him to give more, to communicate better, to be sweeter or more romantic, to take charge or back off in various and unpredictable circumstances that I decided on a whim. And all the while I knew that he could have morphed into anything, into anyone. He could have met every single one of my demands, and it still would not have been enough. I had convinced him that he was lacking because I'd been too selfish and too terrified to admit that, in fact, it was *me* who was not whole. That was the crux of this whole damn thing. I was not whole. And I did not know if I could become a whole person while sharing my life with Brian.

Yet the yellow envelope had shown me that, though giving could be uncomfortable, it came with its own rewards. If I could learn to be vulnerable to strangers for the sake of Michele and Glenn's gift couldn't I also give of myself to my husband in the same way? Couldn't I at least *try*? Didn't he deserve it more than anyone else?

That evening I'd emailed Wendy and explained what had happened in the park. She'd responded in five short sentences:

Everything changed for me when I realized that the only person I could control was myself. I can't control what people do, only how I respond to what people do. You have the same choice. What would happen if, the next time Brian asked for love, you gave it to him?

Her words set off a panic inside of me. What would happen if I allowed myself to love Brian the way he deserved to be loved? It was too scary to think about. I charged on, ignoring Wendy's advice.

The quaint villages of the German countryside sped by as our train raced down the line. Decorated trees held vigil in the town squares and clock towers glowed in festive white lights. "It looks just like you'd imagine in fairy tales," I told my sister over the phone the evening before when I called home on Christmas Eve. "It's a storybook." Christmas in Germany, with the candles burning in the medieval windows and the holiday wreaths gracing the doors, was Hollywood perfect, and I seemed to be hollow by contrast. The emptiness inside of me had spread like spilled oil, leaving a stain of darkness in its wake.

My attention wandered back toward the window, and I

thought of my family across the ocean in Ohio. They were probably gathered in the living room of my parent's house playing board games as a football game blared on the TV. I could almost smell the spread of food on the kitchen table and see my sisters sitting cross-legged on the carpet, plates of appetizers stacked in their laps. I imagined the presents wrapped under the Christmas tree. Back in Peru, Brian and I had mailed home Christmas gifts of alpaca blankets and handwoven hats, and I wondered if they'd opened the packages yet. More than anything I just wanted to be home.

When I stole a glimpse at Brian, he appeared to be deep in thought, his head cocked toward the speeding landscape outside. I knew he missed home as much as I did, yet instead of sharing our sorrow, we'd wrapped ourselves in our individual sadness.

But we'd planned a Skype call with Brian's family from the airport. The thought of the phone call lifted me, and I knew how much Brian looked forward to it. We needed to cast our nets toward home, to catch the familiar and drag it to these distant shores to buoy us for awhile. We needed a reprieve from our sinking.

Three nights back, on our last night in South America, we'd been perched like caged birds on opposite sides of the bed in a sad little standoff. But unlike most nights, that night we hadn't argued. What we'd come to was closer to resignation.

Our arguments, at least, were born of emotion: of hurt, of love, of desperation. But that night we'd waved the white flag of surrender, too exhausted and injured to continue the war. I'd finally told Brian the truth: I didn't know if I wanted to be married anymore. He hadn't even seemed surprised. Instead, I'd recognized a look of relief in his eyes. We'd agreed: There were too many knots in our marriage to untangle. The mess felt simply too big.

Later, as Brian lay breathing the ragged rhythm of the unconscious, I'd slipped out of bed and in the darkness fumbled for my shoes. As I unplugged my laptop and tucked it under my arm, Brian had not stirred. When I closed the door softly behind me, it clicked into place, and the tiny sound was magnified by the utter silence of my surroundings.

On the rooftop patio of our rental apartment I found a weak but steady Wi-Fi signal and sat down at a forgotten rusted table. The clock on my laptop read twenty minutes past two in the morning. Around me the air hung sticky but cool, and above me the black Argentinian sky was pricked with a map of stars. A full yellow moon hung low in the sky. The landscape held a heightened sense of beauty in the way things do during times of raw heartache. The pulse of the earth felt magnified. And I felt both electrifyingly alive and unable to bear the pain of my aliveness.

My eyes burned from crying. I squeezed them shut against the glow of my laptop and counted time zones in my head. It was 2:30 a.m. but only 9:30 p.m. in Portland. I pictured Brian and myself in a rewound home video running backward up the continent toward home and slipping in reverse through our old front door. Portland existed five hours in the past, where we had not yet said the words we said or made the decisions or cried the tears.

As I pulled up my email I scrunched my eyes closed again. Wendy should be home. "Please be there, please be there, please be there," I whispered into the night. I typed *You there?* into the subject line. In the body of the email I wrote: *Can't sleep and really need to talk*. I hit send. I could hardly breathe.

Four years earlier I'd met Wendy at work. She called me one day and introduced herself, her words clacking through the phone at double speed. Then she appeared at my desk, a slim, beautiful girl about my age with a face full of freckles and brown hair that hung down her back. She stuck out her hand, and when I extended mine she pumped it with gusto. "Hi, I'm Wendy. Nice place you've got down here next to the copy machine," she said with a grin. She stuck her head into my cube and saw the shoes tucked beneath my desk. "Are you a runner?" Right away I could tell she was a force of nature. She possessed the sort of intensity that normally caused my introverted soul to turn and run. But we hit it off, bonded by a shared love of running and a mutual disdain for the thumping bureaucracy of government work.

In the years since we met we'd run thousands of miles together, hashing through the details of our lives. She helped me talk through my discontentment long before I'd found the courage to admit my life needed changing. And then, when I saw what had to be done, she cheered me along as Brian and I went about the slow and emotional task of disassembling our lives.

She was the only one who knew I felt that maybe, because Brian and I had come together at such a young age, that I had missed out on something. Not the wild years of dating and promiscuous sex, but something deeper and simpler: an opportunity to become myself.

Wendy knew that I wasn't sure if I'd chosen Brian or if I'd just gotten swept up in life with him. Did I even truly love him? How could I be sure if I had no control group with which to measure my feelings? I trusted Wendy to listen without judgment. She let me say things without being held to them, to try statements on for size. "I love him so much," I'd say, just moments after questioning if, perhaps, I did not know what love was at all. She acted as my sounding board as I talked through my confusion in order to determine what felt false and what felt true.

Wendy possessed a kind of laser truthfulness that didn't allow me to lie. She asked me direct questions I didn't want to answer. She was tenacious. She wouldn't let me hide from myself.

Standing, I pushed my chair back from the table and walked to the edge of the rooftop. Below me the streets were silent and vacant, the streetlamps illuminating nothing but the bugs that batted against them in the humid nighttime air.

Maybe *this* is what it feels like to be alone, I thought, and my throat squeezed with the uncomfortable truth of my desire. I'd lived thirty-one years without knowing what it was like to be alone. And now an essential part of me demanded the freedom and space to define myself.

I needed to find out what I would do if the slate of my life were wiped clean.

From across the rooftop I squinted at my computer. An email had arrived in my inbox.

I'm here. Isn't it the middle of the night?

Quickly, I shut my email and pulled up a chat box and typed:

It's almost 3 a.m.

Wendy wrote back:

What's going on?

We had a talk. It might be over this time. We're so exhausted. We've been dealing with this for months. I'm tired of going around in circles. We can't come to any conclusions. I don't feel happy. He doesn't feel happy. At this point it just seems easier to walk away.

My fingers rested above the letters that would spell out the biggest thing of all.

I told him the truth. I told him I don't know if I want to be married anymore. We've agreed to take some time apart.

My finger clicked the enter key, and the message flew across countries to Wendy. Three little dots scrolled across the chat box. Wendy was typing. They disappeared and then emerged again. I imagined her at home on her couch trying to come up with the right thing to say. Finally, words popped up on the screen.

Oh Kim, what a hard thing to come to. I'm so sorry. I know
you've been struggling with this for a long time. It's a hard
decision to make.

My fingers sat numb on the keyboard and tears welled
in my eyes again. Alone, I nodded into the empty night. The
second rule of the yellow envelope popped into my head: *Share
your experiences.* Finally, I'd done that, and now everything I'd
ever known was crumbling around me. The pain felt physical,
a living, breathing entity that had locked its arms around me,
squeezing.

What do I do? I typed. *I just want to come home.* Wendy's
clarity was more critical to me than the oxygen circulating in my
own blood.

There was a long pause as the circles danced across the screen.

I think the first thing I can tell you is that making the decision to separate is only the first step. Brian is your best
friend. He's someone you've had next to you for the last...
how long?

10 years.

10 years. That's a long time to have someone by your side.
Ending your relationship carries the loss of the possibility
of your future together, the pain of the past, and perhaps
the fear of being alone.

But I wasn't afraid of being alone. Was I? It was something I knew so little about that I didn't have the experience to fear it.

My first advice is to take a minute and either with Brian or by yourself truly identify those reasons that you two are no longer made for each other. Identify tangible reasons you do not want to be with him. You will need those when you miss him. Then think about what, where, and who you want to be in the future. Make sure you know these things so that when you feel weak you can brace yourself with the hope of the future and the happiness that lies ahead. Going back to these things in breakups has always helped me. And as for what to do next, how do you feel? What seems right?

I typed, simply, *Nothing seems right.*

If you really want to come home because you want the strength of those that know you and can support you, then that might be the best option. But maybe you need to just run free for a month. Catch your flight to India, take the rickshaw ride with those girls and see where it puts you. You can always come home at any point. The worst-case scenario if you stay is that you are a complete wreck and end up bailing half way through to come home. But the worst-case scenario if you come home is regretting leaving. Do you have more things to talk to Brian about? Is going home just an escape from the hard work that needs to happen? I think you should come home if you really want to, but I'm not sure that's the right choice.

As I read her words slowly, I imagined her voice saying them to me. Deep down, going home felt like running away, avoiding the problem I had to continue to face. But the relief of it was hard to pass up. It'd be so easy to just step on a plane and lock myself in Wendy's spare bedroom until I could face the light again.

Yeah. I just don't know. It's so hard to tell what I want. I'm just so tired. Everything feels so impossibly hopeless. I want so badly to be by myself, but at the same time I can't imagine life without Brian.

What about just taking a few weeks away from each other to get some perspective? Try being alone. This rickshaw race seems like the perfect opportunity to have some time apart.

And then she typed the thing that nagged me deep down, the thing that I needed above all else but could not see a way to have without leaving my husband.

When was the last time you did anything on your own?

My brain flipped through the pages of my memory but I

could not remember. I did not know if I'd ever done anything on my own. And how could I be a whole person, how could I be a wife, an adult, a full, actualized woman, if I had never done anything alone?

My fingers began typing, but then I erased it, I started again and then erased that too. The screen glowed at me expectantly, waiting for an answer. The whole world seemed to hold its breath.

I wrote:

I've never done anything alone. And I think I will never be content until I do.

The black dots, the waiting.

Then do this thing alone and see how you feel at the end of it.

My eyes processed the words on the screen. She was right. It was not necessary to give up completely. I could take time to do something on my own. Brian could take time alone too. We needed space to see our relationship with clarity, to see if it was worth fighting for, and to gather our strength for whatever lay ahead. I typed:

You're right. Thank you.

Wendy wrote back:

Hey, I'm due for a vacation. No matter what happens, how about I come to India for a visit when you're done with your rickshaw ride? We can go on an adventure, just the two of us.

I need that more than you can imagine. And I'm going to hold you to it.

Raising my face from the light of the computer screen, I looked toward the blackness of the sky. The stars were dead, yet the brilliance of what they had been still gave light. Could something be dead and living at the same time?

Thank you, I typed to Wendy. *I love you.*

You too, she wrote. *Miss you tons.*

As I began to shut the laptop I saw the dots crawling across the screen. Wendy was typing again.

Kim, one more thing: don't think that this time apart from Brian will be anything like your life without Brian. Being alone physically is very different than being alone in your heart. Remember that.

~

"What time is it?" I asked Brian after we'd dropped our heavy backpacks onto the conveyer belt. He glanced at his wrist and told me the time. We'd arrived at the airport hours earlier than necessary to ensure we'd find a quiet place to call Brian's family. But we were also there because we didn't have anywhere else to go. A traveler knows that the airport is always open, even on Christmas Day.

After my talk with Wendy, I'd sat Brian down and asked him if, before making any big decisions, we could take some time apart. Since we'd be separating anyway during the Rickshaw Run we'd agreed to let that physical space serve a much greater purpose. We would take those weeks to ourselves, without feeling greedy or guilty about it, to think through what we truly wanted.

It wasn't clear to me if I just needed a bit of space or if I would discover that I needed to leave the marriage completely. Could I come into my own in the confines of a relationship? I needed to find out. And I needed to give myself permission to come to any decision that was real and true.

⌣

We settled into a hard plastic row of seats by the duty-free shops, and Brian pulled out the computer. Passengers rolled their luggage behind them down the hollow corridors. Despite the holiday decorations and the carols streaming out of the duty-free shops, the collective mood at the airport was somber. No one wanted to be there. The dividedness among us was palpable. Our bodies were in the cavernous terminals. Our hearts were somewhere else.

Brian still fiddled with the computer and I leaned over to look at the screen. "Are you having a problem with the Internet?" We'd done our research and knew that the Frankfurt airport had free Wi-Fi. But there was a pop-up on the screen. "What's that say?"

"It says that I need to fill out a form and then they'll text me the access code to log-on."

"Oh, no," I said. We'd been traveling without a phone, relying on email and Skype to communicate with friends and family. We could not receive a text message.

Brian headed off to the information desk to fix the issue and came back minutes later exasperated. "There's nothing the information desk can do. If we don't have a phone we can't receive the text message, and if we can't receive the text message we can't get online. End of story."

"Can the person at the desk use his phone to get our text message?"

"When I asked he refused. He didn't seem too happy to be stuck working on Christmas."

I sighed. "Well, let's walk around. We might be able to find a café or restaurant that has Wi-Fi."

We took off down the terminal, ducking into every darkly lit airport bar and bright coffee shop that we came across. But everyone told us the same thing. The whole airport connected to the same system, the one that we were unable to access.

Exhausted and annoyed, we resigned ourselves to the fact that we weren't going to get to talk to Brian's family after all.

"I'm sorry," I told him. "When we get to India you can send them an email and let them know what happened."

Brian nodded his head. "I know," he said, and his voice held so much sadness that it made me want to cry. "I was just really looking forward to it."

"I know you were." I felt cracked and helpless and so stupidly far away from home. I wanted to reach out and fix everything: me, us, and that dumb Wi-Fi system. A restaurant sat a few paces away and I pointed to it. "Let's go in there, drink a beer, and forget that it's Christmas."

Our waiter, a man in his early-thirties with wire-rimmed glasses and a nest of blond hair, came up to our table smiling. "Merry Christmas," he said in English, and the little touch of familiarity made me tear up again.

"Merry Christmas," we said, and forced smiles on our faces.

"Are you heading home?" he asked us. "If your flight leaves soon you can make it back to America before the day is over."

My eyes dropped to the table and I shook my head. "No, we're missing Christmas this year. We've been trying to call home from the airport but we can't log-on to the Wi-Fi." I paused. "Is there any way of getting past it? Maybe an Internet café or a coffee shop somewhere in the airport that has Internet of their own?"

"Ah, I'm sorry, there's not," he said in his thick German accent. I nodded unsurprised.

Our waiter left, and I glanced across the table at Brian. "I guess it just wasn't meant to be."

"There were a lot of things I expected about traveling," said Brian quietly. "But homesickness wasn't one of them. I can't believe how hard it is to be away sometimes, especially on days like today."

We were always the outsiders, the foreigners, struggling to grasp the language and the tiny nuances of each culture we found ourselves in. Even on easy days, traveling could be isolating. Now, not even the one solid thing we had, each other, was certain anymore. I gave him a sad smile. "I know."

Our waiter returned a few minutes later with our beers, gigantic steins brimming with a heavy lager. He set them down in front of us.

"You know what?" he said as he stooped to mop up the beer that had sloshed from our glasses. "I should have thought of this before. I'm not going to use my free minutes today. You can use my password code to call your family." He pulled his cell phone out of his pocket and scrolled through the screen, reading his access code to us.

"Are you sure you don't need it?" asked Brian.

"Oh, no, I don't need it today," he said and winked at us. "Merry Christmas."

Across the table my mother-in-law's voice came through the speaker, and Brian's face instantly lifted. From the sound of it, the Christmas gathering at my in-laws' house was in full swing. The distant bustle of their holiday party spilled out into the foreign airport, and my heart swelled with the sounds of home.

After taking a sip of beer, I scooted my chair around the table next to Brian. Our nieces and nephews ran laps around the Christmas tree, and aunts and uncles stood in the kitchen eating cookies and talking with each other. They looked up and waved as Brian's sister walked the screen by them. "Hi Brian and Kim," they called toward the computer. "Merry Christmas."

We talked until our time ran out, and then we were swept through the whole scene again to say our good-byes.

"I love you, sweetie," Brian's mom said through the screen.

"I love you too, mom," Brian replied, his voice cracking just a little.

"Merry Christmas and stay safe. Take care of each other."

Brian glanced up at me. He didn't even try to hide the pain. "We will mom, we miss you. Merry Christmas."

Afterward we sat in silence for a minute, sipping our beers.

"I really needed that," Brian said eventually.

When I looked up at him, his eyes were weary. "I know you did. I did too."

Our waiter approached, and we thanked him. "It means a lot to us that we could make that call," I told him.

He smiled. "It's no problem at all. It is hard being away from family on Christmas."

When we settled the bill, I pulled out the yellow envelope money and left an enormous tip. Brian and I didn't discuss it; I just tucked the money in the checkbook and told him what I'd done. For once I didn't overthink it, didn't worry about how it might be received. Instead, as I set the yellow envelope gift down on the table, I said a silent thank you. The kind waiter had given us something that we needed more than anything: a little piece of home. It is the small kindnesses, so ripe and available yet so rarely exchanged, that turn ordinary interactions into miracles.

An hour later I handed my ticket to the man at the gate before boarding the plane that would take us to India. He flipped through my passport to find my VISA.

"When was your first time in India?" he asked.

"I've never been."

He slapped my passport shut and looked up with a mischievous twinkle in his eye. "Enjoy your stay."

Other travelers had warned us that India either cracks you open or kicks you aside. To survive India one had to embrace it for what it was: an incredible, beautiful, hideous cauldron of humanity as stripped and exposed as a skinned deer. If we tried to control our experiences in India, if we tried to make sense of the chaos, we'd hate it. In order to love it we'd have to accept it just as it is.

In five days Brian and I were diverging. I'd climb into a rickshaw with two women I'd never met before to drive the length of India on some of the world's deadliest roads. Brian would board a southbound train to God knows where. We'd agreed to meet up after the rickshaw race, hopeful that the distance between us would give us the clarity we needed to make sense of our relationship. And yet we had no guarantee that the other person would be there at the end of the Rickshaw Run. We'd given each other the freedom to do whatever needed to be done. Brian might decide to get on a plane home tomorrow, so might I.

Many hours later, we touched down in a wholly different world. India was a country that would shock and transform us, though we didn't know that yet.

INDIA

CHAPTER 9

BRIAN AND I TOUCHED DOWN AT THE INDIRA GANDHI International Airport and caught a taxi to the Delhi Train station. I stared out the window as we drove through the streets, surprised by the relatively light traffic and lack of chaos. We'd been so intimidated by India that, upon landing, we'd sat in the corner of the airport for hours, delaying our departure until the last minute possible. We'd heard stories of travelers being swarmed and harassed and scammed by touts the second they walked outside, but when we finally left the airport, Delhi felt no different than any other major city.

At the train station there were people everywhere, standing in crowds, sleeping in rows against the station walls, and hanging out of the windows of the trains as they arrived and departed. Everything smelled of urine and body odor and spices. We'd reserved two sleeper bunks on an overnight train to Jaisalmer, an ancient fort town southwest of Delhi, where the Rickshaw Run would begin. We wandered through the mass of people until we found our platform and took a seat on a metal bench to wait for our train.

Shoving my backpack between my knees, I watched as a man dressed like he'd stepped off the set of *That '70s Show* hosed down the train tracks. He used the force of the water to push garbage from one side of the tracks to the other. Another man stood across from him and did the same thing. It was like watching a strange version of air hockey. The garbage passed back and forth between them, for what purpose I did not know.

Brian nudged me. "Kim, check it out." Out of the corner of my eye I saw that at least two-dozen young Indian men had gathered around us in a semi-circle. When I looked up at them they jumped back in unison like they'd touched an electric fence.

I turned to Brian. "What the hell?"

"It's like we're animals in a zoo."

"Say something to them," I whispered.

Brian turned to the group and gave them a wide smile, exposing his teeth from beneath his bushy red beard. "Hello."

The men erupted in laughter and wiggled their heads.

Brian looked back at me and raised his eyebrows. His eyes were so wide they looked cartoonish. "They're just *watching* us," he said through clenched teeth.

"Let's just act natural and pretend they're not here," I offered. Pulling my Kindle from my backpack, I began reading, trying to ignore the forty-eight eyeballs that watched my every move.

A few minutes later our train pulled into the station. "*Finally*," Brian said, letting out a hiss of air. "I don't think I've ever gotten so much attention in my life."

Slapping the leather cover of my Kindle shut, I ignored our audience, picked up my backpack, and followed Brian as he pushed his way onto the train.

We found our assigned sleeper bunks, and I crawled into the bottom one and drew the curtain. It was dirty—everything in India seemed to have a film of dust on it—but I pulled out my sleep sack and made myself comfortable. Almost immediately Brian began snoring above me. I tried to let the knocking of the train lull me to sleep, but my mind wouldn't calm. A flutter rose in my chest. *We were in India.*

In my little bunk I laid in silence listening to the cockroaches scuttle across the floor and reading long into the night, leaving only to go to the bathroom to relieve myself through a hole in the bottom of the train, a process that for some reason delighted me. In my journal I marked our arrival. *So, I've made it to India,* I wrote, but then scratched out the sentence to revise it. *We've made it to India. It is us, together, who have made it here.*

Many hours later our train stopped in the ancient desert city of Jaisalmer. Weary-eyed from the long journey, strung-out yet wide-awake, we stepped onto the train platform. Scanning the crowd, I spotted two bohemian women amidst the sea of brown faces and recognized them as my Rickshaw Run teammates. I waved my arms above my head, and a look of recognition illuminated them.

"Hi, honey," Lesley said in a charming Irish accent when I approached. "Nice to meet you in person, finally."

"Nice to meet you too."

Sarah smiled and leaned in to hug me. "Well, here we are," she proclaimed, dropping her hands to her sides. "I suppose we best get on with it."

Brian and I decided that he would stay in Jaisalmer until my departure on the Rickshaw Run. I craved my freedom and wished he would go, but I also clung to him and wanted him to stay. Existing in this emotional in-between was torture for both of us.

I felt massively guilty about sending Brian into India alone. There were certain things that he did not seem capable of doing on his own, and traveling India solo was one of them. But it had been his choice. He could have flown back to the states for a visit. He could have asked someone to join him abroad. He could have done anything he wanted, but he had decided to travel India on his own. He'd made his own plans, and I tried to let that fact absolve me of my guilt.

Lesley, Sarah, and I spent the days leading up to the Rickshaw Run test-driving the rick, and we discovered quite quickly that we were in trouble. For one thing, our rickshaw was prone to breakdowns. During our test-driving sessions we'd be puttering right along and then, inexplicably, our rick would sputter and die. Brian, who was very handy mechanically, tinkered around under the hood. Other rickshaw runners took a look too. But no one could figure out the cause of the breakdowns.

The other thing was, Indians drove on the left-hand side of the road. Lesley was Irish and Sarah Australian, two left-driving countries, but I drove on the right. Though I adapted to left-hand driving quickly, when encountering roundabouts, which seemed to be everywhere in lieu of stoplights, I'd panic over the manic merging—it felt like swan diving into a tank of hungry sharks— and inevitably enter the wrong way, straight into oncoming traffic. To my surprise, no one on the road seemed to think it out of the ordinary, but my teammates would scream, "WRONG WAY! WRONG WAY!" from the backseat of our crappy little coffin on wheels.

The eve of the Rickshaw Run was also the eve of the new year. Brian and I and my Rickshaw Run teammates gathered at the Jaisalmer Palace for the kickoff party. At midnight, the pulsing lights and blaring music suddenly cut out, and the grounds of the palace were engulfed in darkness. From the field behind us fireworks began to explode. Lesley clinked the green glass of her beer bottle to mine. "To our first full year of freedom," she said.

Brian leaned over and kissed me. "I love you," he whispered.

Pulling my head back I squeezed his hand. "I love you too." Right then and there I decided that my New Year's resolution would be to *live* the first rule of the yellow envelope: don't overthink it. As Michele had suggested in her letter, I would listen to my soul and allow myself to be guided by the things that made me come alive. I sat back in my chair and watched the colorful blasts illuminate the sky, and I allowed myself to be happy without wondering what might come next. Many hours later when we walked back to our hotel under a pinprick of stars, I felt on the very verge of something big and true.

The following morning, the first day of 2013, seventy pimped-out rickshaws pulled away from the starting line at the Jaisalmer Palace and into the city streets, blasting music and honking horns. Looking up at the smoggy sky I said a little prayer. *Please, don't let us die.* Then I thought of all of the painful stages between *alive* and *dead* and revised my prayer. *Please, no accidents and no injuries.* I took a deep breath. *And if at all possible, no breakdowns either.*

The processional of rickshaws slowly began to putter out of the driveway. From the edge of the road, Brian waved good-bye and I waved back, wiping away tears. "Be careful!" I yelled toward him. "I love you!" But my words were swallowed up by the street noise. Because the Rickshaw Run had been her idea, Lesley earned the honor of driving first. She steered the rick through Jaisalmer and onto the dusty desert streets. According to Sarah's GPS, the finish line in the state of Kerala was one thousand five hundred miles to the south. It twinkled in the distance, a massive goal we weren't quite sure we'd reach.

In the daylight the sandy landscape of northern India lacked vibrancy, yet the street life exploded with it. Purple-turban-wearing men, their lips curled toward the sky and their beards reaching for the road, sold spicy samosas and bright, beaded textiles. Women walked down the street in saris the color of candy.

The earth refused them color, but they refused the earth its dull-ness. India was a land of paradox, just like everything in my life.

The dirt from the desert swirled through the open sides of our rickshaw and settled on our bodies. I wrapped a red scarf emblazoned with a Hindi mantra around my face. Brian had given it to me as I'd packed up my bag that morning. He'd draped it around my neck and then leaned back to give me a sad smile. "For good luck," he'd said. "And to keep you safe."

As I stared out of the windowless rickshaw, I thought about my departure from Brian. When we'd pulled away he'd looked both heartbroken and brave, like a warrior headed for a battle that he did not want to fight. I'd just left him completely and utterly alone in *India*. It was necessary, I knew, but I also knew how fragile and raw we both felt. I had an adventure and two new friends to distract me, but Brian had nobody. When I pulled away in the rickshaw I'd effectively abandoned him during a time of deep emotional turmoil. *Do not feel guilty*, a voice inside of me demanded. *Do not overthink it. Let things unfold as they will.*

"Uh-oh," Lesley said from the front seat, quickly jerking the rick to the side of the road where it sputtered and died.

"Not already," I groaned.

We climbed out of the rickshaw onto an empty road that cut a straight line through the Thar Desert. Away on the horizon goats grazed at a few scrawny, tangled bushes but there were no other people around.

"Maybe we're out of petrol?" suggested Sarah. She leaned back into the rickshaw and retrieved a funnel and a jerrican of gasoline, two of the many items we'd loaded into the rick before departure. She filled the tank, and Lesley turned the ignition, but the rickshaw didn't respond.

"Shit," I said, and kicked the ground. A billow of dust and dirt rose toward my head.

Raising my hand to shield my eyes, I squinted up the highway. Two rickshaws were approaching in a cloud of dust. Stepping into the road I waved my arms above my head. A blue and green rickshaw slid to a stop in front of us, and two young guys dressed in jeans and T-shirts jumped out. I recognized them as another Rickshaw Run team from the kickoff party.

The driver strolled up to us and untied a bandana from his face. "Are you guys all right?" he asked. "Having problems with your rickshaw?"

Lesley nodded. "It was driving fine, and then it just died. We've filled up the petrol tank, but it still won't start."

"It could be you've got a clogged fuel line. I'll check," he said, and popped the back hatch of the rickshaw to investigate.

Three hours later the largest sun I'd ever seen sank toward the horizon, and our rickshaw was still an immovable hunk of metal on the side of the road. Our road angel had tried everything, including disassembling and reassembling the carburetor, before finally standing up, wiping his hands on his jeans and declaring defeat. "We're about ten miles outside of a town," he said. "I can tow you." So we'd been hauled into the city of Barmer.

The next morning, I pulled open the shades and let the weak morning light filter into our dingy room. Gazing out the window,

I spotted our bright-orange rickshaw—optimistically named Sunny—sitting alone in a gravel lot. Last night the lot had been packed with other rickshaws and the hotel filled to capacity. But this morning we were alone.

Behind me Lesley stirred, raised her arms above her head, and yawned. "What time is it?"

I looked at the bedside clock. "It's 7:30 a.m." I gestured toward the window. "Everyone else is gone."

From the bed nearest the door Sarah asked a question. "Well, ladies, what are we going to do now?"

Plopping down on the bed next to Lesley, I responded. "I don't even know where we are. And it's not like we can call AAA. Do you even have that in Australia?"

Sarah stretched her long dancer's legs in front of her in a V. "We've got something like it in Australia. Much good it does us here, huh?"

⌒

Barmer's mechanic was the oldest man I'd ever seen. He was bent at the waist like a broken limb but moved with remarkable speed as he walked up to me and opened his knobby hand, revealing a small metal clasp half the size of a door hinge that had cracked down the middle like a broken egg.

"That's the problem?" I asked. The man gave a definitive nod and gestured for me to take it. Lesley and Sarah gathered around and we gaped at the miniscule culprit.

"It's so small," Lesley said.

Sarah poked it. "You arsehole."

Taking a deep breath, I navigated our rickshaw onto the streets of Barmer, a city of two hundred thousand people and, as far as I could tell, not a single traffic light. As I steered the rick to the far left side of the road, I said a little prayer to the universe. Before we'd left Jaisalmer we'd propped a small statue of Ganesh, Remover of Obstacles, up on our dashboard, and I squeezed it for support. The reflection of my own eyes stared back at me in the rearview mirror, and I assured myself that I could drive this rickshaw. We would survive. Probably.

During our few days of test-driving, I'd learned of the pecking order on Indian roads, a hierarchy based almost exclusively on size. At the bottom were dogs, goats and humans, and then larger animals like elephants and camels. Next came bicycles, then rickshaws, then cars, dump trucks and buses. And at the top of the order sat the holy cow.

The basic rule of the road was this: anything lower in the pecking order than you had to get out of your way. As a rickshaw driver I could motor headlong into a human, for instance, or a pack of dogs, without worry. If they didn't get out of the way the fault was theirs, not mine. Likewise, if a car, truck, or bus came barreling at me, I had to scramble like hell to get out of its path. And cows were king of the road. They'd sprawl in the middle of the highway like Egyptian pharaohs, ears twitching away flies, while a mass of humanity honked and swerved around them.

An hour down the road the traffic thinned considerably. I

stopped Sunny in a threadbare town so that we could stretch our legs and fill a thermos with chai. Along the side of the road sat a series of shacks selling snacks and samosas. Behind the shacks a dog sniffed piles of garbage in search of food. She was painfully skinny, each rib visible and protruding, and her nipples were ripe and prominent against her matted fur. Somewhere she had a litter of puppies to feed. Crouching down I clicked my tongue at her. "Hey," I cooed. "Hey there." She raised her head and backed away.

I approached the man at the snack shack and pointed toward a plastic cylindrical tub filled with packs of pineapple biscuits. Holding my hands two feet apart I mimed my desire to purchase the entire tub. He picked it up and raised his eyebrows at me. After nodded yes, I ran back to the rickshaw and pulled some yellow envelope money from the bottom of my backpack.

Michele and Glenn were animal lovers just like Brian and me. On the night they gave us the yellow envelope gift they told us a story of a sick and stray dog they'd encountered while on a trip to Greece. They'd fallen in love with the dog but had been traveling with a tour group and were whisked away to their next destination before they'd been able to help.

In my short time in India I'd already crossed paths with a hundred sick and starving dogs. The sheer number of them was too much to bear. From now on, I decided, I'd give all I could to the dogs we passed, even if it was only a scratch behind the ear and a pack or two of pineapple biscuits. My mind drifted back to the waiter in Germany. A small gesture could sustain you, I knew.

Pulling the lid off the tub, I grabbed a few packs of biscuits, tore them open, and crouched down at eye level with the dog again. "Here you go," I called to her, and threw a biscuit in her direction. She took a few hesitant steps toward it and looked up at me with weary eyes. "It's okay," I said. "Feed your babies."

She sniffed the biscuit and then took it gingerly in her mouth, looked up at me again, then swallowed. "It's good, huh?" I threw another biscuit her way. She scarfed it down and looked up at me with hungry eyes. "You can have as many as you want." I opened five more packs of biscuits and dumped them into a pile in front of her, trying to let the energy of my heart send her a message: *I'm so sorry you're suffering. I wish I could do more.* She stood and chewed at the pile of biscuits, and I turned back toward the rickshaw.

Lesley and Sarah were making their way back to the rick, our thermos filled with chai. I raised the tub of pineapple biscuits. "For the dogs. I'll keep it filled and we can feed them as we go." We'd collectively pooled our money to pay for things like gasoline and meals, and in our hotel room the previous night I'd told them briefly about the yellow envelope. "I'll buy the biscuits with the yellow envelope money," I explained. "Michele and Glenn would like that."

Lesley smiled. "That's a lovely idea. How's it going, anyway? Have you given a lot of the money away?"

My eyes fell to the ground. "No, not as much as I thought we would have by now. It's kind of hard, you know? Harder than I thought it would be." Lesley stared at me expectantly so I started rambling. "I'll want to give to someone but then I'll start to second-guess myself, though we were specifically told not to second-guess. Or, I'll feel really awkward because I can't explain the intention behind the money. At first I thought about the yellow envelope all the time, but then it kind of faded into the background. So I'm trying to make a conscious effort to keep it in the forefront of my mind. When I can accomplish that, it's kind of an amazing state of being because I see the world in this new way. It's like, *Here I am. How can I be of use?*" I climbed into the rickshaw and shoved the pineapple biscuits into the space behind my seat. "I wish I could say that I stay present most of the time. But the truth is I've been pretty wrapped up in my own head lately."

"There's no time frame, is there?" asked Lesley. "Like, you don't have to give the money away within the year?"

"Oh no, nothing like that. There are only three rules. Don't overthink it, share our experiences if we want to, and don't feel pressured to give it all away."

"Don't worry about it then. You'll find ways to give when the time is right." Lesley climbed into the rickshaw beside me. "You may not feel like you're doing as much as you should, but those biscuits might have been the difference between life and death today to that dog and her pups."

Sarah revved the engine to life. "We better get moving, ladies." We had at least two hours of driving left before we reached a town on the GPS that we hoped would have a hotel. As we pulled away, I looked back at the shack where the starving dog had been scavenging. She was nowhere to be found, but the pile of biscuits was gone.

~

An hour later our rick broke down again. We were stopped on the side of the road half-heartedly poking under the hatch when two skinny men driving a gigantic and overloaded Goods Carrier truck approached. Without saying a word, one of the men got down on his knees, unhooked our fuel line, and sucked, relieving some blockage within. Gasoline shot into his mouth and he spat and coughed. Lesley, Sarah, and I jumped around shrieking like it had happened to us until I finally thought to offer him a bottle of water. He rinsed his mouth out twice, gave us a gigantic smile, and then climbed back in his truck again without ever saying a word. We called out "thank you" and waved as he drove away.

"It's amazing," I said after the truck had disappeared down the road. "Everyone in India is a rickshaw mechanic."

"Except for us," said Lesley.

Our rickshaw was a dud. Yet, as the Goods Carrier truck disappeared down the road, I wondered if maybe that wasn't a blessing. The teams ahead of us were cruising along without problems, but they were missing out on something incredible: the extraordinary kindness that appeared out of nowhere each time that we broke down.

Before leaving home I'd never needed to rely on the kindness of strangers. Because I'd maintained the same routine for so long, I'd essentially wiped out almost all chance for the unexpected to occur. If my car died I could call Brian or a dozen different friends or AAA. I sent a subliminal message to the universe: *I've got this covered.* And so I never allowed the space in my life for magic to creep in.

But I was learning to enjoy the great swath of possibility that came with uncertainty. Since leaving my comfort zone to step out into the world, I'd been at the mercy of those I encountered, from the cops who picked us up in Ecuador to the Goods Carrier driver. And no one had let me down. When I left on this journey with the yellow envelope tucked into my purse, I thought I had something to share with the world. And I did. But what I didn't realize was that the world had something to share with me too. The people I met were teaching me not just how to *give* the yellow envelope but how to *live* it. The unknown no longer seemed a threat, but a gift. Could it be that the world wanted to help me, if only I'd allow it?

Our breakdown, though brief, had cost us another forty-five minutes. We had hoped to arrive in the next town by late afternoon so that we could find a safe place to sleep before the sun set. Though we didn't feel overtly threatened, it wasn't hard to miss the fact that there weren't too many women out and about, especially after dark.

Just three weeks before we arrived in India a twenty-three-year-old woman had been brutally beaten and gang raped on a bus in Delhi while traveling home from the movies with a male friend. She'd died in the hospital last week. The crime evoked an outcry in India and around the world. Her murder had exposed an undercurrent of rape and sexual violence in India.

In light of that, Lesley, Sarah, and I had set up a few ground rules to protect us. And our number one rule was that we would not stay out after dark. My hackles rose the closer we inched toward dusk.

A giant red sun sank beneath the horizon, and the sky blazed pink and orange. Our rickshaw puttered along weakly down the empty desert highway. The town on the GPS was still at least an hour away. We were three women, alone, with no place to take shelter. We were not going to make it in before dark. I felt both terrified of the encroaching darkness and awed by the stunning sunset. But despite all of the uncertainty, I felt wildly at peace. And for the first time in my life I saw that I could be at ease even while things were crumbling around me. It was possible to be afraid and happy; worried and free. I could be content just as things were.

The road began to deteriorate. Huge holes pocked the pavement. *BAM!* Our rick hit a pothole. *BAM! BAM! BAM!* Over and over we slammed into the street. We were at serious risk of a flat tire or, worse, jarring a spark plug or clip out of place and sidelining us, alone and after dark, in the middle of nowhere. Sunny coughed and began to lose power. Lesley cooed at her. "Keep going, baby, you can do it. Don't die on us now. We need you."

Sunny's single headlight illuminated a thin patch of road in front of us. Suddenly, the piece of pavement we'd been driving on disappeared and our rickshaw dropped into a pit of sand. The engine sputtered and died. "Shit," Lesley groaned, hitting her hand against the dashboard. "Shit, shit, shit."

We climbed out of the rickshaw to investigate. The front

wheel of our rick was submerged in sand. Sarah grabbed a head-lamp and walked up the road. She called out from the darkness that the road picked up again. "I can't tell how long the pavement lasts," she yelled, "but at least there's some up here."

Though the temperature in the desert had dropped consid-erably once the sun had gone, we were panting by the time we finally pushed Sunny back onto the road. Pulling the scarf Brian had given me up around my chin, I climbed back into the rick-shaw. Lesley turned the ignition but nothing happened. "Try it again," said Sarah, but the rickshaw did not even croak.

Before we'd left Jaisalmer, another rickshaw runner had shown us how do a jump-start. "Just put it into second gear and run it down the road, then let out the clutch and the engine should kick on," he'd said. So Sarah and I ran down the road pushing Sunny while Lesley sat in the front seat, hand engaged with the accelerator, prepared to drive if only Sunny would cooperate.

Lesley let out the clutch, and the engine coughed weakly to life. Sarah and I jumped up and down and cheered. Lesley revved the accelerator, and Sunny took off on her own free will like a child who'd just learned to ride a bike.

We'd pulled ourselves out of this mess on our own. I knew that if I'd been traveling with Brian all of the rickshaw repairs would have fallen on him. Above me a thousand bright stars pricked the night sky. I opened my mouth and howled with pride.

It became obvious that the next town on the GPS would take us hours to reach. The road threatened to deteriorate back into sand again at any minute, and Sunny was acting up. She kept losing power and stalling. We knew it was just a matter of time before she died on us completely.

We were breaking our rule and driving after dark because we were out of options. We could park the rickshaw on the side of the empty highway and wait out the night, but that felt dangerous because if a passing motorist discovered us we'd be completely alone and exposed. Or, we could keep driving and hope for some miracle to appear out of nowhere. It seemed unlikely, but in India nothing felt out of the question. Plus, there was safety in movement. We just didn't know how much movement Sunny had left in her.

We drove for an hour in darkness before reaching a ramshackle town, too small to appear on our GPS, at the intersection of two dirt roads. A campfire burned, and we could make out the silhouettes of about a half dozen men warming their hands against the cold of the night.

Sarah spoke up. "Should we stop?"

"God," I whispered. "I don't know." Scanning the village quickly, I looked for other women, but there were none.

The men around the fire watched us, unmoving.

In a lean-to structure near the side of the road a pot of chai burned over an open fire. We decided to stop, order some tea, and discuss our options. A middle-aged man in dusty gray pants and an even dustier gray shirt motioned for us to sit down. Sarah smiled at him and held up three fingers. "Chai, please. *Namaste.*" The man nodded.

A single, dangling bulb hung from the ceiling. The exterior

walls of the shop were made of woven branches like a child's forest fort. The front of the structure opened to the road and a strip of corrugated metal hung as a roof.

Another man, old and skinny, squatted over a low fire, cooking food. The smell of spice and curry made my stomach rumble and I realized that I was starving. The only thing I'd had to eat since leaving Barmer were a few packages of pineapple biscuits that I'd bought for the dogs.

The man delivered our chai, and I pointed to the food cooking on the fire then drew my hand to my mouth. "Can we eat here?" I asked. The man gave another expressionless nod and shouted something toward the cook.

We ate in silence, our fingers clinking lightly against the Thali plates as we scooped the food to our mouths with our hands. The meal was delicious, and as the warmth of it hit my stomach, a bone-deep exhaustion consumed me. Wearily, I looked out at where we'd parked Sunny on the side of the road, illuminated in a thin sheath of moonlight. I did not have the energy to climb back in that rickshaw and ride off into the cold, dark desert. Every ounce of me longed to stay exactly where I was, sitting cross-legged on a dusty lounger chair.

But Sarah broached the topic of sleeping there for the night. "I'll go talk to him," she said, standing to make her way across the dirt floor.

The temperature had dropped near freezing as we pulled our rickshaw behind the man's shop for safekeeping. We dug around in our backpacks and pulled on all of our warm clothing. The sky above us was a crisp canvas slate. Lesley waddled to the front of the rickshaw and looked down at her padded body. "I have to pee," she said, and our laughter burst into the quiet night.

When we returned to the chai stand, the man was laying pads on the thatched recliners we'd just eaten on and heavy blankets for us to sleep under. Standing for a minute, I watched him. He arranged our beds as if he'd been expecting us. But I knew that he did not keep extra bedding just for guests. Somewhere, his family must have been going without.

Feeling guilty for his help, I considered declining the blankets but did not know how. Then I remembered the man on the bus on the way to Puno who'd given Brian and me his CD and how we accepted his gift in the way that we hoped our yellow envelope gifts would be received. This offering, too, I had to graciously accept. So I caught the man's eye and smiled. Then I placed my hands together and gave a little bow, trying to convey my thankfulness.

Uncurling my sleeping bag liner, I burrowed inside it for extra warmth, then pulled the heavy blanket up to my shoulders and the thin fabric of the liner over my face like a veil. Earlier, we had stacked our backpacks on an empty bed that ran parallel to the foot of our beds. From beneath my sleeping bag liner I watched, confused, as the man picked them up and placed them on the floor. Then he sat down on the bed and prepared himself for sleep. He planned to wait out the cold at our feet, I realized with amazement.

My eyes fluttered closed. Never in my life had I been unsure of where I would sleep for the night. Even on weekend road trips around the Pacific Northwest I'd book hotel rooms weeks in advance, operating under the assumption that if I didn't stick my hands in things it would all go to hell. Why had I always assumed that life, left to its own devices, would not play out in my favor? Why had I never before trusted that the world might take care of me?

It seemed a million years ago since we'd left Jaisalmer, but it was only yesterday. It seemed two million years ago that my life was coming apart in South America, but it had only been a week. And my life back in Portland, where I owned a house and worked in a cubicle, where Michele had passed the yellow envelope across the table to me? It felt as though that life had never existed at all. An eon might have transpired in the few days since Brian and I landed in Delhi. I'd lived a lot of years walking down the wrong roads, and those days had compacted like the folds of an accordion, into an inch of time. Now everything expanded. My life was wailing like a beautiful prayer, the moments stretching into hours, the days to years. I could see now that it was possible to live a long life poorly, or a short life well, and that at any moment one might shift their position and, after years of hibernation, decide to crawl out of the den and live.

The morning dawned gray and cold as snow. The three of us folded our blankets and walked to the front of the chai shop to order a thermos of tea. Out on the dirt street a litter of yellow puppies tumbled over each other. Lesley and I fed them pineapple biscuits and they nipped at our heels for more.

Sarah paid the man for the chai and food with our collective pot of money and headed out to our rickshaw. I followed closely behind. "I'm going to give him some yellow envelope money," I told her.

She hoisted her backpack onto the rack atop the rickshaw and turned to frown a little. "I wouldn't. I tried to give him extra money when I paid for our meal, and he wouldn't take it. I'm worried I might have offended him."

It was my biggest fear when it came to giving away the yellow envelope money. In the United States I intrinsically understood our culture of giving. I knew when it was appropriate to give, what to say while giving, and how much was acceptable. But outside of my own culture, the rules were different.

"It's tricky," I said, thinking of the couple with the cow in Ecuador, the man on the bus in Peru. "I guess I won't then."

We climbed into Sunny, optimistic that she would start. Lesley turned the ignition, and miraculously it sputtered to life. We pulled onto the street, leaned out of the rickshaw and waved, shouting thank you as we drove away. The man stood in the street and watched us go.

CHAPTER 10

DRIVING THROUGH INDIA WITH TWO WOMEN I'D NEVER met before was strange. We barely knew each other, yet we'd been thrown together into an intense and physically intimate situation. During the day, we sat for hours in the rickshaw, close enough to touch. At night we shared beds. We talked about ourselves a bit, but we also existed in our own silos. And while on some level I hoped that we would become the best of friends, chatting like we'd known each other forever through a one thousand five hundred-mile, girls-only road trip, I was equally okay when it became evident that it would not be that way.

Because Sarah and Lesley had both explored India extensively, at times I felt like a child traveling with her parents. Few things ruffled Lesley's feathers, so I adopted her laid-back attitude. Sarah naturally took control, so I sat back and let her make decisions. For the first time since my trip began, I could simply exist without feeling like it was necessary to stay on my toes or worry about making decisions that would please Brian. I really and truly stopped overthinking it. It was *glorious*.

We arrived in Udaipur, a beautiful tourist town sometimes referred to as the "Venice of the East" or, less dramatically, the "City of Lakes," hoping to find a guesthouse and settle down for *sixteen whole hours* after four days of driving on India's maniacal roads.

Somehow I managed to weave us through the dense city traffic, winding along single-lane alleyways best suited for pedestrians and cows. We ended up at a lakeside overlook with a view of the Lake Palace, a sprawling luxury hotel plopped on its own private island. It was stunning, but it's not like we could sleep *there*.

So we flagged down a rickshaw driver and asked him to lead us to a more affordable guesthouse. He nodded enthusiastically and then took off like his ass was on fire. I chased after him, driving much too fast in order to keep up.

Which is how I hit a motorcycle. A *parked* motorcycle. Sunny made a terrible crunching sound as she scraped against the bike. When I realized what had happened I hit the brakes, blocking traffic, and screamed "Oh shit. Oh shit. *Oh shit*." My mind flashed to a scene from the novel *Shantaram* where a driver responsible for a traffic accident was promptly pulled from his vehicle and beaten.

Cussing, I sat in the driver's seat and waited for an angry mob to descend. Sarah jumped from the rickshaw to check the damage and returned with the news that the accident had sounded worse than it actually was. The motorcycle looked *fine*, she assured me, and our rickshaw was undamaged too.

So I drove away. Quickly. Because not only had I just crashed a bright-orange rickshaw into somebody's motorcycle, but I'd done so without carrying my International driver's license *or* my Oregon driver's license, both of which I'd managed to leave in Brian's backpack before we parted ways in Jaisalmer.

The rickshaw driver paused ahead of me, and I caught up to him again, screaming for him to slow down before I killed myself, my teammates, someone else or, God forbid, a cow. My hands held the wheel in a white-knuckled death grip, and my heart slammed into my breastbone from the pure stress of it all.

Finally, the rickshaw driver pulled into a claustrophobic alley and pointed to a two-story guesthouse with a blue door. We nodded thank you, abandoned Sunny on the side of the road, and carried our bags to our room. Forty-five minutes later, Sarah remembered that we hadn't paid the driver for his time. She ran outside to find him leaning against his rickshaw, chatting on his phone, completely unbothered by the wait.

In the shower I unsuccessfully tried to scrub the funk and road grease from my arms and face. After changing into clean clothes, I wandered over to a coffee shop across the street where Sarah and Lesley had already claimed a table.

Thoughts of Brian preoccupied me. He'd emailed to say that after I'd left him in Jaisalmer he'd gone on a camel safari into the desert, and it'd given him a lot of time to think. But he hadn't elaborated on what that meant.

I missed him. It felt *good* to miss him. The truth of what he'd said in Argentina became clear to me. He couldn't be the person I wanted him to be because no one could be that person. The real problem was that *I* wasn't the person I wanted to be.

But I was becoming her. I was proud that I'd had the guts to follow my heart and take this trip. And though it was brutally hard, I was also proud that Brian and I were no longer ignoring the problems that plagued us. But what if Brian discovered something different? What if time and distance helped him to see that I'd been unfair and unpredictable for far too long and life was easier without me?

A strong feeling told me that I didn't want to lose Brian. But an even stronger part of me was okay with any outcome. The thing I cared about most was that whatever happened in the future was real and true.

From across the table Lesley spoke and pulled me from my thoughts. "You know what? Driving in India is a metaphor for life."

"How so?" I asked.

"Well, as we are well aware, driving here is just crazy. There are rickshaws, cars, buses, bicycles, motorbikes, people, dogs, and cows in the street."

"Don't forget the elephants and camels," said Sarah.

"And elephants and camels too. It's the biggest headache trying to keep up with it all. The traffic flows in a million directions; it seems impenetrable, but then, somehow, a little spot opens up, and we make it through."

A few hours later Sarah realized she couldn't find her phone. Losing an expensive phone is a pity under any circumstance, but a flat-out emergency given our current state. We'd been using the GPS on that phone to find our way around India. Without it, we were pretty sure we'd end up in Pakistan or, at the very least, crying on the side of the road as we tried to navigate the chaotic madness of every Indian city.

We tore through our bags and hotel room and scoured the rick, but the phone had disappeared.

"The only thing I can think is that the phone fell off of my lap when I got out to check the damage on that motorcycle." Sarah said.

It sounded probable. Lesley suggested we return to the scene of the crime. "Maybe the phone's still there?" she said.

"I'll go with you," I told her, but a voice inside my head quipped: *There's not a chance in hell we'll find that phone.*

We retraced our route through the alleyways, dodging the same crazy traffic on foot that we'd encountered hours before in the rickshaw. I was weary about returning to the accident scene but even wearier about driving another one thousand two hundred miles without GPS. Back in Portland, I'd often get lost driving to Wendy's house even though I'd been there a hundred times. To put it mildly, I was navigationally challenged. Without the help of modern technology, I'd be useless driving to Kerala.

Luckily, Lesley did not suffer from the same condition. Somehow she managed to lead us back to the location of my hit-and-run. We searched the area where we suspected the phone had gone missing, but no phone, smashed or otherwise, graced the shit-strewn street.

Because *really*, even if the phone had slipped out of the rickshaw, what were the chances it had survived the fall? And even if it had survived the fall, what were the chances that it was just lying on the ground waiting for us to find it? And if someone else had found it, how would they track us down to return it? Besides, the phone was worth four hundred dollars, more money than many of the locals made in a month. Finding that phone was like finding gold.

But just to cover our bases, we asked a few of the nearby shopkeepers if anyone had turned in a phone. They all shook their heads no. By the time we reached the third shop I knew we were wasting our time.

"Has anyone turned a phone in to you?" Lesley asked. "We lost it this morning."

"No, no, not to me," said the shopkeeper. "Were you here earlier, in an orange rickshaw?"

"Yes, we were," I said with a bit of skepticism. It felt a little too good to be true.

He pointed across the street. "Go, to the police station; someone put a phone there."

Swiveling at the waist, I glanced at a crumbling, nondescript building. "That's the police station?"

"Yes, that's it," the man said, wagging his head up and down.

Lesley shrugged. "It's worth a shot."

Inside the station, six policemen eyed us. We stood in the doorway feeling awkward and out of place. Finally, a man seated behind a desk spoke up. "What is your purpose here?" he asked. Lesley launched into our story, explaining about the phone.

The men listened, expressionless, and then spoke to each other in Hindi. "Is it a Motorola phone?" asked the stone-faced deskman.

We nodded, hardly believing it possible. "Yes, it's black."

"Go to the room next door," barked the deskman.

Next door we sat in two metal chairs while Lesley explained the whole story again. Again, we were asked to describe the phone. Again, the officers discussed among themselves in Hindi. Again, we were sent next door, back to where we'd come from.

"Why does it seem like they don't want to give us the phone?" whispered Lesley.

Fear thumped against my ribs like a caged gorilla. I knew why. I'd hit a motorcycle and driven away. The shopkeeper witnessed my crime and reported it to the police. Now I'd stumbled obliviously right into their trap. No one had our phone. This was a ploy to arrest me.

Back in the first room the men made phone calls and talked in hushed voices to each other. Lesley and I sat in silence, our hands folded neatly in our laps while I calculated my next move. It was probably too late to escape, but maybe I could bribe them?

The door to the station opened and two serious-looking policemen entered holding hands, an Indian expression of friendship that never failed to disarm me. *Those are the men that they've sent to arrest me*, I thought. Following the two men with my eyes, I barely noticed the tiny old man in a brown sweater that trailed behind them. Lesley nudged me and pointed to the old man. In his hand he held Sarah's phone.

"Oh my God," I said to Lesley. "I cannot believe it."

Lesley smiled like she'd expected it all along. "Another miracle upon miracle from the people of India," she said.

The old man handed the phone to us, and we hopped up out of our chairs. Then the whole room of sober-faced policemen erupted into cheers. They clapped and smiled and wobbled their heads like we'd just walked into our surprise birthday party. Lesley and I blushed and thanked the old man over and over again. He just nodded at us, smiling.

We headed back to our guesthouse, the phone clutched in my hand. Bells chimed from a nearby temple, and a call to prayer echoed over the city. Something inside of me vibrated like a thrummed string. I was still a free woman, getting freer by the day.

Back at the coffee shop we relayed the story to Sarah. While telling her about the old man who'd found her phone it dawned on me that I should have given him some yellow envelope money. In the moment, I'd been so consumed by my own deluded thoughts of jail time that I hadn't even thought of it.

That evening the three of us had dinner on the café balcony overlooking the Ghats of the Ahar River. The haunting sound of bells rang out into the nighttime air. While sipping chai I amazed over how long the day felt. The rickshaw accident had just happened that morning, but it felt like a week ago. It was always the phenomenon when you lived a day good and well, I thought. You were rewarded with more time, or so it seemed.

Lesley leaned across the table and asked about Brian. "I miss him," I told her. "But I have no idea if he misses me. I wish I could know what he is thinking. It's terrible wondering if he's happier without me."

Lesley and Sarah knew about my problems with Brian. On our second day in the rickshaw, feeling an intense desire to be untethered, I'd removed my wedding ring. My ring represented my life with Brian, and I needed to know how it would feel to be without its symbolic presence. Lesley and Sarah probably would not have noticed its absence, but I felt it profoundly, so I'd briefly filled them in.

It was so refreshing to speak honestly about my troubles with Brian. Until recently, I'd been afraid that if I admitted them to anyone other than Wendy they'd feel too big and real. But the opposite had happened. The more I talked about the struggles between Brian and me, the less insurmountable the problems seemed. Lesley patted my hand reassuringly. "I'm sure he misses you, honey. You guys just needed a little room to breathe."

On our way out of the café, the owner stopped us. "Where will you park your rickshaw?" he asked. We'd been avoiding the question all day. Every place we'd slept so far had parking lots, or something like them, but tonight our only option appeared to be leaving Sunny unattended in the middle of the busy alleyway. We'd hauled our bags and our tubs of gasoline up to our room but it was

Sunny herself that we worried about. If we left her unprotected on the road the odds were good that she'd be gone by morning.

The café owner pointed to his houseboy, who had been running dishes to and from the kitchen since we'd arrived many hours ago. Now that the café was closed, the boy pulled a dirty sleeping mat to the front of the shop near the door to watch over things for the night.

"You pay me three hundred rupees, and my boy will watch your rickshaw tonight," he said. We had no other option. Lesley dug into our collective pot of money and paid him. Then we climbed the stairs to our guesthouse and collapsed into bed.

We woke the next morning before dawn and wandered out into the cold, dark day. A call to prayer echoed out over the river. Sunny sat untouched where we had left her.

When we approached the rickshaw we found the houseboy asleep on the floor of our rickshaw, curled like a cat into an impossibly tiny ball. He wore pants and short sleeves and was without even a blanket to keep him warm. My assumption had been that he would come out periodically to check on things, not spend the whole night outside guarding Sunny.

I did not understand then, and I still don't now, the complexities of poverty in India. But I had heard that there were tens of thousands of street children illegally employed by hotels and restaurants all over the country. Oftentimes, these children were exploited, treated as virtual prisoners, mistreated physically and emotionally by their employers. If that was the case with this boy I do not know, and I will never know.

Rousing the boy awake, I whispered above him, and small clouds of condensation puffed from my lips. He sat up with a start, a metal pole clutched in his hand for protection.

"We are leaving," I whispered into the silence of the morning.

Remembering the old man in the police station the day before, I knew my thank you had not been enough. I would not miss out on another opportunity to give.

My backpack still hung from my shoulders. Lowering it to the ground, I pulled out the yellow envelope money. My fingers counted the bills and then I pushed them into the boy's hand.

"For you," I said. My index finger poked gently into his skinny chest. "You. Yours. Thank you." He nodded, and a half-moon smile spread across his face.

We hoisted our backpacks on top of the rickshaw and covered them with a plastic tarp to keep the dust out. Then we secured them with bungee cords to keep the bags in place. Sarah sat behind the wheel and turned the ignition. The sun began to drain the darkness from the sky.

We wrapped our scarves around our necks to fight the chill of the morning and drove Sunny away from Udaipur, pointing southbound to that distant finish line in Kerala, still over one thousand miles away.

CHAPTER 11

WE TOOK TURNS DRIVING IN ONE-HOUR SHIFTS, THE MAXI-
mum length of time we deemed tolerable before the stress shot
our nerves completely. Poor Sarah was stuck behind the wheel
as we navigated the terrible traffic of Ahmedabad. She sat stark
straight, trying not to stall in the stop-and-go chaos as cars and
buses and motorbikes whizzed by us in all directions. From the
back of the rickshaw I noticed tears running down her cheeks.
Leaning forward, I squeezed her arm for comfort but knew there
was nothing I could say. The stress of driving on crazy Indian
roads had pushed all three of us to our limits. When I hit my
breaking point I cussed. Lesley detached. Sarah cried.

We were driving through Gujarat, an industrial state that
we'd been warned to avoid altogether. But we didn't have the
luxury of avoiding Gujarat because we were behind schedule,
and we couldn't afford to pay the hefty fee if we returned our
rickshaw late.

The beauty and magic of the first few days of the Rickshaw

Run felt like a distant dream. We'd been driving for more than a week, and the novelty of navigating India in a rickshaw had not retained its charm. In Gujarat we saw a different side of India. It was dirty and ugly, and the level of poverty was profound; everywhere people and animals suffered.

We drove past people living on the side of the highway in shanties made from tarps and branches. In a rural village I saw a girl, aged about twelve, skeleton-skinny and working naked in a field. There was garbage everywhere. Cows and goats, their ribs as bowed as cathedral arcs, stood on the roadside chewing plastic wrap and chip bags.

As we drove down a crowded highway, we saw a starving dog standing over the bloated corpse of another dog, eating it. Later, I saw a dog heaving and bleeding on the side of the road, heartbreakingly close to death. Actually, the dead dogs were everywhere. We passed too many to count.

Our collective mood darkened. Each time we ran out of gas, broke down, or got a flat tire, I had to suppress my urge to kick the ever-loving shit out of the rickshaw. I knew exactly where I wanted to kick her, too, right in that mockingly perky orange posterior door.

Many miles passed as I contemplated my years with Brian, and many more passed while I sat suspended in a kind of unthinking awareness, staring out of the rickshaw and dreading my next turn to drive.

India was taking her toll on me. In the mornings, when many Indians burned their garbage, the pollution became so thick and invasive that the caustic smell of scorched plastic burned my throat. I'd developed a hacking cough from our twelve-hour days in the rickshaw.

We'd been subsisting on pineapple and Parle-G biscuits, India's ubiquitous best-selling cookie, and I hadn't pooped in nine days. I felt like hell, but I also felt guilty for my minor and temporary suffering. There were so many people in India just trying to survive, who lived every day with no escape from the discomforts that were temporary and fleeting to me.

And yet the beautiful color of the women's saris as they trudged down the roads carrying pots of water on their heads cut through the bleakness. The waving children and the manic motorcycle drivers who'd weave in and out of traffic, pull up so close they could touch us, and yell, "HELLO! WHERE YOU FROM? WHAT COUNTRYYY?" almost made me blind to the hardships of the people I encountered. Many suffered, yet they seemed happy and open and available in a way that I had never been. Before arriving I thought I understood the way things worked, but India was pulverizing all of that. Each molecule of my body felt like it had evaporated in a grand and transcendent explosion, and I could no longer make sense of the world.

We were twenty miles outside of Pune, another huge industrial city we were dreading driving through, when a Café Coffee Day appeared out of nowhere like a mirage. At first I barely believed it but Lesley yelled "Oh my God, a Café Coffee Day!" Then Sarah shrieked and made a spontaneous turn into the parking lot, almost sideswiping a truck.

Café Coffee Day was India's version of Starbucks. It had air conditioning and served machine made lattes and individually wrapped sandwiches that were displayed on glass platters. A Western toilet glistened in the bathroom. Fighting off the urge to drop to my knees and kiss the ground at Café Coffee Day, I locked myself in the women's room and turned the hot water on, filled my cupped hands and splashed my wind burned face.

As I studied my left ring finger in the steam of the sink, I pumped soap into my hands and tried to scrub away the grime that had settled on my skin and underneath my fingernails. It felt good to have an unmarked hand, no ring to claim me. *I could keep it this way*, I thought, and the idea simply sat there like a waiting dog as the water swirled black down the drain.

From the interior of my backpack I pulled out a roll of toilet paper and dried my skin, then leaned forward and looked into the mirror. A thick layer of dirt and pollution had settled on my face. Leaning closer, an inch from the mirror, I stared hard into my own eyes. They looked bluer against the tone of my skin. "Hi," I whispered, and my breath fogged against the glass. Raising my index finger, I tapped my reflection in the mirror. "Hi." My eyes stared back at me, unblinking. I felt silly. What the hell was I doing talking to myself in a bathroom mirror? Stepping back, I stared at the bust of my reflection and the smile curled on my lips.

A weird thing had happened to me earlier in the rickshaw. While staring at the landscape as we bumped down a rural road, I'd fallen into a trance-like state. My mind was far off and wandering when I had a dream-like vision of Brian and I standing across from each other in a field. From across the bending grass I yelled to him. He waved and yelled back, but when he opened his mouth to speak my voice had come out.

Suddenly, all of my beloveds were standing in the field. My sisters, Wendy, and even me as a young girl, dressed in a navy blue dress I'd once worn. When I saw child-me I ran toward her, picked her up, and told her that I loved her. And somewhere deep inside of me some truth clicked into place. I was still that little girl, lovable and loved, worthy of the bounty of the world.

One by one I ran toward each person in the field and embraced them. But when I got to Brian I wasn't sure if I should run to him. My body froze, unsure of what to do. And then a truth washed over me. I did not have to run toward him if I did not want to. The choice was mine. And suddenly, empowered with that choice, I realized that I *did* want to. As I reached his arms, I knew that I had made the right decision.

When I finally emerged from the bathroom, cleaner than I'd been in days, I found Lesley and Sarah huddled at a table with a collection of cups, sandwiches, and cakes spread out around them. "We bought everything," said Sarah.

"I can see that." Sliding down into a plastic chair, I picked up a piece of iced cake and shoved it into my mouth. "Oh my God," I moaned, "this is so much better than those stupid Parle-G biscuits." I turned to face them both. "Let's just sleep here tonight, at the Café Coffee Day. We'll stay until they close and then we can sleep on the patio. Or maybe they'll let us sleep under one of those." I pointed to a row of pristine booths lined like perfect white teeth against the wall. "Either way, I don't want to leave."

"Neither do I," said Lesley. We fell into silence, stuffing our faces with baked goods and washing it all down with chai.

In the parking lot, the staff of the Café Coffee Day had gathered around our rickshaw. They were snapping pictures with their cell phones. One of them approached us. "Is this your rickshaw?" he asked.

I nodded. "Sort of. I mean…yes. For now. We're driving it to Kerala. We started in Jaisalmer."

The boy's eyes grew wide. "Noooo," he let out a long moan. "How is this possible? You are crazy!" he exclaimed, wobbling his head.

Returning his smile, I wobbled my head back at him. "Tell me about it!"

An hour later I reluctantly sat down in the driver's seat and turned the ignition. Sunny sputtered to life and then made a terrible sound like a weak cough and died. I turned to look at Lesley and Sarah, who were getting situated in the back seat.

"That did not sound good," I muttered as I cranked the ignition again. The rickshaw barked weakly to life and then sputtered out.

"Maybe she just needs some rest?" suggested Lesley. My eyes caught Sarah's in the rearview mirror and she shrugged. Our rickshaw had already been resting for an hour. But I loved Café Coffee Day so much that I just let myself believe the lie. We walked back in and ordered another round of drinks. The sun was setting. We didn't even talk about what to do.

A wealthy family pulled into the parking lot and climbed out of their SUV. They looked amusingly from the rickshaw to the three of us slumped around our coffees. The father called out to us. "Is this your rickshaw?"

We nodded in unison. "It's broken," Lesley said.

"Oh, that's too bad. What is the matter with it?"

"We don't have any idea."

The family quizzed us. What were we doing in India? Why were we driving a rickshaw? Where had we started, and where were we going, and what did we do when we were not risking our lives navigating the subcontinent in a bright-orange, busted-down rickshaw?

They called us over and took our picture, and then they wished us luck. "Where will you sleep tonight?" the mother inquired.

"I don't know," I said.

She looked toward her husband who looked at the ground. They wanted to help us, but something held them back. Silently I envisioned their big house with plenty of spare room, their bathroom with hot water, and how nice it would be to have a safe place to sleep for the night. I thought of the man whose shack we had slept in. He did not have much, but he gave what he had, freely and openly and without, it seemed, even a moment's hesitation.

Yet I understood the dilemma that played out in the minds of the family as they stood in the parking lot wondering if they should help us; it was the same internal debate that stopped Brian and me from giving yellow envelope money when we knew we should. Even before traveling, I'd been in a similar position half a dozen times over the years back home. What had stopped me from helping in those situations? Had I worried about being taken advantage of or of opening myself up to some sort of danger? Was I overscheduled and simply did not have the time? Or had I never truly learned that in order to make it in this world we needed to be able to rely on each other?

A few other customers had come out to the parking lot to take photos of us, and the rich family used the distraction to bid their farewells.

"Good luck," said the woman as she climbed back into her SUV. "I hope it all works out for you."

Overhearing our discussion, a young, college-aged man offered to take a look at Sunny for us. He fiddled around with the spark plugs for a moment and then asked, "Do you need a mechanic? My friend is a mechanic."

We *really* needed a mechanic. It was getting late, the daylight nearly gone, and we were stranded.

"Probably," I said, feeling ambivalent about our predicament.

"I'll pick up my friend and bring him here," said the man. He climbed on his motorcycle and headed off in the direction that we were supposed to be moving in. We sat down once again and waited for the mechanic to return.

A man in his early thirties emerged from the shop clutching a coffee and struck up conversation with us. He wanted to know what we were up to but, more importantly, he wanted us to know what he was up to. He was self-employed and driving to Khadki for business, he told us. He read a self-help finance book that he kept face up so that we could see the title. He asked about the broken rickshaw.

"It happens all the time," I muttered. "The good news is that every time we break down someone comes along to help us."

He looked disgusted and leaned across the table to scold me. "It has been your luck, but you should not depend on luck."

"Okay," I said, and turned away to ignore him.

But he insisted that I know the number to the police department and how to change a spark plug. (Okay, he had me there.) He squinted his eyes into a scowl as he told me that I should know people in every city that we were driving through so that I'd have someone to call when I got myself into trouble.

An uncomfortable feeling scratched inside my chest. He was so mistrusting. We'd been relying on the kindness of strangers for days, and not one of them had done us wrong. This guy acted as though we ought to be dead by now. He was so paranoid that I felt my own paranoia creep up my spine and settle tightly on my shoulders.

But just then, as if to disprove him, the young man returned on his motorcycle with his friend, the mechanic, seated on back.

"Hey, look," I said smugly.

The mechanic fiddled around in Sunny's bowels and reported that her gasket had blown. In order to get her running again we'd need a new part. But due to the hour most of the shops were now closed.

I turned to Sarah and Lesley. "I guess we're sleeping at Café Coffee Day after all."

But the mechanic insisted that he might be able to track down the part that we needed, tonight, in a neighboring town.

"Are you *sure?*" we asked him.

"Yes. Yes. Do not worry. It is no problem."

"Okay," we said. "All right. Thank you."

The self-help-reading, self-employed Rich Guy, however, was appalled at our willingness to trust the mechanic. He inserted himself into our conversation, talking gruffly to the men in Hindi.

There was something off about Rich Guy, and I didn't want his help. He made me uncomfortable with his insistence that we not trust anyone. "There are many bad people out there," he told me, and I began to fear that he might be one of them.

The mechanic and his friend drove off into the darkness before we were even able to give them money to buy the gasket. "If those guys don't come back it's because Mr. Rich Guy over there pissed them off," said Sarah, nodding in his direction.

I was drinking my third cup of coffee when the power went out. Everything for miles and miles became cloaked in a deep, black darkness. It became suddenly apparent how truly alone we were, stranded at an isolated Café Coffee Day with creepy Rich Guy and two male employees.

"This does not feel right," I whispered to Sarah across the inky expanse of our table, quiet enough that Rich Guy couldn't hear me.

"I know," she said, "Mr. Rich Guy gives me the creeps."

For the first time on the entire journey, I felt unsafe. Rich Guy gave off a terrible vibe. Why was he still hanging around?

We gathered our things and took refuge in Sunny, though she didn't provide us any real protection. From my perch in the rickshaw, I watched with relief as Rich Guy finally climbed into his car and reversed out of the parking lot. As I let out a deep breath I hadn't even realized I'd been holding, I whispered to Sarah, "Thank God."

But instead of driving away, Rich Guy reentered the parking lot and pulled his car up to our rickshaw so close we could touch it. He'd blocked us in. Music blared from his radio, a popular American song, *And tonight's gonna be a good night. And tonight's gonna be a good, good niiiight.* Suddenly my brain issued a red alert. Every cell in my body fired a warning. It was so dark out there.

Before Brian and I had parted ways, he'd handed me his Leatherman tool and shown me how to extract the knife. "Listen, I know you probably won't need to use this, but you should have it with you just in case." I'd balked, but he'd insisted. "Just take it," he'd said. "It will make me feel better."

I dug through my backpack and found the tool. Mr. Rich Guy watched me through his open window. My nerves were firing double time as I flipped up the blade and clenched it in my right hand, just in case.

~

We were still waiting for the mechanic to return when the lights came mercifully back on. A little bit of light made a huge difference, and I felt myself relax a little. Rich Guy was still sitting in his car, but he'd taken the hint and stopped talking to us. He played a video game on his phone, blowing things up.

I began to lose hope that we'd ever see the mechanic again. Café Coffee Day would be closing in less than an hour, and Rich Guy did not appear to be going anywhere. We were stranded and out of options, again. The best plan I'd formulated was that we could sleep in shifts in the rickshaw, alternating turns holding the knife.

But then, like a superhero, the mechanic-on-the-motorcycle came swooping back into the Café Coffee Day parking lot. In his hand he held a small cardboard box, and inside that was a gasket. I stole a glance at Rich Guy who still fiddled with his phone. It felt like all of India had been vindicated by the mechanic's return. *See*, I wanted to tell him, *people are good*.

It took the mechanic less than three minutes to replace the gasket and resurrect Sunny once again.

Mr. Rich Guy, seeing that he'd done his job, gracefully took his leave. We thanked him with muted enthusiasm before turning our attention back to the mechanic, who was milling about with the motorcycle driver. These guys had spent their entire night sourcing parts for us and fiddling with our rickshaw for no discernable reason except for that we needed them to.

When we asked the mechanic how much we owed him, he told us that the gasket had cost 150 rupees (three dollars). Otherwise, we should pay him only what we could. Lesley, Sarah, and I huddled together to discuss what we should do. Nothing seemed enough to express our gratitude. Lesley counted the money from our combined funds and folded it in her hand.

"Wait," I told her, "let me add some yellow envelope money." I dug it from my backpack, and Lesley handed it all to the mechanic. He didn't count it. He didn't need to. We thanked the mechanic and his friend—we were getting good at thank-yous—and puttered down the road in search of a hotel.

～

Our brake pads had completely disintegrated, and duct tape held our spark plugs in place as we limped through the finish line in Kerala five days later. We pulled into a grassy lot where a few other rickshaw teams loitered about. A man sold chai from the back of his bicycle. We unceremoniously signed the arrivals board. There was an utter lack of enthusiasm among the three of us. We'd driven over one thousand five hundred miles through the rural villages and roaring cities of India in a rickshaw, and we'd arrived where we intended to arrive with all of our limbs still attached to our bodies. We'd survived! But we were too road weary and exhausted to enjoy our accomplishment. I only wanted to get the hell out of the rickshaw. And then I wanted a shower, a nap, and an ice-cold beer.

The rickshaws of the teams that had arrived before us were parked in a row near the back of the lot. Some of them were banged up and bashed in and made Sunny look like a shiny new floor model in comparison. "Did anyone die?" I asked the woman collecting rickshaw keys as I slid ours across the table to her.

"No," she said, "not this time."

Later in the evening we caught a ferry to a small man-made island where the organizers of the Rickshaw Run were throwing the after party. They'd built a dance floor in the middle of an open field, and buffered it on three sides by two buffets and a bar. Dozens of round tables were sprinkled about the yard and draped with clean, white tablecloths. It looked like an upscale wedding reception filled with hundreds of guests who had black grime caked to their skin and rosy, wind-burned cheeks.

In the buffet line I ran into the rickshaw runner who'd saved us on that first night by towing us into Barmer. I told him about our breakdowns (too many to count) and about the man who let us sleep in his chai shop, about losing Sarah's cell phone and then finding it again, about the dogs we fed and the countless people that came to our rescue time and time again. Though it felt like an important piece of my Rickshaw Run experience, I didn't mention the yellow envelope. This time I followed the second rule and kept it in my heart.

A starless, humid sky stretched above us. It turned 1:00 a.m. and then 2:00 a.m., and we were drinking beer and laughing. I felt giddy with happiness and freedom. Everyone at the party had completed the same daunting task, but we all had such different experiences. One thing, though, we shared: the people of India had taken care of us all.

The following day I said good-bye to Sarah and Lesley and caught a taxi to the airport. A few days earlier Brian had emailed to tell me that he'd rented an apartment in the southern state of Goa and asked if I would meet him there. It was not easy to get things done in India, and I couldn't imagine renting an apartment had been simple, but he'd done it on his own. He was capable of more than I'd given him credit for.

My nerves fizzed like exposed wires as my plane flew south, bringing me closer to Brian. A mixture of emotions bubbled inside of me when I thought about our reunion. I was excited to see him again but also anxious, comforted by the thought of him but equally stifled by it. The scale of my heart seesawed with dueling desires. I had no idea what it would decide to do.

CHAPTER 12

BRIAN OPENED THE APARTMENT DOOR IN HIS TATTERED Ganesh T-shirt and stained khaki shorts. I hugged him big, and he hugged me right back, and it felt right to be together. As he held me, I realized how much I missed him. There was no doubt that I loved him, but I was not yet sure if that was enough.

Brian broke our hug and stepped back to look at me. There were tears in his eyes. "Welcome home," he said, and held the door open so I could walk through. "I'll give you the tour."

The apartment was a light-filled, open space with a couch, a glass table for eating, a thin strip of kitchen with a stovetop and a small refrigerator, a bedroom with a bed as stiff as a broom, and a single, sparkling bathroom.

"A Western toilet!" I exclaimed when I saw it. I could not have been happier if it spat out hundred-dollar bills when it flushed. "I've gotten pretty good at the squat toilet though," I bragged.

"Me too," he said. "I prefer it, actually."

As I ran an admiring hand along the length of the kitchen counter I asked, "This place is amazing; how'd you find it?"

Brian shrugged. "It took some work."

I reached toward him and squeezed his arm just above the elbow. "I missed you."

He leaned in and brushed his lips against mine. "Same here," he whispered, then picked my backpack up from where I'd dropped it near the couch. "Let's get your things put away."

In the bedroom, I settled cross-legged on the floor and folded my clothes into the bureau while Brian sat on the bed watching me.

"Well, how was it?" he asked.

My lungs filled in a deep breath. How could I describe the dust-filled emptiness of the Thar Desert and the maniacal chaos of Barmer and Pune and the dozen other big cities we drove through? How could I explain the heartbreak of seeing the starving dogs and the hopeless poverty? How could I convey that despite all of that my drive through India had been beautiful and uplifting and transformative? That it had shown me that many people have hard lives but a hard life is very different than a bad life or a life without purpose and meaning.

"I don't even know where to start."

"Okay. I get that," said Brian. "How about I tell you about one of my days first?"

"Yes, do."

"Well, after the camel safari, I took the train to Jodhpur and decided to find a few of the bazaars that I had read about. I didn't really know where they were, but I figured if I wandered around long enough I would find them. So I started out and was walking down the streets and felt like I was on the verge of a panic attack."

"Oh, God."

"I'm not saying that to alarm you. I've realized that is the norm for me when I wander the streets in India. But this day was especially bad. My anxiety was so strong that I felt light-headed and had to stop for a moment to gather my bearings.

"So it wasn't going so well at first. After about twenty minutes of walking, I found myself in the Old Town district of Jodhpur, which I had wanted to explore. It was nice there, quieter and more residential. Somehow I ended up at a small lake, which was really peaceful, so I hung out there for a while. While I was there a couple of teenage boys came up and asked me if I wanted to feed the fish with them. At first I thought there was a translation problem, but when they started throwing little balls of wheat into the lake I joined them. Then they showed me a small Hindu temple that was nearby, and that was neat to see.

"After parting ways with these boys, a guy about the age of sixty stopped me. He had a two-year-old in his arms, and I shook hands with both of them. He invited me into his house to have tea, which I accepted. He introduced me to his entire family. During tea he told me his hobby was collecting friends. We talked for about twenty minutes, and then I left."

I laughed. "Collecting friends?"

"Right? How great is that?" He continued. "I was feeling good because I hadn't felt good at the start of the day, and my anxiety levels had been really high, but I fought through them and met some people who were really nice."

"That sounds like a great day," I said, happy that it had not ended with Brian locked in some dingy hostel bedroom trapped in bed fighting panic attacks.

"I'm not done yet."

"Oh, sorry."

"Then I was hit by a motorcycle for the second time that day. The first person clipped me on the arm with their handlebars on the elbow. It wasn't a big deal, but it did kind of hurt. The second person hit me in the calf from behind, which took out my leg. I nearly fell, and it kind of hurt, and the guy didn't stop, which pissed me off.

"This totally ruined whatever good feeling I had from the people I'd met earlier. So I headed back to my hostel to read a little bit, listen to some music, and begin packing up my stuff. Then I headed out to dinner.

"On the walk to dinner I was stopped by a number of people wanting to chat. People were just being nice, but I didn't want to tell everyone my name and what country I was from and my age and whether or not I liked India. One of the guys who wanted to chat stopped his motorbike to talk to me. We ended up going to a bar to get a few drinks. We talked about things ranging from music to what we thought life was about to the girlfriend who'd recently dumped him. It turned out that he lived in Goa and was headed down there on his motorbike. But he told me that only after I told him I'd planned to go to Goa. So I didn't know if the guy was honest or full of shit.

"I left the bar and went to a restaurant, alone, and ate a delicious curry. The owner's dog curled up at my feet, and it was a pug in a puffy coat, if you can believe it."

I let out a little laugh, "Now, that's one thing I haven't seen here yet."

"It was just another day in India, and I felt a range of emotions, from wanting to fly away ASAP to loving it and everything in between."

"Wow," I said when he'd finished. He'd managed to capture the experience of traveling in India in a single story.

"At this point I have no idea what to make of this country. It has tried and tested me in so many ways. The only way I can really describe it is exhausting. It's both good and bad, but I can't tell which it is more of."

Good, I wanted to say, but Brian's feelings about India were more convoluted than my own.

"Also," he added. "This is the first time in my life I have experienced real culture shock. Some days I can do a good job of letting things just roll off of my back, but other days everything starts to jade me." Brian sat back on the bed and seemed overwhelmed just at relaying the story. "We've only been in India for three weeks, and there's a lot more to learn, but at this point it confuses the hell out of me."

"Me too," I said. "But that's what I love about it. India demands that you are fully present. You have to be all here, just while walking down the street. It kind of pulls you out of your own head."

"That is the truth."

While unpacking my backpack I'd pulled out the yellow envelope and sat it atop a stack of my clothes. I held it up toward Brian. "Hey, did you give any yellow envelope money away?"

He shook his head. "To be honest, it was the furthest thing from my mind. What about you?"

I told him about the dogs and the pineapple biscuits, about the boy who guarded our rickshaw and the magical mechanic in Pune. "There were so many others—" I stopped midsentence, thinking of the man at the chai shop who'd slept at our feet and the dozens of kind strangers who'd tinkered with, jump-started and changed tires on our rickshaw.

"I know," Brian said, and I knew he did.

As I shoved my empty backpack beneath the bed I looked down at my left hand; my wedding ring was still tucked away in my wallet.

"Brian, I..."

"Wait," he said, and held up his hand. "I know we have a lot to talk about. But can I just enjoy you for a few minutes, just enjoy having you here, before all of that begins?"

Surprised, I sat back in the bed, sensing a change in him. He was more confident, more self-assured.

"You seem different."

"Huh," he gave a small laugh and looked down at his ratty traveling shorts. "Same old me."

I looked him in the eye. "No, something is definitely different."

He shrugged. "Maybe I am different." Then he paused before saying, "Or maybe you're the one who has changed?"

⌒

Our apartment sat at the edge of Colomb Bay, a peaceful blip of a village that seemed to be barely winning its fight for existence against the encroaching jungle. The single-lane roads were covered in thick red dirt, and the palm trees and tropical plants were so dense that monkeys could swing from tree to tree without ever touching the ground.

That evening we set out on a fifteen-minute walk from our apartment to the beach. Following Brian down the skinny roads, I swiveled my head from side to side as we passed colorful houses painted lime green and fuchsia. Chickens clucked aimlessly around in the dirt yards, and clotheslines slumped between trees, draped heavy with laundry.

A warm breeze blew off the ocean and bent the palm trees away from the water. We settled in at a beachfront restaurant constructed of palm fronds and tarps, and sat at a plywood table lit with a single flickering candle. The sand was still warm from the heat of midday and I buried my bare feet beneath it. Brian leaned toward me. "Remember that email I sent you about the camel safari? How I told you it gave me time to think?"

My heart began to pound. *This is it*, I thought, *he's going to tell me he's not happy anymore.*

"Kim, I realized something when we were apart. We sold the house and all our stuff; we left our jobs and everyone we know behind. All of a sudden we're spending every minute together in foreign countries. Everything about our lives has changed, but the way we approach our relationship hasn't changed at all. It's crazy to think that we can go through all of that change and not change our relationship too. We're not on vacation, this is our *life.*"

Our waiter arrived and slid a paneer masala dish and a steaming piece of naan in front of me. I ripped tiny pieces of it off and gave it to a begging dog; grateful for the few seconds the interruption gave me to think.

During the last day or two of the Rickshaw Run, I'd tried to wrap my head around my feelings about our relationship and what I wanted moving forward. And I hadn't come to any definitive answer. But Brian was right about this. Our entire lives had changed. If we wanted our relationship to work it would have to change too.

But did I want it to work?

It was all so goddamned confusing. I had the urge to run straight into the ocean and swim toward the enormous glow of the moon, to listen to the embryotic swish of the waves, stare up at the stars, and let the salt of the water pound my body until life made sense again.

After taking a sip of my beer I said, "Brian, I had a lot of time to think during all of those hours in the rickshaw. But the truth is, I'm still confused." I took a deep breath. "I wanted this so badly." I waved my arm in the air to indicate all of it: travel, freedom, the time and space to craft a life I wanted for myself. "I just assumed once we hit the road I'd be happy and that we'd be happy together. I never even considered that it wouldn't be that way." I remembered the anxiety I used to feel back in Portland, how fearful I'd been that my future was already mapped out. I'd thought traveling would change all of that, and it had. But I'd just swapped one set of problems for another.

"But I'm not happier than I was before. Truthfully, I'm less happy. But I also feel closer to living the life that I want. And that confuses me, because if I'm closer to the life I want, shouldn't I be happier?"

Brian stared off into the black ocean waves and did not respond.

"So much of my unhappiness I've blamed on you," I continued. "Unfairly. During the Rickshaw Run I realized that my unhappiness doesn't have anything to do with you. I love you, but that's not what this is about."

After the Rickshaw Run I'd called my parents from my hotel room to let them know I'd survived. Through the crackling static of Skype my dad had asked, "You're on a journey of self-discovery, so what have you learned about yourself?"

"Dad!" I'd said. "That's ridiculous!" His blunt statement had embarrassed me, but he'd been right of course. I *was* on a journey of self-discovery. In the beginning I hadn't seen that, but I could see it now.

Breathing deeply once again, I dug my feet deeper into the sand.

"I just need to figure out who I am, Brian, who I am on my own without being defined by you, without relying on you. We've been together for so long. I can't imagine myself without you. And that scares me because I'm afraid that I will never know who I am as an independent human being while we are together."

When I looked over at him he would not meet my eye. It

was such a beautiful evening, so much like the evening when we'd roamed the streets in Buenos Aires, back when things were just beginning to fall apart. Just like then, a large part of me wanted desperately to be content. But a more insistent piece of me kept pushing for the truth.

Brian let me take his hand. "I know this sucks. Maybe I'm asking too much by hoping you'll stay here and wait while I figure it out. I don't expect you to wait, if you don't want to."

Brian was still watching the ocean. His face remained unreadable.

"The thing is, I feel stuck in so many of my old ways. I want to grow. But I don't know if that is something that I can do with anyone else, or if the only way I can do it is on my own."

Brian blinked and turned his head toward mine. "Kim, have I ever asked you to be anyone other than who you are? Have I ever held you back from anything you wanted to do? Have I ever discouraged you from anything? I mean, I'm here, aren't I? I'm sitting on a beach with you in India because you wanted to see the world. You just got back from driving a rickshaw through the goddamned country. Did you ever think about how that made me feel? How worried I was about you? And how jealous I was too? I would have liked an adventure like that." Brian shook my hand from his and gripped his beer.

He was angry. Any normal person would be angry. But I was angry too. Because I didn't *want* it to be the way it was. I wanted it to be easy. I wanted to be happy. But I'd ignored the truth, and it'd gotten me nowhere. This was the only other option.

"If I could just snap my fingers and have it back the way it used to be I'd do it in a second. But this is something we have to go through, I have to go through, so that, whatever happens, I know I faced it. I need to know that I didn't just let life happen but that I chose the direction. I just need to Brian. *I need to.*"

Brian finished his beer and stood up to leave. I looked down at his meal; he hadn't touched a bite of it. "There's nothing I can say to that, Kim. You do what you need to do. But don't forget who you're dragging through the mud with you."

~

Two weeks later Brian and I caught a taxi to the Goa airport in the early hours of the morning and stood around waiting for Wendy to arrive. She bounded through the exit doors and bellowed, "HELLO," and I felt myself almost buckle with joy at seeing a familiar face after so many months among a crowd of strangers.

It'd been almost a year since I'd seen Wendy, and I was surprised at how rocked I was by her sudden appearance. In the whirlwind of the last crazy months, it felt like our entire life back home had been washed from the map. But here stood Wendy, flesh and blood, proof that it all still existed. Enfolding her small frame in my arms, I told her how great it was to see her. Then Brian and I ushered her toward our taxi.

The three of us shoved into the back seat. "Hello!" Wendy bellowed again. She tapped at the glass of the window. "Wow! India!

"How are you guys?" She gave me a look that I knew meant,

We'll talk all about that later. "I can't believe I'm finally here! It's so good to see you!"

"Put on your seatbelt," I warned. "And hang on for dear life." Our driver hit the gas, and the three of us shot backward as our driver sped south toward our temporary home.

An hour later the taxi dropped us in front of the apartment. "Wow, look at this place," said Wendy as she stepped from the cab to look up at the bright-yellow building. "It's so, *sunshiny*."

I laughed. "Right? Very tropical."

Behind us, a herd of dusty water buffalo were lumbering down the road toward an open field where they grazed each morning. Their rough and wrinkled skin looked prehistoric; their horns curled from the side of their heads like hooks.

"These are our neighbors," I said, and fanned my hands at them. "Try not to get in their way." Then I pointed to a red moped parked in front of our building. "That's our scooter. Brian rented it so that we can drive to the nearby beaches." From beneath a palm tree, a black and white dog, curled between two other dogs, raised her head and barked. "And *that* is Sheera. The other two are Stewie and Juan."

"How do you know their names?"

"I don't. But we've grown pretty fond of these little guys, so we named them." I walked up to Sheera and scratched behind her ear. "They spend all day sleeping beneath this tree. We use Michele and Glenn's yellow envelope money to feed them." Wendy nodded. She knew all about the yellow envelope, had run dozens of miles with me my final week in Portland listening as I daydreamed aloud about all of the ways we might give the money away.

That afternoon, after Wendy had settled in, we plotted out a whirlwind tour of India. Since I was still trying to refuel from the Rickshaw Run, I would have been content to spend the three weeks of her visit lounging on the couch watching movies on my laptop. But Wendy had not flown all the way to India to stare at the white walls of my apartment. So two days later we were back at the airport to catch a flight to Delhi.

A crowd gathered at our departure gate. The swarm of bodies stood hip-to-hip and elbowed for position to board our plane. Wendy and I held back and watched the madness from a distance. "I'm so confused," she said and looked down at her boarding pass. "We've got assigned seats, what's the rush to get on the plane?"

I laughed and shrugged my shoulders. "I have wondered that many times. One thing I've learned is to try not to apply Western logic to Eastern thinking. Just sit back and enjoy the ride."

Onboard I tracked down my seat. A large man sat near the aisle in my row, and I scooted past him, folded myself next to the window, and stole a glance in his direction. He wore florescent hipster sunglasses, a long, embroidered sherwani jacket that looked like it'd been bedazzled by an over-sugared ten-year-old, and rings on all of his fingers. His long, straight hair hung down past his shoulders, and he was huge, easily six-foot-five with a body as big as a linebacker. He looked like a Bollywood star.

After shoving my bag beneath the seat in front of me, I dug

out my Kindle and began to read. But the in-flight announcements
came on, and I switched my Kindle off again. The man, seeing an
opportunity for conversation, turned and introduced himself.

"Are you from America?" he asked.

"Yes. Are you from India?"

"Mumbai." He ran his giant fingers elegantly through his
hair. "I am a devotional singer. I travel all over India, and sometimes internationally, performing."

"Are you traveling to a performance now?"

He shook his head purposefully. "No." I waited for him to
continue but he said nothing more.

Our plane rose. Outside of the window a layer of cloud swallowed up the thick green jungle below. When we emerged, the sky
was blue, the ground a memory below us. Flying was not my forte,
but I always loved the moment when the plane broke through
the gray into a perfect, sunny sky. Back in Portland I'd think of
it often during the endless days of winter rain. Somewhere up
there, I'd tell myself, the sun is shining, and the sky is as blue as it
is in early autumn.

Removing my journal from my carry-on bag, I began writing, trying to sort through my thoughts about Brian. It was so
much easier for me to comb through my issues when we had
physical distance between us. I'd grown tired of living in a state
of upheaval. I wanted a resolution to this mess, so I'd write until
some kind of truth popped through.

The devotional singer leaned over in his seat and began to
read my scribbling. Shooting a look at him I snapped my journal

shut. He held his hands out in front of him, inspecting his rings. "Tell me," he said. "What do you think God is?"

Bringing up God was the Indian equivalent of asking someone back home what he or she did for a living, and it no longer surprised me when Indians wanted to talk philosophically. I shifted in my seat so that I could face him. "What do I think God is? That's a complicated question, don't you think?"

"No, I think it is very simple. God is vibrations. God is emotions. Whenever you feel something you are not far from God."

"Huh," I said. "Well if that is the case I've been very close to God lately."

He smiled, pleased to hear it. "Now, let me ask you. What is religion?"

A beat of time passed and then he continued without waiting for an answer.

"I am Hindu, but what is that? I do not believe in caste, religion, or money. I believe in soul. The soul is what I believe in."

Remembering the conversation I'd had with Carver way back in Peru, I told him, "Me too. I believe in the soul."

Our plane began to bump with turbulence, and I gripped the armrests. The devotional singer looked unfazed. He turned toward me again and changed topics. "How old do you think I am?" He removed his sunglasses and folded them into his enormous hand.

"Thirty-eight?" I guessed.

"No, I am thirty."

"Oh," I said, embarrassed. "I'm really bad at guessing ages. How old do you think I am?"

He stared at me. "I think you are between forty and forty-five."

Wincing, I instinctively touched at the corners of my eyes where the slightest of wrinkles was beginning to form. "No, I'm thirty-one. Wow, you think I look forty-five?"

He stared me squarely in the face. "I'm sorry. I did not mean to hurt you. Sometimes I am wrong."

How easily those words flowed from his lips. Had I ever apologized so directly, so sincerely, to anyone in my life?

"Don't worry about it," I muttered, and touched the corners of my eyes again.

Directing my attention back to my journal, I laid my arm across the page to keep the devotional singer from reading it. A half hour later, the flight attendant delivered boxed lunches to us, and I opened mine and scanned the contents. Vegetarian. God bless India.

The singer picked up his sandwich and offered half to me, saying, "I think you have had hard times recently."

Surprised by his gesture, I turned down his sandwich but ignored his remark.

He pointed to my journal. "May I show you something?"

"In my notebook?"

"Yes, I must write something down for you."

Flipping to an empty page, I handed it to him. He nodded toward my pen. "I need that too." I slid it across my tray table. He pinched it between his enormous fingers, then bent over my journal and wrote GOD IS NOWHERE.

"What does this say?" he asked.

Was this some kind of joke? Glancing behind me, I checked to see if I was being filmed by an Indian version of *Punk'd*, but no one was watching. "It says God is nowhere."

"No!" he exclaimed. "Look again."

My eyes scanned the paper again. "It definitely says God is nowhere."

He picked up the pen again and drew a line through the last word. GOD IS NOW | HERE. "You see," he said, and tapped his finger on the page. "It says God is now here. God is *always* here; it is just a matter of looking."

"Ah," I said. "Very clever."

"No, not clever, just true. Kim," he continued. "Challenges are from God. They are a *test* from God. We can't learn and become without challenges."

Had I told him my name? I scanned my clothes, my journal, and the bag at my feet to see if my name was visible, but it wasn't.

"Are you a teacher?" I asked him.

"Oh noooo." He drew out the 'o' in a long breath. "There is only one teacher. The rest of us are students." He looked at me and stroked his long hair; the sunlight streamed through the window and glinted off of the rings on his fingers. "All is written," he said. "God planned to put me in this seat next to you."

~

The Taj Express train deposited Wendy and I in Agra. We shrugged off the touts pushing taxi rides and Taj Mahal tours and stepped into a small restaurant outside the western gate of India's most famous landmark. I was quieter than usual, replaying my conversation with the devotional singer. How did he know my name?

We sat down at a table near the window. After ordering a banana *lassi*, I stared out at the street scene. Cows wandered aimlessly down the dusty alleyways and people on foot, in rickshaws, and on motorcycles zipped around them. I adored the reverence that Indians had for cows. How odd, I thought, the things we assign meaning to; something mundane to one person was holy to another.

Inside the restaurant, a group of Indian women were gathering at a table across from us. The flash of their colorful saris caught my eye, and I looked up at them. They were giggling at us.

Looking down at my shirt, I felt self-conscious. That morning I'd dressed in the nicest thing I owned, a hand-beaded tunic that I'd bought from a textile shop back in Barmer while Lesley, Sarah, and I were waiting for the mechanic to finish work on our rickshaw. Were the women making fun of me? *A white woman in an Indian* kameez, *how funny!* I blushed at the thought and wished I'd dressed in my Western clothes.

"So," said Wendy. "How are you *feeling?*"

My head dropped into my hands. "I am so confused," I told her. "I love Brian. But I'm not sure if I can become who I need to become unless I'm on my own."

Wendy took a sip of her lassi. "All right," she said, "then let me ask you this. Who do you need to become?"

"I—" I stopped to think about it. Who did I need to become? I began to speak again, and then stopped. "God," I said finally. "I have no idea."

My eyes were drawn back to the table of women. One of them stared at me. She smiled and called out, and I shifted in my chair, annoyed. I did not want to engage in yet another conversation with a stranger while I tried to sort through the biggest crisis of my life.

But she held my gaze and beamed the brightest smile. She had dark eyes, deep pools that danced like light on water, and I could see that she radiated a maternal kindness.

From across the room the woman spoke to me again and I cocked my head to the side like a dog. "I'm sorry," I told her. "I don't know what you said."

A girl sitting across from her spoke up. "That is my mother. She is speaking to you in Punjabi. We are from Punjab."

"Oh," I nodded distractedly. "Hello."

"My mother just loves you. She is saying hello to you in our language."

I repeated it back, the word. The woman laughed, and the rest of the table laughed with her.

Turning my attention back out the window, I watched a young boy chase a bicycle tire down the street, desperate for some uninterrupted time to think through my thoughts. Wendy's question stomped through my brain. Who did I need to become? Who did I need to become?

From the corner of my eye, I watched the woman rise and approach our table. I shot a look at Wendy. Was she going to ask us for money? Try to sell us a tour? As I muttered a tentative hello, the woman reached down and cupped her hands around my chin like you might do to a child. She said to me slowly in lilted English, her palms warm against the cool of my cheeks, "You make me so happy." Hap-E! The end of the word pronounced in an upswing, like a celebration.

Shocked by her touch, I stared right into her eyes. She stared back deeply into mine. "You make me so hap-e!" she said again.

And then she turned and walked away. My hand rose to my chin and I stared at the space next to our table that the woman had just occupied. My heart pounded, and tears welled in my eyes.

The strangest sensation settled over me. I *believed* her. Suddenly I knew that I was cherished and that everything, including me, was perfect, and I had nothing to worry about at all. Wendy had asked, "Who do you need to be?" And, inexplicably, I felt an answer rising up from the truest part of me. I was already everything I needed to be.

CHAPTER 13

FIVE DAYS LATER WENDY AND I ARRIVED IN HAMPI, AN ancient city, historical and sacred, settled among boulders in the bright-green Indian state of Karnataka.

On the day of our arrival, we dropped our backpacks at our guesthouse and sat down cross-legged in an empty restaurant. Cows sauntered past the gate outside. Monkeys jumped around in trees.

An amazing thing had happened since we'd left Delhi. The deliberations in my head had suddenly, mercifully, silenced. In their place a feeling of peace had settled. Mentally I felt like I'd traveled from Times Square to some silent cave at the edge of the world. It was such a relief to be free of the maddening chatter of my own looping brain.

We had three days in Hampi, and we spent them wandering around crumbling ruins beneath the relentless sun. In the evenings, when the town cooled, Wendy and I would sit on the rooftop of a restaurant called Ganesh's, drink chai, and talk about our lives. I hadn't felt so happy in months, in *years*, actually. Somehow, a feeling of contentment had arranged itself inside of me in the same space that all of the questions had so recently occupied.

"I feel so weird," I said to Wendy.

"How so?"

"I don't know. I feel clearheaded, I guess. I feel happy. I feel *whole*." I took a sip of chai. "For years I've been worried that Brian held me back. Like, there was someone I wanted to be, and I wasn't her, so I blamed Brian because it was easier than blaming myself. God, that makes me sound like a terrible person."

Wendy shook her head. "Kim, a lot of us have been there in one form or another."

"This weird thing happened to me when I was doing the Rickshaw Run. While I was zoning out, watching the world pass by, I had this vision of Brian. He was standing across from me in a field, and I had to choose whether to run toward him or not. I had a *choice*. And I *chose* to embrace him. We've been together for ten years, but until that moment I don't think I'd fully committed to him. I'd always kept the door cracked just a little, so that I'd have enough space to squeeze through and make my escape if I wanted to."

Wendy picked at the *pakora* in front of her, listening.

"When we split up during the Rickshaw Run I told myself I could leave if I wanted to. But I didn't want to. Actually, I realized that I'd never wanted to leave. I'd only wanted to know that I was the driver of my life and not just a passenger along for the ride. I'm ashamed to admit that, but it's true." I took a deep breath. "With

Brian, I needed to know that I stayed with him out of choice and not just convenience or habit. And for myself, I needed to become someone I took pride in being. It sounds crazy, but I feel like, all of a sudden, both of those things happened. But *how?*"

Wendy shrugged. "Sometimes change happens really fast."

"We've been traveling for nine months, and they've been the hardest months of my life. This was not what I expected when we left Portland. But they've been the most important months of my life too. I'm a different person now. I don't even know how to explain it."

"Nine months," said Wendy. "That's funny."

"It is? Why?"

"Because it's our gestational period. We grow for nine months, and then we're born."

"Huh." I looked out over the rooftops of Hampi and down at the empty street below. A lone stray dog pawed at a pile of garbage. The evening seemed to let out a deep sigh. Goose bumps formed on my arms, and the slightest breeze blew at the nape of my neck. "I never thought about it like that before."

The following day, our final day in Hampi, we crossed the Tungabhadra River where we met the rickshaw driver whose windshield shattered. I'd given him yellow envelope money, and he'd thanked me, and then Wendy and I had climbed back into a boat to cross the river once again.

As we walked back to our guesthouse, Wendy spoke. "That rickshaw driver loved you," she said. "Even though you haggled him to death in the beginning. Even before you gave him the yellow envelope money."

I'd noticed our connection too. "It's weird, but giving him yellow envelope money felt different than it has in the past. I didn't feel awkward or worry about what he would think. Back in South America I overthought it so much that giving felt burdensome. But it doesn't feel that way in India."

"I wonder why?"

"I think the only difference is that I feel more comfortable now."

A dog trotted at my feet, and I bent down to pet it. I'd kept up the habit of carrying pineapple biscuits in my purse, and I fed one to him.

"I've noticed something," said Wendy. "People in India are attracted to you." She nodded toward the dog. "Even the animals are attracted to you. I think they sense that you're open, that you're willing to let them in."

I thought about the man on the plane, the woman in the restaurant. What had changed?

"Do you think so?"

"Yeah," said Wendy. "I've never seen anything like it."

That evening we took the overnight bus home again, wedging our bodies into our sleeper compartment, happy to let the cool breeze blow in through the window. The bus bumped away overnight, stopping at intervals so that passengers could pee. Wendy and I filed out and squatted by the side of the road under the moon's unblinking eye, laughing at the pure Indianness of it all.

We were dropped at an intersection on the outskirts of Colomb Bay in the quiet hours before sunrise. We walked back to my apartment through the empty streets, and the dogs barked in the distance.

"India sleeps!" said Wendy. "I didn't think it was possible."

It was a magical time to be awake. Everything around us zinged with energy. It felt like I walked the roads back to our apartment for the very first time. I noticed a colorful one-story house set back in the field where the water buffalo grazed, and banana trees, whole groves of them, next to a beaten path that wound behind a white and red temple. Those things had always been there! But I had never seen them. The same was true of everything in my life. I'd upturned so many rocks, scavenged like the starving for the missing pieces of myself, just to learn that I'd held them all along.

Wendy and I crept into the apartment, and I crawled into bed beside Brian's sleeping body. Tucking my frame against the outline of him, I intertwined our fingers. Brian hardly stirred. "I love you," I whispered into the darkness. I was speaking to us both.

When we woke later that morning, the heat throbbed oppressively. Wendy and I headed to the ocean in the late afternoon, bought Tuborgs, and chatted on recliners. As the sun made her daily departure from the sky, we swam out into the ocean and dove beneath the waves, feeling as free and as playful as dolphins.

The setting sun glowed a brilliant pink, and its light reflected on the water. I floated in the rose-colored afterglow. Wendy bobbed next to me in the Arabian Sea. "You seem happy," she said. "Lighter."

The last blazing moments of sunlight were skipping across the water. I called out over the turning of the waves, "I am."

The following morning, we caught a taxi back up to the airport. As I encircled Wendy in my arms, I told her that I'd miss her. She waved good-bye at the security gate, and Brian and I waved back, watching her go. And then we turned to find a ride back to our apartment. We were alone in India again.

Well, we were not completely alone.

One of the dogs that spent his time curled up at the base of the palm tree outside our apartment door, a black mutt of about forty pounds that we named Stewie, had charmed us so much that he now had both a water and food bowl on permanent residence in our apartment. We let him in for long naps under the couch or short ones spread-eagle on our tile floor, dozing in a strip of sunlight that shone in through the patio door. Our neighbors, Indian women who spent an inordinate amount of time sweeping their porches so that they could watch us interact with the dogs, were horrified that we allowed an animal inside of our apartment. But it felt great to have a dog curled up at our feet.

On the afternoon that Wendy left, I sat Brian down and told him about my revelation. I apologized, not because I felt wrong for doing what I had to do, but because I felt terrible for hurting him.

"It's been a shitty year, Kim," he said. "But it's also been the most incredible year of my life. I'm not going to lie and tell you that I don't feel some hurt and resentment, but I know that whatever you were struggling with was going on inside of you. It was *you*, not me."

"What other choice did I have?" I asked him, feeling a bit defensive. "Did you just want me to ignore it? In a perfect world I'd have worked through all of this before meeting you. But we met too young. I never had the chance."

"I know, I know. I'm not saying you didn't do what you needed to do. I'm just saying that you can't expect me to be completely okay that you held our relationship hostage while you did it."

A part of me wanted to argue, to defend my actions and myself once again. Instead, I took a deep breath and said, "I understand. I would be mad too."

A strange energy rose up between us. From my seat on the couch I stared out of the window into the green of the palm fronds beyond. Brian had given me the room I needed. A lesser person would have jumped ship months ago. I owed it to him to give him the room to feel however he needed to feel.

"Just know that I love you," I told him. "That was not a question."

"I know," he said. "I love you too."

All of the things I'd stopped doing in South America I began to do again. Each morning I'd wake early and go running. In the afternoons I'd read and write. Brian made friends and went off on adventures, driving our rented motorbike to distant beaches and climbing through canyons in the jungle. In the evenings we'd reconnect to eat dinner at the thatched roof restaurants on the beach, feeding pieces of naan to the begging dogs and talking idly about our days.

It felt so good to run again, my heart pounding and my breath finding its rhythm, my legs stretched out and carrying me past the smells and sounds and bright colors of India.

My favorite running route took me on a single-lane road that wound through our small village, past a colorful temple, and up a jungle highway. On this highway, next to the garbage dump, was the crumbling green building that housed the local Animal Rescue Center.

The first day I ran past the rescue center I'd been alarmed as a dozen mangy dogs sprinted from the building toward me. "Whoa!" I'd screamed and frozen in place as the group yelped and barked around me.

From that day on, each morning when I ran past the rescue center, the pack of dogs would join me. Some of them would playfully race ahead of me, while others would trot at my side. We were a total freak show: a Western woman and a pack of misfit, disfigured dogs, dodging manure and motorcycles and water buffalo.

Many of the dogs had terrible ailments. Some were missing limbs. Some had been beaten or starved down to just the bones. All of their hips were rubbed bare from the time they spent pent up on their haunches. But when they ran with me they were happy and free, and I was happy and free, my laughter rising up out of the click of their nails and the pounding of my own feet on the pavement.

For six weeks we lived in the peace of simple routine. Rise, run, and work. I wrote and wrote and wrote, happy because I could finally focus on what I loved and commit my time and energy where I wanted. My contentment was so encompassing that I could have stayed in Colomb Bay forever. But the oppressive heat and stifling rains of monsoon season were on the horizon. One afternoon, while riding on our moped, we were caught in the first of the torrential rains. Water poured from the sky with such intensity that my face stung and I had to close my eyes against it. In a matter of seconds every part of me was drenched. I grabbed tight to Brian's waist as he steered us toward safety.

As the tourist season came to a close, the little shops and restaurants on the beach were being deconstructed one by one. Another disappeared every day. It was time for us to go too.

One afternoon as I typed away at the computer, hidden in the relative coolness of our apartment and making plans to leave India, an email from Michele arrived in my inbox.

Hey you guys! So we wanted to plant an idea as you are planning your extended adventures.

Bicycling through Vietnam is on my bucket list, and there is a trip that Glenn and I have been thinking of doing for several years. It is a two-week bicycling trip from Ho Chi Minh City to Hanoi. It is an organized adventure trip... So, there are guides, hotels, meals, bikes, support vehicles, etc., all included. You sort of show up on day one... Along with other folks who booked the trip...and you don't have to worry about anything else until the end of the trip.

Glenn and I would love to take you guys on this trip. And, by that, we mean pay for it. We have some money put away for just this purpose...and without giving you the sordid details, it isn't money that we have worked for and saved, but rather money we have been lucky enough to acquire that is intended for our amusement. And we can't imagine anything more amusing than bicycling through the rice paddies and hot jungles of Vietnam. Right??!

So, before you listen to that little voice in your head that says "We can't let Glenn and Michele pay for us to travel through Vietnam, they have already done so much for us," please understand that we would get far more out of this than you. We think it would be a blast and would be absolutely thrilled to make it happen. Truly and honestly. We wouldn't offer if we weren't 100 percent sure it wasn't something we wanted to do.

Everything I have read about Vietnam makes it sound

like an amazing place to visit. I have no idea if riding a bicycle as a means of travel is even remotely on your list of things to try. Although, after some of your epic bus rides and the rickshaw, it might seem like a pleasure…sore butt and all!

So think about it. We were thinking maybe November or December. Some of the timing might depend on Glenn's ability to get enough time off (vacation, etc.). He doesn't get much and used it all recently, so he needs to build it back up again. Ahh…remember those days?

We totally understand if (1) you aren't interested in visiting Vietnam, (2) you aren't interested in riding a bicycle every day for long distances (ten to seventy-five miles) in hot weather, (3) the timing isn't right, or (4) you aren't excited by the idea of traveling with strangers (much less us) for a couple of weeks. (Admittedly, there are always some interesting/challenging personalities.)

We would still plan to come visit you on your travels… so it isn't like we are saying it's "biking through Vietnam or nothing." It was just an idea we had and wanted to toss it your way to think about as you ponder where your journey takes you next.

Cheers!

Michele (and Glenn)

Brian and I hemmed and hawed over the decision for a few days. It felt wrong to allow them to do this for us when they had already done so much. But when I told a friend about it she said,

"Give Michele the gift of accepting her offer with grace." Giving yellow envelope money had taught me how scary it could be to extend a gift and how nice it felt when that gift was accepted with an open heart. I didn't want to bat down Michele and Glenn's generosity. And there was no question about *wanting* to go, it sounded like an amazing experience. So we said yes. Suddenly, Vietnam appeared on our radar.

～

We had train tickets booked out of Colomb Bay and plans to travel a few more weeks around India. But the idea exhausted us. A few months ago we would have just stuck with our plans, but we were more in tune with what we wanted now. We canceled our train tickets and developed a new plan. We'd fly to Nepal and trek through the Himalayan Mountains, fulfilling one of Brian's biggest dreams.

The day we left India, a driver picked us up at our apartment. "Before we head to the airport we have to make one final stop," I told him.

He steered the car along my running route, through the windy village roads and past the colorful temple, up the jungle hill, and around the forested bend to the Animal Rescue Center. Earlier in the morning we'd said good-bye to Juan, Stewie, and Sheera. We fed them extra biscuits and rubbed behind their ears. "Hold down the fort until we can get back here," Brian told Stewie. Stewie rolled on his back, looking for a belly rub.

Our taxi stopped in front of the crumbling old building. The dogs were out in the yard running about. They barked when we approached. "I can't go running today," I told them. "Sorry guys."

Inside, a volunteer fed liquid food to a starving dog through an eyedropper. "He's eating," she told me, "but he isn't gaining weight." I thought about the dozens of starving dogs I'd fed pineapple biscuits to over the past few months and the dogs that begged at our beachside tables each evening. Outside of the window, my eyes fell on my wild pack of mangy dogs out playing in the yard. I wanted to save them all.

"We want to make a donation to the shelter," I told the volunteer. She nodded and put down the eyedropper, walked to a tiny wooden desk in the corner of the room, and pulled out a small receipt book. When I filled out the donation form I wrote "Michele and Glenn Crim" in the donor box.

The volunteer looked down at the receipt and then back up at us. "Thank you, Michele," she said to me. She turned to Brian. "Thank you, Glenn." We nodded and smiled and thanked her for the work she did. She handed me a pink slip of carbon paper and I folded it into quarters and slipped it into my wallet. The receipt was the first definitive proof I'd have to show Michele and Glenn of their kindness. The rest was only in pictures and in the stories that I would one day tell.

We climbed back in the cab, and our driver pulled onto the two-lane local highway, racing us toward the airport once again. Soon the swampy jungle heat of Colomb Bay would be unimaginable. We were about to trek hundreds of miles around the highest and most dangerous mountains in the world.

NEPAL

CHAPTER 14

BRIAN AND I CHECKED INTO A DAMP ROOM IN AN ANCIENT teahouse. A single, dim bulb hung from the ceiling like a head in a noose, and bugs threw themselves at the glowing light, buzzing and bombing in a suicidal dance. A poster hung on the otherwise bare wall above one of the single beds. It said, *Enthusiasm is faith set on fire.*

It had rained all day. I dropped my new-to-me trekking poles and knockoff North Face backpack, which we'd picked up for cheap in Kathmandu before starting our trek, on the floor. Then I peeled off my hiking clothes and wrung them out over the squat toilet, changed into a dry outfit, and walked into the dining room. In the corner a wood-burning stove pumped out heat, and a handful of trekkers huddled around it. Above the stove someone had strung a clothesline the length of the room. I draped our slopping socks and muddy pants to dry. Then I held my red, raw hands in front of the fire, and the sting of the warmth brought them slowly back to life.

Brian and I sat down at a heavy wooden table next to a woman. She looked up from her book and nodded at me. "Pity about the weather," she said. "I haven't seen the mountains since I started walking."

"Where'd you start?" I asked her.

"Besisahar."

"Us too."

When the Tibetan bread and potato soup I'd ordered from the old Nepali owner of the teahouse arrived, I cupped my hands around the bowl to warm them again. Brian devoured *dal bhat*, rice with lentils, which the porters we met on the trail claimed gave you "twenty-four-hour power." As I ate, I stared out the window and willed the thick mountain fog to disappear.

The Annapurna Circuit was a two hundred-mile trekking route around the Annapurna Mountain Range that we'd started walking five days ago. It crossed two river valleys and wound through Hindu and Tibetan villages. At its height, the circuit crossed Thorung La pass at almost eighteen thousand feet—three thousand feet higher than any mountain peak in the contiguous United States—and touched the edge of the Tibetan Plateau.

Despite the weather, the structure of trekking felt so deliciously right. Brian and I were always at our best in the mountains, and it was wonderful to move at a human pace, to experience the villages and countryside of Nepal on foot instead of inside of a taxi or bus or even a rickshaw. Moving my body freed my mind to wander, and because the looping indecision of my brain had silenced in India, it finally felt great to be alone with my thoughts.

There was no Internet out there, no television, and no cell phone reception—not that we had a phone. With none of the distractions of the modern world I had time to process all of the insights I'd experienced in India, and Brian and I had hours alone on the trail to talk. We were connecting in a way we hadn't connected in years. We'd been right to come to Nepal.

Through the dining room window I could see the clouds were beginning to clear on the horizon, revealing patches of blue sky. Pulling my hat onto my head, I stepped outside for a better view. In the distance, the seventh-highest peak in the world, Dhaulagiri, appeared through a shroud of clouds, 26,795 feet tall. The Sanskrit name of the mountain, translated, meant *dazzling white beautiful mountain*. I gasped as it appeared and dug into my pocket for my camera. I'd never seen anything so beautiful.

After snapping a photo, I ran inside the teahouse and tapped the woman at our table on the shoulder. "You can see Dhaulagiri!" Then I dragged Brian outside without even letting him put on his shoes. We were both mountain fanatics, and now one of the grandest of them all appeared like a mirage in front of us. "Look," I said, and pointed toward the shadow of Dhaulagiri. It was such an incredible mountain that I felt a twinge of fear as it broke through the fog, humbled by its grandiosity. We stood silently in awe until the clouds thickened and blocked our view again.

An hour later the rain let up completely. "Do you want to go check out the village?" asked Brian.

My legs ached from the eight hours we'd walked, mostly uphill, climbing slippery stone steps that had been chiseled into the slope of the mountain. But our tiny room was much too cold and damp for relaxing, and I was getting anxious in the teahouse dining room. "Yes," I told him.

We walked from one side of the village to the other in under ten minutes. Terraced stone walls held the earth at bay around the perimeter of town. A handful of stone buildings leaned at unnatural angles, slumped with the force of gravity and the settling of their dirt foundations.

A group of boys were lofting a basketball toward a netless rim on a dirt court in front of the village school. We stopped to watch. One of the boys pinwheeled his arm at Brian, gesturing for him to come play. Brian looked at me and gave my arm a little squeeze before stepping onto the court. "Come on."

"Nah, I'll sit this one out."

Sitting on a flat rock, I watched from the sidelines. The basketball slapped rhythmically on the ground, echoing against the mountainside in the waning evening light. The boy passed the ball to Brian. He threw it at the rim and we all watched as it circled once, twice, and then dropped through. "Whoo!" we shouted in unison. I added sports to the mental list I'd been keeping of common languages. So far the list included smiling, laughter, food, music, dancing, and fawning over small babies.

The sky hovered gray as a ghost as we left the village the following morning. On our walk out of town we passed the school again. The windows were dark and the door locked shut, but two preteen boys stood in front of it soliciting donations.

Behind them, a handwritten sign explained that the school had been damaged in a recent earthquake and was too dangerous to enter. They were seeking donations to repair it.

We stopped and stared up at the empty school.

"Do you think that's true?" asked Brian, pointing toward the sign.

"I don't know. There's no way for us to know."

Brian dug his hand inside of his pocket and dropped a wad of rupees into the donation bucket.

"We'll donate in good faith," he said. "Should it be from the yellow envelope?"

I shrugged my shoulders.

There'd been many times that we'd tipped cab drivers larger sums for their friendliness or bought food for hungry children. And each time we'd debated over whether the gift should be attributed to the yellow envelope or if it was a gesture we were making on our own. The lines between what came from *us* and what came from the *yellow envelope* were blurred. Eventually we'd agreed that it didn't really matter. The yellow envelope made us more aware of opportunities to give, and that awareness made us more charitable. Whether we were giving yellow envelope money or our own felt less important than the fact that we were giving at all.

One of the boys held out a notebook. The page was filled with the names of donors from all around the world. Brian propped the notebook against his thigh and wrote, *Michele and Glenn Crim, USA.*

The morning was misty and the trail slick. The path out of town descended steeply. I balanced myself with my trekking poles and watched my feet, worried that even a second of distraction would result in a sprained ankle. As I focused on my steps, I contemplated the rules of the yellow envelope, running through Michele and Glenn's letter in my head. They applied oddly well to my life at the moment.

The first rule of the yellow envelope was *Don't overthink it*, which was another way of saying, *Listen to your gut*. I'd listened to my gut during that momentous run in Forest Park, but I hadn't been able to face the most painful questions it posed right away. So I'd tiptoed into a new reality, peeling back truths as I could bear them, following the path that my gut nudged me down. In that sense I'd *needed* to overthink it. It had been necessary to prod and till the landscape of my innermost longings, to pluck through every insistent question until I felt content with the answers. The overthinking had been necessary. But now I was done with all of that. I felt content with my choices because I could finally see that they had always been my choices. I controlled my life. I always had.

The second rule was *Share my experiences*. Following this rule from the beginning could have saved Brian and me a lot of pain. I'd been ashamed of my feelings, so, instead of voicing them, I'd tried to bully them into alignment with the life I already had. It was only when I shared my experiences, when I *told the truth* about how I felt, that I started down the road to finding peace.

And the third rule, *Don't feel pressured to give it all away*, was the most relevant rule of all. Somewhere along the line I'd developed the false belief that in order to grow up, I had to leave behind the parts of myself that made me feel alive and free. I'd thought that adulthood should feel like sacrifice, so I'd given the most essential parts of myself away, and then I'd blamed Brian for my missing pieces. But I'd been wrong about that. I'd been wrong about so many things.

As Brian moved quickly down the slippery steps in front of me, I called out to him. "You know, the rules of the yellow envelope are surprisingly relevant to our life."

Brian stopped and turned toward me. Surrounding him on either side of the trail were gigantic rhododendrons exploding with magnificent pink blooms. "What makes you say that?"

Cautiously, I stepped down the trail and stopped when I reached him. "I don't know; I was just thinking about it."

"But you're not supposed to overthink it," Brian teased.

I rolled my eyes and smiled at him. "No, really, they're kind of applicable in all kinds of different scenarios," and I explained my reasoning.

An hour later we were white-knuckling our way across a perilous suspension bridge made of four ropes adjoined by wobbly slats of wood. "This is how people die!" I screamed at Brian. Beyond my feet I could see a muddy river raging two hundred feet below. "And if we die, *it is nobody's fault but our own.*" I paused to catch my breath. "This is crazy!"

In response, Brian bent his knees and jumped. The impact echoed backward and the bridge swayed under my feet. My hands grasped the ropes tighter and I squeezed my eyes shut. "Never mind," I screamed again, louder, and with an edge of panic in my voice. "If we die, it is definitely only your fault!"

Brian called back behind him, "So, how does *this* relate to the rules of the yellow envelope?"

Slowly, I stepped my way toward the safety of solid ground. After finally reaching it, I took my backpack off and dropped it against a rock. Then I sunk into a sitting position and looked back at the rickety bridge. "That was stupid," I said, glancing up at Brian.

He looked down and fixed a smile on me, his eyes twinkling with adrenaline. "Where's your sense of adventure?"

Lowering my head into my hands, I tried to slow the pounding of my heart. "It's only an adventure if we live to tell the tale," I muttered. "Otherwise it's called a tragedy."

Brian raised his head toward the sky and spread his arms out in the morning breeze. "But look at this. If we've got to go down somewhere it might as well be here."

The gray mist of the early morning had disappeared, and an orange sun crept into the sky, illuminating the mountains that surrounded us in a stunning, peachy light. It *was* beautiful. But death had never felt as close as it did in Nepal, and I didn't want to tempt fate by joking about it. "Don't say that," I said.

When we first arrived in Nepal, while we were waiting for our trekking permits to be processed, Brian and I had gone on a rafting trip down the Kali Gandaki River, *the mighty Kali*, named after the Goddess of Destruction. The Kali Gandaki was one of Nepal's most holy rivers, and I could see evidence of that everywhere; her banks were dotted with colorful puja, offerings to the Gods.

We'd paddled past temples and statues of Krishna. Calls to prayer rang out over the water, and colorful prayer flags clung to the mountainsides high above us. Onshore, groups of people built funeral pyres. Bodies lay nearby, wrapped in orange shrouds, prepared for burning.

On the second day of our trip, we went through a rapid that spit us out with force near the riverbank. And there, floating face up in the doldrums of still water between two giant boulders, bobbed the body of a dead woman. I'd blinked at the body, astounded. My brain knew what it saw, but my mouth could form no words.

"Is that a human body?" Brian sputtered.

The others in our raft were as wide-eyed as we were and craning their heads toward the bloated and discolored corpse. But in a matter of seconds we were floating off again, rushing away from the body. It had happened quickly. The body was there, we saw it, the raft moved on.

Our guide had treated the corpse as though it was as mundane as an apple in a tree, so I'd tried to let it go. But for the next few hours as we rafted toward camp all I could think about was the body. I wanted to know more about the woman and how she ended up in the river. She had probably been Hindu, and I knew it was customary for Hindus to burn the dead in funeral pyres. Perhaps the woman's family could not afford a pyre so they put her body in the river instead? Or maybe she'd slipped while washing clothes and drowned? Maybe she'd jumped in?

Later as we pitched a tent along the rocky riverbank I asked Brian if we should report it. "Kim," he said. "Who would we report it to?" The Kali Gandaki was an isolated river that had carved one of the deepest gorges between the highest mountains in the world. There were not even roads in this region, just a string of rural villages connected by footpaths worn into the mountainside. Brian was right, there was no one to report it to.

We rafted the Kali Gandaki for three days, and when our trip ended we ate lunch on the riverbank. The rafts and supplies were packed into a bus, the heavy things hauled from the river to the road by porters.

A group of children crowded around us as we ate. A little boy with a brutal burn on his leg pointed to the food on my plate and I nodded yes to each item, an apple, a cookie, and he put them in his mouth. Looking at his scar, I noticed that someone had gathered the skin around his burn and twisted it closed. The result was gnarly; his leg had puckered and deformed. For a moment I considered the yellow envelope, but giving money seemed futile in the face of such immediate needs. He wanted food, so food was what I gave him. Brian sat down beside me, and the boy ate from his plate too. As I watched him gingerly pick food from Brian's plate, I thought that the point of the yellow envelope was not to spread money but *kindness*. So although we were not giving the boy money, we were still sharing the intent of the yellow envelope with him.

From my seat on the riverbank I watched the porters, thin as bone, carrying the heavy supplies up to the bus and thought about how hard life was on them physically. I thought of the woman in the river, of the oxygen-starved altitude, the landslides and the earthquakes that constantly threatened the area. It felt like Nepal's boarders backed right up to the uncomfortable void of death. It made me deeply aware of my aliveness and conscious of how quickly it could all disappear.

In India, too, I'd been exposed to the slim margin between life and death. It wasn't really the presence of death that shocked me but what it represented: that there were customs of dying I'd never considered before and, by contrast, customs of living as well. There were so many ways of being in this world. Of course I'd always *known* that, but to experience it firsthand had rocked me.

I held the thought of India in my mind. What was it about that country? Something big had happened to me there, an inner shift from one way of being to another. India had forced me to surrender, I realized, to uncurl my fingers, loosen my grip, and let go. And the world had not crumbled around me—just the opposite. The world had come to my aid and shown me that I could be so much more if I let my guard down and revealed myself.

The next day we walked away from the Hindu lowlands and climbed into the Tibetan plateau, the land of the Buddha, the awakened one. I, too, vowed to be awake while walking, to *remain* awake, to *really see* the brilliant skies and the old Mani walls, to *really hear* the tinkling of the bells that hung around the necks of the brown packhorses as we passed them. I vowed to be awake to the flap of the prayer flags, to the warmth of the sun on my skin, to the stretch of the day as the hours rose around me.

I vowed to be awake to my aliveness and to the hum of my own inner voice, because I did not want to lose the lessons I'd learned in India. "Be here," I chanted to myself as we walked.

The dirt road we'd been following dwindled to trail. We hiked switchbacks up the side of a mountain, stopping frequently to catch our breath and pet panting, thick-coated dogs. In the distance a Mani wall appeared, a thousand Mani stones propped against it. The stones were decorated with hand painted mantras that had faded from exposure to the elements. Tattered prayer flags blew around it in the wind. Majestic snowcapped mountains rose in all directions.

My heart beat fast as we approached. I ran my hand along the wall. "This is incredible," I whispered to Brian. He nodded, silently, and I knew he sensed the sacredness of the place. We'd passed dozens of temples, Mani walls, *gompas*, and monasteries during our first week on the Annapurna Circuit, and each one had stopped me in my tracks, compelled me to peek through their windows or run my hands along their holy bones. Never before had I been drawn to religious artifacts, but up here on the Tibetan plateau, in the shadows of the Himalayan Mountains, I felt tugged toward them by some unseen force.

I wandered to the side of the trail and dug a small rock from the ground with my fingernail. Just like I'd done on Amantani Island, I would leave this stone as an offering. Though I thought of asking for the same thing I'd asked for on top of Pachatata Mountain, my heart urged me in a different direction. I rolled the rock between my hands and closed my eyes, squared my shoulders toward the sun, and planted both of my feet on the ground. Then I whispered the most important prayer of all, that blessing of the blessed: "thank you."

We reached the village of Upper Pisang in the late afternoon. A wall of prayer wheels marked the center of town. I dropped my backpack and stared up at the snowy peak of Annapurna II. A mighty giant of a mountain, it blocked the dropping sun.

Behind me, a weathered old woman walked clockwise around the wall, reciting the *Oṃ maṇi padme hūṃ* mantra and spinning the wheels. Turning, I watched her for a moment. She looked up at me, and her dark eyes settled on my face. They were warm eyes, and kind, but I felt like an intruder and looked away. It seemed to me that out here you could not tell where spiritual practice stopped and life began because they blended together so completely. The act of living was devotion. I wanted my life to be more like that.

The village of Upper Pisang clung to the mountainside in tiers. Ahead of me, Brian climbed an uneven stone staircase toward a scattering of teahouses. Hefting my backpack onto my shoulders, I followed.

At the top of the stairs a woman, her cheeks a ruddy pink against her dark Tibetan skin, swept the stoop in front of a single-story building. "Seven hundred rupees," she said. We paid her and dropped our backpacks in our windowless room, then climbed a set of dusty old steps even higher above town to a five-hundred-year-old *gompa* to watch the sun set. Brian settled onto a bench—a plank of wood nailed to two tree stumps—and I sat down next to him and looked out over the village toward the mountains beyond.

"It's so beautiful up here," I said in the same revered whisper I'd used at the Mani wall. The sky behind the mountains dripped in cold blues and purples. I zipped up my coat and buried my chin inside for warmth. A biting wind had begun to blow, and a strand of prayer flags whipped from the top of the *gompa*.

"I know," said Brian. He closed his eyes and held his face up to the sinking light, then shoved his hands deep into the pockets of his coat. "It's incredible." He dropped his voice and said, "I never thought I would be here."

"How so?" I asked, unsure if he spoke literally or metaphorically.

"Well, you know, I grew up in the suburbs in Ohio. Everyone I knew lived in Ohio. My family vacationed in Indiana, and sometimes, if we were traveling far, to Michigan. I didn't know anything about the world."

"Yeah," I said. I'd had a similar childhood, though my family had not really vacationed at all.

"When we moved to Oregon I remember that I could physically feel the distance between me and everyone I had ever known. Oregon was as exotic to me as landing on the moon."

"Yep, me too." We'd discussed this all before, our origin stories.

"But now we're in Nepal, sleeping in beds that smell like sweat in rooms without electricity, shitting in squat toilets, and walking through some of the oldest civilizations in human history. And the world feels smaller and less scary to me now than it did back then when the entire boundary of my life stretched from Ohio into Indiana."

That was the irony of travel. The bigger the distance between you and the familiar grew, the smaller and safer and friendlier the world felt. As I sat there among the Himalayan Mountains, it wasn't the first time I'd considered how grateful I was that life could be so much bigger than our own confining perceptions of it.

When the sun disappeared, we reluctantly made our way back down the steps toward our teahouse. Candles flickered in the common room where other trekkers sat sipping tea and talking in low voices. Brian went to join them. Lingering in the doorway, I turned my face toward the sun's soft afterglow and watched until the stars emerged like torches in the sky, offering light until the sun returned again.

That night we huddled down in our separate, single beds. Our room was so void of light that I could not see my hand though I held it inches from my face. There was something I needed to say, something I should have already said. The darkness made it easier to say it.

"Brian?" I whispered.

"Yeah?"

"I'm sorry."

"What?" he ruffled around in his sleeping bag and rolled his body toward mine. "For what?"

My eyes scanned the darkness searching for his, though it was too dark to find him. Earlier in the day, I'd walked a good number of miles thinking about the devotional singer on the airplane to Delhi, how he'd so easily and sincerely apologized to me when he'd wrongly guessed my age. When I was wrong my stubbornness often kept me from admitting it. But I wanted to be the kind of person that apologized when I hurt people. "For everything I've put you through," I said. "I never wanted to hurt you. You're the person I love the most in this world." My voice cracked. "It's not fair that I hurt you."

Tears formed in my eyes and I buried my head in my sleeping bag. I wasn't looking for sympathy, and I knew Brian would try to comfort me if he thought I was upset.

"Are you crying?"

"No."

In the darkness I heard Brian unzip his sleeping bag and take four quick steps across the room. He settled on the edge of my bed and I scooted over to make room for him.

"Hey," he said. "I'm not mad about it, okay? I know you were only doing what you needed to do." His hand probed the bed like a blind man's until it landed on my hip. "The truth is," he continued, "I needed that time too. I wouldn't have had the guts to ask for it, but I needed it too."

"Yeah, but…" I swiped my sleeve across my eyes. "I forced it on you. I forced this entire trip on you."

"Yeah, you did. And you know what? It's the best thing that I've ever done. I'm grateful that you insisted on this trip. I'd never have done it on my own." Swallowing my tears, I waited for him to continue. "Listen, we both hurt each other. Okay? We had our own ways of doing it, but both of us are to blame."

I shook my head against my pillow; it was the only sound in the room. Since our reconciliation in India I'd been carrying around a question that needed answered. "Brian?" I swallowed hard. "Why didn't you just leave?"

He sighed and shifted his weight at the edge of the bed. "I almost did," he said. "But when I thought about it I realized that I love you, and we'd built this whole life together, and if we were able to work through the mess that our relationship would, hopefully, be better for it. Things were bad, but not so bad to quit. Because that would be final…" His voice trailed off before he said, quietly, "and I wasn't ready for that yet."

Patting the bed next to me, I unzipped my sleeping bag and spread it over us like a blanket. "Lay down." I burrowed my head into the pit of Brian's arm and spoke into the warmth of his skin. My words were muffled, "I'm sorry," I said again. "I just need to say it."

Brian tightened his arm around me. "I'm sorry too."

CHAPTER 15

THE VILLAGE OF MANANG HAD ONE ROAD, A HANDFUL OF teahouses, and five skinny horses that milled about. Though it had a population of only six thousand five hundred people, it was one of the largest cities on the entire Annapurna Circuit. Other trekkers told us that Manang had at least one teahouse with hot showers and a bakery that served real coffee. It sounded like the perfect place to take a break.

We were celebrating an important day. Exactly one year ago I'd attended my last day of work. From the dusty streets of Manang we squinted upward and could just make out a splash of color, Praken Gompa, perched like an eagle's nest against the Tibetan brown of the mountains. A holy woman lived there. Those that made the effort to visit her received a blessing for the bargain price of one hundred rupees. It seemed like the perfect way to mark the occasion.

The trail up to the holy woman was so steep that we had to bend forward almost ninety degrees or risk falling backward. My calves screamed at the effort. "So much for a rest day," said Brian when we stopped to catch our breath.

We trudged upward in the thin air. I kept an even pace, breathing so intensely that I could feel the full capacity of my lungs as they expanded inside of my body. As we climbed, I was aware of every tendon, every muscle, and the blood that pumped with purpose through my veins.

A weathered wooden gate eventually greeted us, cracked as though expecting our arrival. The *gompa* was carved from the mountainside, like a cave, and a white *stupa* stood proudly in front, prayer flags waving in the wind. The view from up there was tremendous, the Annapurna range snow-covered and mighty, and the village of Manang looked like a miniature model of itself far below.

We ducked beneath a low door frame to enter the *gompa* and climbed a flight of uneven stone stairs toward a small room. At the top, we took off our shoes in silence and peeked our heads inside. A woman, a Buddhist nun wrapped in a crimson robe, waved us in. She motioned for us to sit on the floor across from her.

She offered us warm tea. The air in the room was spiced with incense. There were no sounds but my breath, Brian's steady breath beside me, and the clinking of our teacups as we placed them on their saucers. Because silence was a state so clearly natural to her, I felt at peace. Had it been a year ago, I would have tried to take control of the situation. I might have said, "Hello, we've come because we heard that you give blessings."

But now I was content to wait and watch, to let things unfold without my intervening.

An altar filled the southern wall of the room, overflowing with burning candles and photos of the Dalai Lama. Gifts from around the world were piled near it: a calendar four years out of date, a clock in the shape of Australia, and, inexplicably, a navy lanyard with the name of a corporate conference printed in a serious white font.

The holy woman sat cross-legged in front of a rustic table. How strange to live on a mountainside, I thought, sitting in silence, waiting all day for people to arrive. Was she alone up here? Was she lonely?

After some time, I broke the silence. "Do you get many visitors?" She said yes and gestured to the altar and then to a metal bowl that sat on the table, filled with folded rupees.

"People come a long way to see you," I said. "We have come a very long way."

She only nodded.

We fell into silence once again. When I finished my tea I set it beside me on the floor. Seeing that my cup was empty, she called me to the table to receive my blessing. As I kneeled in front of the holy woman she tied a colorful string around my neck. Her lips moved, chanting a prayer, and her hands held a holy text. She reached out and touched it to my forehead while pointing to the string around my neck. "For good luck," she said and waved her hand in the direction of the mountains. "This keep you safe."

"*Dhanyabad*," I replied. Thank you.

Exactly one year ago I packed up my desk and bid farewell to my coworkers. Certainly I prayed for good luck that day, anxious in my office chair, perched on the very edge of changing. Then, I couldn't have guessed that with a full rotation of the earth I would be here, on my knees before a holy woman on a Himalayan mountaintop. "Good luck," she said, and they were the same words I received from my coworkers a year before as they paraded me out the door with cupcakes and email addresses and tokens of safekeeping, the same words that Michele and Glenn had written in their yellow envelope letter. "Good luck," they'd said. "Good luck," she said. I bowed my head in reverie to receive it.

We walked for days, rising early with the sun, eating banana porridge and Tibetan bread, smearing zinc onto our noses to protect us from the sun. All of the days were the same, and all were different, as we put one foot in front of the other.

Sometimes we talked and talked, about our life back in Portland, or the people we gave yellow envelope money to, or our trip and what we hoped for when the trip ended. Sometimes we did not talk at all, but the silence between us was so different than the silence that had haunted me in South America, the silence that had screamed *you're lonely* and had only served to illuminate the great distance between us. This silence was warm and filled with understanding. I am here, and you are here, and between us is a place we both belong.

One afternoon we came across an old monastery, set so inconspicuously off the dirt road that we almost missed it completely. But the makeshift fence caught my attention, and I wandered over to take a look. "There's a sign that says all are welcome. Do you think we can go in?"

"It doesn't look open," Brian said, peeking through a slot in the wooden fence with me.

He pulled back from the fence and surveyed our surroundings. I turned too but saw no one, just a chalky, vacant road that disappeared into the horizon. Brian made up his mind. "It wouldn't hurt anything to go in," he said, and then stepped through an opening in the fence where a board hung loose. He disappeared completely behind the wooden barrier before I stepped through the slats after him.

The floor creaked as we walked into a cavernous, musty room. I blinked in the low light, trying to make out the shadows around me. Above me, red and blue textiles hand-stitched with the mantra *Oṃ maṇi padme hūṃ* waved hauntingly from the ceiling. A giant golden Buddha sat cross-legged behind glass in the back of the room, and large, framed photographs of the Dalai Lama hung on the walls. Candles burned in iron goblets and cast jumping shadows on the ground.

"Brian, come look at this," I said, turning to wave him over to the glass case I faced. Inside it were stacks of documents bound by wooden blocks and weathered string.

"I wonder what they say?"

Behind us a smooth voice responded, "Those are ancient Tibetan prayers."

Brian and I both jumped at the unexpected sound and turned to see a young monk standing ten feet away from us, barely visible in the shadows. He stepped into the center of the room, moving as silently as a ghost.

"The Dalai Lama stayed at this monastery sixty years ago when he fled Tibet," said the monk. "He escaped on foot through the mountains. And those documents were smuggled out of Tibet with him." The boy gestured toward the north. "Today the journey would take five days in a jeep."

Brian and I both nodded, stunned by his presence and feeling awkward about our trespassing.

We stood dumbly in our puffy coats and hiking pants and stared at the monk. Staring back at us, the monk, in his orange robe, stood like a dancer—straight and light. "I'm sorry we came in without permission," I said finally. "Is it okay that we are here?"

The boy smiled. "This room is where we pray every morning. You can come tomorrow and pray with us if you'd like. We begin at 6:00 a.m." He paused before adding, "Everyone is welcome here. We are glad you have come."

I looked up at the boy and studied him. He was perhaps fourteen years old with glowing skin, sharp cheekbones, and deep brown eyes. His black hair was cut into a stubbly buzz. Around his neck hung a black bandana printed with white skulls and crossbones.

When Wendy and I were on our whirlwind tour of India we'd visited Dharamsala, the home of the Dalai Lama and the Tibetan government in exile. We'd been lucky, arriving, by accident, just two days before Tibetan Uprising Day. On the day of the celebrations, a sea of monks dressed in orange robes had gathered in front of the Dalai Lama's monastery. Up on a temporary stage, a group of men clutched Tibetan flags, gave speeches, and sang songs.

Many of the monks pulled out cell phones and iPads to snap photos, and I'd been surprised and a little sad that the modern world had encroached upon such ancient traditions. But I did not get to decide who withheld from modern conveniences and who partook in them. Monks could have iPads just the same as a girl from Ohio by way of Oregon could board a plane and find herself at the home of the Dalai Lama among a sea of monks.

Over his orange robe this young monk wore a striped knockoff sweatshirt that I'd seen sold at the tourist shops in Kathmandu. He was a twenty-first-century teenager living a fifth-century tradition. And just as I'd been at the Dalai Lama's monastery, I was struck again with the sense of how little I knew about the world and all of the lives that are lived within it.

"Do you live here?" asked Brian.

"Yes, I do."

"And you study here?"

He nodded. "Our monastery is five hundred eighty-two years old. For hundreds of years, monks from the Mustang villages studied here. But over time the monasteries closed and the monks had to travel to Kathmandu or India to pursue their spiritual studies." The boy walked into the center of the room and pointed toward the door. "And once they left most of them did not return. But two years ago we built a school here. Now the monks do not have to leave."

"Is this where you learned to speak English?" Brian asked.

The monk nodded again, and his cheeks flared pink, clearly pleased and suddenly bashful. "Come upstairs," he said. "I have something to show you."

We climbed an old wooden staircase and stepped gingerly onto the sagging clay roof of the monastery. "This is the best view in the village," said the monk.

"Oh, wow," I uttered as I walked to the edge of the building. Beyond me, colorful prayer flags flapped in the crisp evening air, frayed and dulled by the relentless mountain wind. The stone houses of the village below looked miniature from our vantage on the rooftop. The Annapurna and Dhaulagiri Mountains rose up in imposing beauty toward the south. And to the north sat the sweeping expanse of Tibet, lost now and maybe forever to the churning wheel of China.

Brian walked to where I stood and looked out over the village with me.

"I have never been anywhere so magical," he said. We stood shoulder to shoulder and watched the light play on the mountains. Brian put his hands in his pockets and produced two pieces of candy. He handed one to me, and a silent knowing passed between us.

Earlier, as we'd walked into town, two young children had followed behind us calling, "*Namaste! Namaste!* Sweet?" We'd grown used to the kids we encountered asking for candy—that type of begging was fairly common but discouraged in Nepali culture—so I'd barely glanced behind me to say, "No, no sweets." Still, they followed us. "Hello? Hello? *Namaste*. Sweet?" But when I turned, ready to rebuff them again, I saw that they were not asking but *offering* us sweets. In their chubby hands they held out two wrapped pieces of toffee.

I knelt down to accept them. "Thank you, thank you," I said to the children. They giggled and scurried away without asking for anything in return.

Taking the candy from Brian, I unwrapped it slowly and placed it on my tongue feeling humbled. Brian held his toward the twilight as if to make a toast. "To the beautiful people of Nepal," he said, and slid the candy between his teeth.

Once again I looked toward the mountains. I realized I felt close to something that I had wanted to be close to all my life. I felt insignificant and yet essential, rooted, like my legs had sprouted and grown all the way to the center of the earth.

The monk led us back to the entrance of the monastery in the waning evening light. A small table stood in the corner near the door, stacked with pamphlets about the school, and I picked one up. *We urgently need stable sources of funding*, it said, *to meet basic day-to-day expenses. Our school lacks reliable funding support because our donations are irregular and unpredictable. Your pledge to help, no matter how small, inspires us deeply.*

I handed the pamphlet to Brian. He slipped his shoes on and wordlessly headed out to the fence where we'd propped our backpacks. He dug through mine and grabbed the yellow envelope. When he returned he handed the money to the boy. "A donation," he said, "for the school." The monk put his hands together and bowed to us in gratitude. We did the same.

Money seemed like a trivial way to show our thanks for what the people of Nepal, their culture, and their landscape had offered us. But that was what we had to give, so we gave it.

As we walked away I hoped that in one hundred years, our great-grandchildren might stumble upon this special place and find it filled with young monks. Maybe they would walk through the cavernous rooms and hear the monks calling their prayers and they, too, would feel the undercurrent of a timeless energy. Maybe they would one day be lucky enough to learn what Brian and I had learned during our weeks of walking in Nepal: that they are standing in the presence of something that must never be lost.

The tinkling of a bell was the first sound I heard the next morning, louder even than the roosters that crowed unapologetically just below our teahouse window. Outside, the sun sat fat and glowing on the horizon. Two men were herding baby goats on the hillside. A group of schoolgirls in brown sweaters descended a stone staircase, their black hair flying behind them like capes. By the looks of it, the world was alive and thriving. So were we.

It was the one-year anniversary of the day we'd left Portland. I sat back from the window and turned to Brian, who remained asleep beside me. When I nudged his shoulder his eyes fluttered awake. "It's been a year," I told him. "Can you believe it?"

A small smile emerged on his lips, and he rolled over to swing his arm around my waist, burying his head in my lap. "We made it," he said softly.

I smiled. "We did."

"Hey," I nudged him again. "We missed the morning prayer with the monks at the monastery."

Brian pulled his head back and looked up at me. "That's okay," he said. "This entire year has been one long prayer."

Burrowing back down in bed, I closed my eyes and remembered pulling out of town on that rainy Portland morning. I thought about how tears had filled my eyes when I'd read Wendy's text message, "There's a reason why Portland cries today." Back then I'd wondered if we were making the right decision. Now I had no doubt.

The past 365 days had been some of the most challenging days of my life. There had been loneliness and uncertainty and heartbreak. But there had also been so much joy and awareness, like the year had allowed me to peel open the layers of my life and expose the very center of my being.

There'd been many times when I'd wanted to give up on traveling, on Brian, and on my own search for whatever the hell

I was looking for out here. But even the worst days had been streaked with an undertone of blessing. I had only to see the yellow envelope in the bottom of my backpack to remember how lucky we were.

Our weeks of walking were giving me the chance to reflect on all of the changes that had taken place inside of me. South America had emptied me, drained me like a leaky tank, and India had plugged the hole and refilled me with a new kind of fuel.

"You can do so much with a year," I exclaimed to Brian hours later as we hiked, wondering if we were even the same people that had piled into the car that wet spring day. I recalled a sentiment I'd read recently in Peter Matthiessen's book *The Snow Leopard*: "This experience has moved me. As in, I'm moved in such a way that I can never go back."

Up ahead of me, Brian walked through a bright-green field of wild marijuana. His broad shoulders and strong arms swayed as he navigated the stepping-stones beneath his feet. My heart swelled with the sight of him.

In Japanese culture there is an art of fixing broken pottery with gold or silver lacquer. The lacquer highlights the pottery's flaw as a celebrated part of its history. Because the piece has been salvaged and repaired, pulled back from the edge of destruction, it is considered even more beautiful for having been broken. We'd been broken. And then we'd been pieced back together. The turmoil had been meaningful because now there was gold where the cracks used to be.

I thought back to the second day of our trek. We'd walked

all day through a humid valley and eventually stopped for the night at a faded teahouse in a village so small we could stand on one end of town and watch what happened on the other. In the dining room that evening we'd met a French woman. As Brian and I sat on the benches sipping Nepali tea, we'd told her about our roaming, and it pleased her to hear it. At sixty-five, she'd lost her job three years back and took to traveling herself. "I only wish I'd done it years ago," she said, not sadly, but with the satisfaction of someone who lived the way she wanted to now. "Enjoy this wonderful space in your lives."

I watched Brian step carefully from stone to stone, his head bowed in concentration. He aimed toward a stand of trees and whatever lay beyond them. Perhaps we would sit down there like Buddhas in the afternoon sun. "Enjoy this moment," I told myself. "Enjoy it, enjoy it, enjoy it."

~

Two weeks later we emerged from the trail and caught a cab to Pokhara, a small tourist town at the edge of the Annapurna Mountains. We tracked down a guesthouse on a street of guest-houses named for other countries, ours being Iceland, and were shown to a room by the owner, a cheerful Nepali man. The lovely room had two big windows and two small beds, a bathroom, and a full-length mirror nailed to the wall near the door. I dropped my backpack beside my bed and stood in front of the mirror, noting the differences in my body after thirty-four days of trekking in the mountains. The pudginess I'd discovered during my time with the mirror in Peru was gone. Brian walked up next to me and we stared at our reflections. "Look at us," I said.

Brian winked at me, "We look good!"

I laughed. "We do." We were fitter and stronger than I had ever seen us.

We took warmish showers and dropped our stinky trekking clothes off at a roadside stand with a handwritten WASH sign hung crookedly from the canopy above it. Back in our room, we pulled our laptops from our bags and connected to the Internet for the first time in over a month.

When I opened my email I cringed at the hundreds of unread messages, scanning through them in search of news from home. At the bottom of my inbox my eyes landed on an email with the subject THE YELLOW ENVELOPE. I clicked it open.

Hi Kim,

I stumbled upon your blog while looking up world travel online. My husband and I plan to ditch our current lifestyle and travel the world in a couple of years once we get everything in place. I love reading about your story and how you got started on your journey. My husband and I have discussed ways in which we could help people and give back to others as we travel. I was very touched by your story of the yellow envelope and was wondering if I could send you money to be added to the envelope?

I'd love to live vicariously through you until we are able to start our own travels.

Jaimie and Will

I'd shared Michele and Glenn's letter on my blog hoping that their generosity might inspire others, but I never imagined that anyone would actually offer to add to the yellow envelope. "Brian!" I shouted. "You will not believe the email I just got." Walking over to his bed, I sat down excitedly beside him. "Read it!"

He squinted at the page. "Oh wow," he said. "Do you know them?"

"No!" I exclaimed. "What should I tell them?"

"Tell them they can add to the envelope! Why not?"

I wrote back, and for the next few hours I felt high from the unexpected generosity of Jaimie and Will's gift.

Later that evening, back in our room after a dinner of chili *momos*, I turned to Brian and asked, "What now?" The bike trip to Vietnam with Michele and Glenn was still a few months in the future, and there was no place that we needed to be before then.

"Let's go back out there and walk the Annapurna Circuit all over again," he said.

Stretching my legs in front of me, I looked down at them. "Don't tempt me. I'd *move* into those mountains if we could get Internet connection. Maybe we should go trekking somewhere else?" I pulled up my browser and typed in a search for flights to the Alps, and the rates popped up on the screen. "Uh, maybe not."

Brian leaned over to look at the prices. "Yeah, definitely not."

"How about the beach?" I offered. "We could soak our legs in warm water after all that walking."

"I could be convinced…"

I typed in a new search. "Oh," I said. "What about Indonesia—*Bali?*"

"Bali," Brian said, rolling the word around on his tongue.

"You know, I've heard great things about Bali," I told him. "And the price is right."

"Okay, do it."

"Really?" I squeaked.

"Really!"

I pulled up the flight options. "We'd need to get to Kathmandu the day after tomorrow to catch the flight. Is that too soon?"

Brian smiled. "Nope."

So I bought the tickets, the thrill of a new country tingling in my spine.

INDONESIA

CHAPTER 16

LIKE A DREAM, THE TRAVELERS ON OUR AIRPLANE FILED OUT of their seats and into the aisle one row at a time, no thrown elbows or WWE wrestling maneuvers like we'd grown used to in India and Nepal. "Getting on this plane is a full contact sport," Brian muttered under his breath as we loaded onto our plane in Kathmandu. But now, like magic, those same pushy people had transformed into line-forming, personal-space-giving, model passengers.

After five months in India and Nepal, the airport in Jakarta, where we were grounded on a twelve-hour layover, sparkled shockingly clean and modern. Feeling suddenly self-conscious, I ducked into the bathroom to splash water on my face and run my fingers through my greasy hair.

The immigration officer smiled at us while he stamped our passports, and the kid at the coffee shop gave us each a free donut. "Where are we?" I said to Brian as we made ourselves a spot on the airport floor.

"I don't know, but I like it here."

Besides the donut, we hadn't eaten since the modest break-fast our guesthouse had served that morning. My stomach began to rumble. "You hungry?"

"Starving." Brian dug around in his day pack. "We're out of snacks."

By now we should have known better than to embark on a travel day without a backpack full of food. "We never learn!" I said, exasperated that after a year of full-time travel we were still making rookie mistakes. I stood and wiped the airport floor crud from the seat of my pants. "I'll find an ATM and buy us something for dinner."

As I walked through the terminal I passed a wall of windows. Palm trees were planted in a tidy row just outside. Beyond them, heat shimmered off of the runway. I was still dressed for the mountains in jeans and a long-sleeved shirt, but it looked to be a hundred degrees outside. It occurred to me that instead of over-thinking things like I used to do, now I barely thought through them at all. I was getting *too good* at the first rule of the yellow envelope. We'd spontaneously booked plane tickets to Bali and then shown up at the airport without considering that we'd need food for the long flight and clothing for the tropics.

At the ATM I pushed a series of buttons until I found one that read *ENGLISH*. How many Indonesian rupiah would I like to withdraw? I realized I had no idea of the exchange rate. Swiveling my head in all directions, I searched for some frame of reference. Down the way, a kiosk sold soda and snacks, and

I squinted toward it but couldn't see the prices. The screen beeped at me. Did I need more time? I typed in 50 and hit enter. INSUFFICIENT ENTRY. Scanning my brain, I tried to remember how much money we had in our checking account. I did not want to overdraw. 500, I typed. INSUFFICIENT ENTRY, the screen said again. I added another 0. INSUFFICIENT ENTRY. Cringing, I typed in 50,000. It seemed like an awfully large number. The machine made some beeping sounds and spit out a wad of bills. I shoved them in my pocket and raced back to Brian.

"I think I might have just overdrawn our account."

"How much did you take out?"

"50,000 rupiah."

"50,000!"

"I know! Shit." We did not keep large sums of money in our checking account in case of robbery or fraud. In India the exchange rate had been 50 rupees to every dollar, and in Nepal it was 100. If Indonesia was anything like that I'd just withdrawn way more money than we had in our account. "I started with 50 but it kept telling me my entry was insufficient so I just added zeros until it gave me money."

"Kim—"

"I know, I know," I interrupted him. "I panicked."

Brian stood up. "Watch the bags. I'll go see if I can figure out the exchange rate."

He returned a few minutes later with a piece of paper in his hand. "Listen," I said. "I'll call the bank as soon as we can get on

Skype. Hopefully they'll understand and waive the charge. I'll move money over from our savings account ASAP."

Brian smiled. "No need." He held the paper in front of him. "You withdrew a grand total of…" He squinted, trying to decipher his own scribbled handwriting. "Three dollars and sixty-seven cents."

I laughed. "You're kidding me?"

"Not at all." Brian handed me a Coke. "And here is your dinner. The ATM won't let us make another withdraw, so this was all we could afford." He dropped a few silver coins, the remainder of our money, into my hand.

We found a quiet corner of the airport and settled in for the night before our flight at ten the next morning. I drifted off to sleep for a few hours, but my growling stomach woke me up again. Beside me, Brian read in his sleep sack. Snuggling deeper into mine, I pulled out my Kindle, but just as I switched it on, an announcement came over the loudspeaker informing us that the airport was closing.

I shot a glance at Brian, unsure if I'd heard it right. "What'd that say?"

"The airport is closing."

"But airports don't close!"

In fact, the airport was not closing, but our terminal was. We gathered our belongings and left to find a spot in a twenty-four-hour terminal where we could spend the rest of the night.

Though it was near midnight, a heavy humidity clung to the air. We walked along a covered, open-air corridor to the next airplane terminal. Almost immediately my shirt became drenched in sweat. "I miss the mountains," I whined. "It's so freaking hot." Alongside the walkway whole families were sleeping, their suitcases stacked in tall piles around them, seemingly unbothered by the heat.

We entered the airport again through the front doors of the main terminal. A small woman in a navy suit and a walkie-talkie hitched on her belt stood guard in the lobby. Digging my ticket from my backpack, I showed it to her.

"No," she said.

"No?"

"No."

Sweat puddled in my bra and beaded at my temples. I dropped my backpack. "But *see*." I pointed at our flight number. "We have tickets."

"No," the woman said again, and my pulse began to quicken in anger. Was that the only word in her vocabulary?

Baffled by her response, I was repeating it again, "But we have tickets—" when Brian stepped in front of me. He handled these situations better, patiently and calm.

"We're flying out tomorrow morning," he explained. "See?" He held the ticket up for her to see it.

"*Tomorrow*," the woman said, emphasizing both the word and how completely clueless we were. "Not now. You come back *tomorrow*."

"Can't we just come inside now?"

"No."

"But where are we supposed to go?"

The women shrugged her shoulders to indicate that she did not care where we went but that we could not stay there. "Outside," she said and shooed us toward the door.

Exhausted and hungry, I was irrationally pissed at the tiny tyrant who'd denied us admittance to the airport.

"She's just doing her job," Brian grumbled.

"Yeah, I get that. But what harm would we have done?" People in Nepal and India would never bother with such rules, I thought, feeling nostalgic for the chaos.

We walked along the covered corridor and looked for a place to park it for the night. My backpack felt like it weighed a hundred pounds. In these conditions I would not get a minute of sleep.

But then, like a stream in a desert, a miracle appeared. "A food court!" I exclaimed as we walked by a cavernous room lined with restaurant stalls. "Let's go in there. Maybe it has air conditioning."

The food court smelled like fried chicken and, though I did not eat chicken and thought, in fact, that chicken was downright foul, my stomach grumbled at the smell. After I dropped my backpack into a booth, I laid my head down on the table and buried my face in my arms. Given the airport policy with which we were already acquainted, I doubted that we were allowed to loiter in the food court either. But I was willing to push the boundaries until they kicked us out. The teenage employee at the fried chicken shop stared at us from behind a rotating spit of poultry but said nothing. "Let's sleep in shifts," I suggested to Brian. "One of us has to stay awake to watch the bags."

"You go first. I'm too hungry to sleep."

Tossing and turning in the uncomfortable plastic booth, I pulled a sleep mask over my eyes and plugged my ears—my airport sleeping ritual—but my neck screamed and my back ached. Every muscle in my body felt heavy with exhaustion, but sleep eluded me. Finally, I sat up and sighed in surrender.

"What time is it?"

Brian looked at his watch. "Almost 3:00 a.m."

"Ugh." I looked up at the chicken stand. It remained open, and the teenage boy was slumped in a chair and scrolling through his phone. Who bought fried chicken at 3:00 a.m.? "I'm going to the bathroom," I told Brian.

The ladies room was located down a long hallway lit with florescent bulbs. As I lumbered down it, blinking in the harsh light, I noticed a door, half ajar, with a mound of shoes piled in front of it. A sign above the door said *Musholla Room*. Inside, a dozen sleeping bodies were curled up on the ground.

I practically sprinted back to Brian. "I found the sleeping room!"

"The sleeping room?"

"Yeah. Follow me." I began gathering up our bags. "It's by the bathroom."

We added our shoes to the pile outside of the door and tiptoed into the room. Four dim overhead lights cast a weak glow on the sleeping figures before us. A partition split the room in two. In the silence I pointed to a space between two sleeping women large enough to fit us both. "There," I whispered.

A woman curled up in the corner of the room raised her head to look at us. She lay it down and then looked up again, eyes bulging, as if she couldn't believe what she saw. But I was used to the attention that Brian's bright red beard drew, and I was way too tired to assign much meaning to her wide-eyed staring. We rolled out our sleep sacks, crawled inside, and fell immediately asleep.

It felt like only ten minutes had passed when my sleepy subconscious registered a sound. A man was singing loudly. *How rude*, I thought, *can't he see we're sleeping in here?* I pulled my sleep sack over my head and rolled away from the noise. The singing continued. "Damn it," I grumbled and raised my head to see what the hell was going on.

The entire side of the room we were sleeping on had cleared of—what I noticed with dawning horror—had been all women. On the other side of the partition a dozen men were kneeling on mats and a man stood among them and called out a prayer. I blinked as the situation fully registered in my mind. The men were praying. We'd fallen asleep in some kind of airport mosque.

Bubbles of panic burst inside of me as I realized the full extent of our mistake. Not only had Brian broken a religious tradition by sleeping on the side of the room designated for women, and not only had we both, I was sure, defied another religious rule by sleeping next to each other *in a prayer room*, but now I was the sole woman left in the room occupied by a dozen praying men. I shook Brian awake, frantic. "Brian!" I whispered. "Wake up!"

"What is it?" he mumbled, and rolled onto his side.

"Get up *now*," I hissed. "We're sleeping in a prayer room."

Brian's eyes blinked open. "What?"

"Look!"

He sat up and looked toward the praying men who were now all on their knees, bent at the waist, kneeling toward mecca.

"Oh my God," he said. "Oh *shit*."

I scrambled out of my sleep sack and balled it in my fist. Brian did the same. We fumbled around, making an extraordinary amount of noise in our haste, hefting our backpacks onto our backs and gathering our day packs in our arms. And then we fled the room, stepping over three praying men, while mumbling, "Sorry, sorry, sorry."

Just outside of the door we dug through the pile of shoes to find ours. Grabbing mine, I fled down the hallway, but when I reached the food court I turned to see Brian still bent in front of the door trying to jam his feet into his shoes.

"Brian!" I hissed. "What are you doing?"

He looked up at me, half awake.

"Just pick up your shoes and get out of there!"

"Oh my God," Brian said when we'd stepped through the doors of the food court into the soft light of dawn.

"You slept on the women's side! We slept next to each other! It was a prayer room!" I blurted, unsure of which embarrassing fact to freak out about first. I buried my face in my hands. "I thought it was a sleeping room. I am such an idiot!"

Brian dropped his backpack and bent down to tie his shoes. "I cannot believe that just happened."

"Me neither."

"Oh God, I feel so guilty," Brian moaned. "I must have made those women feel so uncomfortable."

"I know! And can you imagine what the men must have thought when they saw me? Obviously I wasn't supposed to be there. All of the other women had left."

"This would be a good time to have an invisibility cloak," said Brian, as he slung his backpack onto his shoulders.

"Hopefully they'll let us into our terminal now. We need to get as far away from that room as possible."

A few hours later we sat at our gate waiting to board our flight to Bali. Brian stared off into the distance, eyes glazed, replaying the events of the morning in his head.

"The more I think about it the worse it gets," he said.

"I know," I agreed. "I mean, if those men were devout enough to pray at an airport then I'm pretty sure my presence was practically sacrilegious. Why didn't someone wake us up? Why didn't one of those women tell us you were on the wrong side of the room?"

I wanted to melt into the floor. All morning I'd been unable to raise my head and meet anyone's eye, sure that every single person looking our way had seen our faux pas in the prayer room. I felt both humiliated and guilt-stricken. We hadn't meant to be disrespectful. I buried my head in my hands again. "And just when I felt like we'd finally figured out this traveling thing."

Our flight was announced over the loudspeaker, and Brian and I sheepishly took our place in line. As we inched closer to the jet bridge, I noticed a rectangular plastic box, about waist high, filled halfway with money. A sign said that we could donate our unused foreign currency to a charitable cause. I dug out the few paltry coins left over from our Coca-Cola dinner and dropped it guiltily in the box, wishing I had one hundred dollars to shove in there. It wouldn't have mattered if I gave our money or yellow envelope money, I just wished I had something, *anything*, to hand over as penance for our guilt.

⁓

Our kamikaze taxi driver jerked down the twisting roads of Bali, hitting the brakes at random for no perceivable reason at all. Brian stared intensely at the windy road we were barreling down, and I silently prayed for him to hold it together. He'd barfed on buses and in taxis all over the world, and this was the single worst ride we'd experienced. In a gesture of solitude, I patted his knee, and he gave me a quick, pale-faced grimace meant to convey that I should not touch him under any circumstances until we were out of the taxi.

"Do you think this is payback for the prayer room?" I joked, but he just fixed a laser stare at the road ahead of us and ignored me.

I turned my head away from him, too nervous to watch his demise. Even I felt like rolling down the window and hurling into the intense green foliage that rushed by outside.

We drove through village after village of palm trees, rice paddies and roadside shops selling Buddha statues in all shapes and sizes. There was not much break in the development, just shop upon shop hocking woodcarvings and rock carvings and furniture and handicrafts.

Our taxi driver finally dropped us on the main street of Ubud, the cultural capital of Bali. Other travelers had told us how popular Ubud was with Westerners, but I was still shell-shocked by just how touristy it really was. It seemed like there were spas on every corner, vegetarian restaurants, yoga studios, twenty-dollar T-shirt stands, chakra-readers, and crystal-sellers. It was like a shopping shrine to the New Age, very different than the spiritual Hindu paradise I'd been dreaming about when we bought our tickets in Nepal.

We slung our backpacks onto our backs and walked the side streets, stopping at guesthouses to check availability, but they were all full.

"There isn't a free guesthouse in all of Ubud," Brian said after our sixth failed attempt.

"Dammit, I know." I stopped in the middle of the street to readjust my backpack. Walking in tropical weather with a forty pound potato sack strapped to my back never failed to put me in a crappy mood. And to top it off, I still wore my winter clothes from Kathmandu. "What should we do?" I was so hungry and hot and exhausted that I just wanted to sit down on the curb and refuse to go one step farther like a toddler throwing a tantrum.

Just then a motorcycle weaved by us and skidded to a stop fifty feet beyond. An old woman sat sidesaddle on the back of it. "You need guesthouse?" she yelled.

"Yes!" we yelled back in unison.

Brian shot me a look that said, how the hell did that happen? I shrugged my shoulders and laughed. After my experience on the Rickshaw Run I'd begun to rely on the serendipitous nature of these things.

The woman hopped off the motorcycle, and it sped away like her only intention had been to find us.

"Did we interrupt you?" I asked, and when she didn't understand I said, "Were you going somewhere?"

She flapped her hand to wave off the question. "To temple. I go later."

She motioned for us to follow her. She could not have been more than five feet tall and her flip-flops slapped on the pavement as she wound her way through the walled alleyways back to her guesthouse.

When we reached her home she showed us a room with a queen-sized bed covered in mosquito netting, a bathroom, a sink, and a lopsided ceiling fan to circulate the heavy air. A patio off the room faced a dense, buzzing jungle. We accepted the room and threw our bags down on the floor. My cotton shirt dripped with sweat. "Where can we buy food?" I asked, nearly desperate with hunger.

"Food? You relax. I make you something."

"You will? Thank you so much."

She waved her hand my way again. "No problem."

Ten minutes later she returned with two perfect omelets. I devoured mine in less than five bites. Then Brian flipped the switch for the overhead fan. As it creaked to life we crawled into bed and slept for sixteen hours straight.

~

The following day we hit the streets of Ubud determined to find out why everyone loved Bali. We walked the windy streets over to the main stretch of town filled with restaurants, juice shops, and jewelry stores. It felt like everyone was trying to sell us something. Taxi drivers yelled out a nonstop prattle of "TAXI TAXI TAXI TAXI. YOU NEED TAXIIIII?"

Ubud had a split personality. Nearly every home had intricate stone temples in their front yards where locals prayed and left offerings first thing in the morning. When I'd stepped onto the patio of our own guesthouse upon waking, I'd seen that the guesthouse owner had placed a tray of delicate flowers and burning incense near our door. Businesses also placed offerings, colorful flowers and fruit wrapped in palm leaves, in front of their shops each day. The temples and offerings were beautiful and evoked a sense of holiness. Yet at the same time, walking down the streets felt like one big hustle as we fought off a constant barrage of pushy taxi drivers and restaurant and shop owners. I felt like a blinking dollar sign with legs and a passport.

Near the edge of town, where development trickled into rice paddies, we ducked into a restaurant to escape a particularly persistent taxi driver who had stalked us for blocks trying to sell us a tour. We slumped into a table under a ceiling fan, and I closed my eyes and took deep breaths, trying to quell the growing frustration I felt at the entire island population.

A petite woman with dark hair to her shoulders and wrists the size of bird bones approached and took our order. "From Australia?" she asked.

"No, America."

"Oh! Far away!" she exclaimed. "Honeymoon?"

Brian and I chuckled. "No, we've been married for six years."

"Long time!" she exclaimed again. "You have kids?"

"Nope," said Brian at the same time I piped, "Not yet!"

She looked from Brian to me. "Sound like you need discuss!" She laughed at herself. "What you do? For money?" I smiled awkwardly and looked at Brian. He snickered at her directness.

"I'm a writer," I said.

Our waitress grinned widely. "Oh, *Eat, Pray, Love!*" she cried. "You write about *my shop!*"

Smiling, I said, "Maybe."

Her restaurant was blissfully empty, and I would gladly face intrusive questions about my personal life if it meant I could escape, even temporarily, the harassment that awaited us just beyond the doors.

The waitress returned with a tray of drinks and set it down in the middle of our table. "This one for me," she said, and held up a smoothie. She leaned toward us and sipped from her straw. "Tomorrow," she said, more of a demand than a request, "you come to my house. We have new temple. We have party for temple."

Oh God, I thought, not her too. I threw a look at Brian, hoping that he'd bat down her advances.

He looked back at me and raised his eyebrows. *What should we do?*

I shook my head no.

"Uh, I don't know," he finally said. "I think we might be busy tomorrow."

She threw her head back and laughed like that was the most hilarious thing she'd ever heard. "No, no. Trust me. This better!"

Brian requested the bill and she handed it over. "My nephew Nyoman pick you up tomorrow. Eleven in the morning." She gave the address of the local supermarket and waved as we walked out the door, cheerfully ignoring the fact that we'd not actually agreed to go.

"What happened in there?" I asked Brian as we walked back to our guesthouse. "Did we just agree to go to our waitress's house tomorrow?"

"Yeah, I think so."

"Do you think we should go?"

"Do you?"

Positioning my body away from the busy road, I stopped walking and squinted up into the sunlight toward him. "I don't know…"

"We should go," Brian said, making up his mind. "What's the worst that could happen?"

"Oh, I don't know, we could do something culturally and religiously insensitive and offend her entire family like we did in the Musholla Room."

Brian laughed. "No! We learned from our mistake. Let's go. When will we get a chance like this again?"

He was right. "Okay, let's do it." I slipped my hand in his, and we retreated to our guesthouse for the rest of the day.

CHAPTER 17

THE NEXT MORNING, WE STOOD IN THE PARKING LOT OF the supermarket waiting for Nyoman to pick us up. It dawned on me as we scanned the crowd looking for someone who looked like they were looking for someone, that the whole undertaking was completely stupid. We had no idea what Nyoman looked like or what kind of car he drove or if our waitress had even been serious.

"This is a bad idea," I said to Brian as 11:00 a.m. slid into 11:15, and there was still no sign of Nyoman. "We should get out of here. At least we tried."

But at that moment, a tattooed, long-haired man screeched his white minivan to a halt right in front of us and leaned his head out of the window.

"Nyoman?" I asked.

"Uh, yeah, I'm Nyoman," said Nyoman. He looked like the kind of dude that might pierce the navel of your underaged best friend in a back alley or steal your Honda Civic, and I hesitated for a second. He reached into the back seat and pushed the door open. "Get in."

Nyoman sped through the busy streets of Ubud, past the restaurant where we'd met the waitress, and into the open countryside beyond. Ten minutes later he turned off the paved road onto a dirt driveway. "We're here," he said. "I've got clothes for you to wear inside the temple." The doors of the minivan popped open behind me.

We climbed out of the van, and Nyoman handed us each a sarong and a sash to tie around our waists. He plunked a headdress down on Brian's head and then walked off in the direction of the waitress's house. It took a second for us to realize that we were supposed to follow him.

Once inside our waitress greeted us. "You here!" she smiled.

"We here!" I said. "Thank you for inviting us."

A beautiful child offered us peanuts and some kind of mushed vegetable wrapped in a banana leaf. Briefly, I looked down to accept it, and when I raised my head again, our waitress had disappeared into the crowd.

We entered a courtyard between three small buildings. A row of plastic red chairs lined the entryway like spectators along a parade route. The whole place smelled of incense, and the sound of banging drums and dinging xylophones filled the air. Underneath a thatched roof of dried palm leaves a concrete temple blazed the color of fire, and elaborate carvings that looked like dragon's breath were etched around the window frames. In the center of the courtyard, two traditional Balinese dancers dressed in colorful costumes and bug-eyed masks stomped a wild, entrancing dance beneath the open sky.

Brian and I sat down sheepishly in two of the plastic chairs. I felt a bit intrusive and out of place, but an older man with teeth like crumbling tombstones pulled Brian into conversation, and I relaxed a little. Before me, the dancers bucked and spun, every movement of their bodies in control, right down to the fluid motion of their fingertips.

Nearby, a group of young women weaved banana leaves into offerings, and a holy man chanted with the band. Kids chased each other, men laughed, and the older women gossiped, I was certain. People were content because they belonged to each other. No one seemed to notice me.

Brian's conversation ended, and he turned to watch the dancing. I gestured at the man with tombstone teeth. "What were you guys talking about?"

"Well, it was hard to communicate since I don't speak his language, and he doesn't speak mine, but the gist of the conversation was that people, at their core, are good."

"You discussed that big important topic with hand gestures and grunts?"

Brian shrugged. "Yeah. And the funny thing is I'm pretty sure I understood almost all of what he said."

On the drive back to our guesthouse, Nyoman glanced at us in the rearview mirror. "Did you have a good time at the temple?" he asked. I had been staring out the window, watching the bright-green rice paddies zoom by, building up the nerve to give Nyoman yellow envelope money as a way to say thank you for bringing us to the temple.

Brian spoke up. "Yes, it was beautiful. Thanks for having us." We'd not seen the waitress who'd invited us since our brief encounter with her upon our arrival, and during our visit I kept wondering why she had asked us there. I'd been expecting to pay some kind of fee or to give a donation, but there had not been a chance. Finally, I just chalked it up to friendliness.

Nyoman nodded into the rearview mirror and then pulled his car to the side of the road. He swiveled to face us in the backseat. "I'm an artist," he said, reaching into the passenger's seat and handing a box filled with paintings of intricately drawn scenes of Balinese life back to us. "Buy one," he said flatly.

So this is why we were invited to the temple, I thought with a rising sense of disappointment.

Brian took the box and began awkwardly flipping through the paintings. They were beautiful, and I knew Nyoman was just trying to make a living, but I suddenly felt trapped and manipulated. I also felt a little guilty. Wasn't the cost of Nyoman's painting worth the price of admission to the temple?

"Ah, we don't really have room for a painting," I told Nyoman as he eyed me in his rearview mirror.

Nyoman pretended he hadn't heard me. He swiveled 180 degrees in the driver's seat and reached between us. His thick, tattooed arm shook the box of paintings. "Look at them all," he ordered. "There is one in there that is right for you."

Brian handed the box to me and I pulled out a black and

white drawing of three men standing in a field, bent at the waist, harvesting rice. "Okay," I said. "We'll take this one."

"Good choice," Nyoman said.

After I paid him, he steered the car back onto the road. My good mood soured. I'd decided to give Nyoman yellow envelope money, but then we'd been pressured to buy a painting, and now I wasn't going to give it anymore. Why, when I was exchanging money for a painting, instead of just giving, did the interaction feel disingenuous? Was it just because Nyoman was pushy?

We arrived back in the busy tourist section of Ubud, and Nyoman dropped us at the same grocery store he'd picked us up at a few hours earlier. We said good-bye and walked back toward our guesthouse feeling hoodwinked.

We slept through the hottest part of the afternoon and woke as the moon appeared. Before falling asleep I'd propped Nyoman's painting on the bedside table, and I turned to look at it. It *was* beautiful, maybe even more so in the muted light of dusk. But I resented it.

We found a noodle shop hidden far off of the main road where we could eat in peace and took a seat at a small, wooden table out front. I was happy to be away from the harassment of touts and the overtly Western stores disguising shopping as New Age spiritual enlightenment.

"I think I have a serious case of culture shock," I said to Brian. "I expected Bali to be more like India and Nepal than the U.S., but it isn't, and I wasn't quite prepared to reenter the Western world."

"Agreed," Brian said. "Bali is not what I expected."

"Even that thing with Nyoman. Normally something like that wouldn't bother me, but for some reason I'm so irrationally *pissed* about it." I looked out toward the quiet street. "I expected to pay to go to the temple, and I like the painting Nyoman forced us to buy. I'm *glad* we have it. But the way we got it just makes me angry."

"He was just trying to make a few bucks," Brian responded. "It's hard to fault him for that."

"Maybe I just need a few days to adjust." I crossed my legs beneath the table and looked out into the quiet night. My eyes fell on the shop vendor across the street. From the metal rim of the awning that hung above his shop swung a dozen tiny bird-cages stuffed with colorful songbirds.

From our table I could hear their sweet singing. A wave of rage swelled inside of me. I wanted to run over and fling open all of the miniature doors and shove the shop owner inside of the cage instead. During our travels I'd seen many suffering animals, and all of them had affected me, but for some reason this injustice infuriated me more than the others. What was wrong with humans that we thought it okay to keep animals born to fly trapped in small cages for the sake of our entertainment?

My skin felt itchy. I stared at the tiny birds in their tiny cages and wanted off of this damn island. "I don't want to stay here any longer," I blurted to Brian.

He looked like he'd been expecting me to say it. "Me neither," he agreed.

The following day we shoved into a white minibus filled

with other travelers and wound our way toward the coast. The world raced by outside of my window. Though the rice paddies had all been harvested for the year, they were still the most intense and luscious green that I had ever seen. The stone temples in the yards and on the sidewalks of every Balinese home were as common as suburban mailboxes.

I could see why this island had earned the nickname *The Island of the Gods*. Bali was a stunning place, but tarnished, I thought, from the influx of tourism. But I was a tourist too, of course, and I wrestled with that problem in my head. What made me any different from the thousands of vacationers that landed on the island? It occurred to me that so many of those vacationers never left home, even while away. They wanted the comforts of home repackaged in a foreign land. They had traveled to a different country, but they wanted to stay in a world they knew. Travelers wanted to enter other worlds. That was the difference.

The bus finally dumped us at the dock and swarms of fruit vendors gathered around us. "Pineapple! Snake fruit! Pineapple! Snake fruit!" They yelled like hotdog vendors at a baseball game. I bought pineapple and held it up each time a new vendor stopped to yell in my direction.

When we arrived a few hours later on Gili Meno, the quietest and least developed of three small islands off of the coast of Bali, I knew that we had come to the right place. We jumped from the boat onto the dock and stepped off the dock into warm white sand. A few people lazed around in open-air huts that were built out over the intense aqua blue ocean. Brian and I hailed a horse-drawn cart (there were no cars on the island) to clomp us the two miles to the beach hut we had rented.

Gili Meno was a haven of sand and shrubs. One could walk the circumference of it in less than two hours and, we learned quickly, there was nothing to do there. Within two days of our arrival we fell happily into a lazy, blissful routine. Each morning we'd wake early, claim a cabana on the beach, drink coffee, read for awhile, and eat breakfast. Then I'd go for a run, shower in the outdoor shower, drink a watermelon juice, and rejoin Brian under the cabana. Repeat for lunch and dinner.

The highlight of each day came in the afternoons when we'd rent snorkeling equipment from a lady who owned a fruit stand next door to our beach hut. We had to make sure we arrived to claim our snorkels before 1:00 p.m., when she disappeared behind her stand for an afternoon nap in her hammock.

The ocean shone a soul-lifting blue, so clear that I could tread water and watch the disjointed image of my legs kick beneath the surface. With our snorkel gear attached snugly to our faces, we'd swim out about one hundred fifty feet from shore and hover above the most intensely beautiful underwater world that I had ever seen. Bright schools of fish darted below us. Yellow and blue and red fish but also schools of fish in a shock of florescent colors. One day we spotted an octopus, its spindly legs moving in divine slow motion from under the security of a rock. Past us, where I did not dare to venture, the shelf of the ocean dropped like an underwater cliff, plunging downward into a dark and deep crevice. When I reached this deep place I could feel the cold water rising from it, and I'd turn back toward the safety of the warmer and shallower sea.

We snorkeled for hours each day, the backs of our bodies turning red from the sun despite our liberal application of sunscreen. The indentation of our masks left pink lines on our faces well past dinner. They remained even after we watched the bright orange ball of sunshine dip behind the horizon, leaving a drizzle of pink and peach in its wake.

We could not seem to leave Gili Meno. Originally we'd planned to stay for just a few days, but we kept extending our trip. Sheepishly, we'd approach the owner of our beach hut to ask if he had availability for three more nights? For four? One day, I looked up from my journal to ask Brian if he knew what body of water we were on. He didn't know. Such was the disorientation that our nomadic ability to go anywhere could sometimes cause. Eventually I asked our beach hut owner, who told me we'd been swimming in the Bali Sea.

One afternoon while out snorkeling, I spotted a sea turtle resting on the white crushed coral of the ocean floor. Screeching with joy into my snorkeling mouthpiece, I popped my head above the surface of the water to scan for Brian. But he floated too far away, his head submerged in his own underwater world, for me to grab his attention. So I put my head back into the water and glided over that amazing sea creature. She scooted along the bottom of the ocean, munching on sea grasses until she finally swam off toward the deep ocean and that dark immense of blue.

She moved with such grace and ancient wisdom that I swear it was like snorkeling with the Buddha himself.

Brian and I also learned from our beach hut owner that Gili Meno rose from the water near the Wallace Line, where the Indian and Pacific Oceans met. The turtles liked to swim those ocean currents, and a great number of them came from as far away as Mexico and South America. Gili Meno was like the United Nations of sea turtles. All of them were endangered.

While out snorkeling the next day I searched like crazy for the sea turtle, and just when I began to give up hope, I spotted her again, or she spotted me. This time Brian floated much closer, and I waved him over. Together we bobbed there in wide-eyed meditation, watching the beautiful turtle move through the water. She knew that we were there but did not seem to mind the attention.

We bobbed and watched. She floated in the amniotic fluid of the sea. Brian lost interest and swam away, but I could not take my eyes off of her. Sea turtles had lived for over one hundred fifty million years. They'd survived and adapted to a world that had killed the red gazelle and the western black rhinoceros, the saber-toothed cat, and every single one of the dinosaurs.

The turtle swam toward the surface for air and floated right by me. She seemed unthreatened by my presence. She passed by so closely that I stared directly into her green-yellow reptilian eye. I sensed a mild curiosity from her, like she'd seen something like me before but wasn't quite sure what to make of me. She glided to the surface and popped her head above the water and I lifted mine. Her mouth took a gulp of the other world, my world, before she swam back down again.

It sounds crazy, but when she looked at me I felt connected to everything in the entire universe, like I was witnessing the divine in those ancient turtle eyes. It was a gift to float at the top of her world. It was, I realized, the kind of authentic experience that I hoped for while traveling. In order to better understand the world, I wanted an unmanufactured glimpse of lives that were different from my own and I'd found one, right below the surface of the water.

On the other side of the island Brian and I tracked down a turtle sanctuary where a local man named Bolong, one of the few people who lived on Gili Meno year-round, made it his life's mission to save the endangered sea turtles.

Bolong had a small concrete office constructed right on the sandy beach and inside it a desk piled with literature about saving the turtles. Right outside of his office, a hundred baby turtles swam in open-air tanks. When we approached, a young woman introduced herself as a member of Bolong's family. She explained that the sanctuary saved the turtle eggs from predators and then allowed them to hatch naturally, giving the turtles a better chance of surviving in the wild. Brian and I oohed and ahhed over the adorable little turtles, and the girl gave us a bashful smile, clearly proud of the work her family did.

She walked inside the office and came out with a sheet of

paper that explained that the turtles were raised for one year before they were released to the sea. They were fed fresh, raw fish every two hours from sunrise to sunset, and Bolong and his team pumped water from the sea into the turtle tanks every three days. The sanctuary also cared for injured turtles, nursing them to health before rereleasing them. It was a lot of work for a small, family-run operation.

After their release, the turtles were under threat in many ways. They were caught for food, harvested for oils used in the cosmetic industry, and their shells were made into jewelry. They drowned in fishing nets and suffocated by ingesting plastic sea pollution that they confused as food. They fell prey to large fish, sharks, and killer whales.

"Man, the cards are really stacked against those little guys," said Brian. "It's amazing that any of them survive at all."

But it was in their nature to survive. Bolong and his family, by sheer force of will, were helping.

Before leaving our beach hut for the turtle sanctuary, Brian and I decided to donate yellow envelope money to Bolong. The turtle I'd seen while snorkeling had made a big impression on me, and I wanted to honor her in some way. So we made our little pilgrimage to the sanctuary with the yellow envelope money shoved into the pocket of Brian's swim trunks.

Brian leaned toward the girl and told her that we'd like to make a donation. She said, "Yes! Okay!" and explained that, in return, we would be allowed to name a turtle. It was a symbolic gesture, like naming a star, but I loved it just the same.

"How about Honeydew?" I suggested after Brian and I had lobbed around names for five minutes straight. It was the name of Michele and Glenn's yellow lab that they had raised from a puppy into a guide dog.

Brian wrote *Honeydew* into a lined, spiral-bound notebook, and the girl handed me a receipt that I folded in my hand to save for Michele and Glenn. I could hardly believe it, but we would see them soon.

As I watched the turtles blow bubbles in their little saltwater bathtubs, I hoped they would make it into adulthood, through all of the circumstances and environments that made them vulnerable.

I thought about the turtle I saw while out snorkeling and wondered if someone like Bolong had raised her. Or maybe she was one of the rare few that survived incubation and hatched in the sand and then scrambled like mad toward the glistening sea, somehow surviving her vulnerable years to grow into the most magical and beautiful creature. Either way, of the millions of lives clambering from their place of birth to the great world beyond, she, against the greatest of odds, had managed to thrive. When you looked at life like that it was all such a miracle.

~

We had to leave Gili Meno because, to the sadness of both of us, we could not stay forever. On our last night on the island, Brian and I sat under a beach cabana in the moonlit darkness, drinking Bintang and listening to the waves roll into shore.

Every time we left a place I felt nostalgic because I did not know if we would ever return again. Each new country, city, or island we traveled to taught me something new, and I always felt a deep sense of gratitude upon leaving. This was true even of the places I did not love and especially true of the ones I did.

Brian must have been feeling the same kind of nostalgia because he folded his legs beneath him and said, "Remember how scared we were landing in Ecuador? We didn't know what we were doing, and there were all those policemen with guns. We didn't want to leave our room."

I laughed. "Yeah, and I wanted to give the cops some yellow envelope money." I slapped my palm against my forehead. "What was I thinking?"

"You didn't know. Hey, in India that would have been totally legit."

"I wonder what we would think if we went back now?"

As I reflected back over our travels, I'd thought about that a lot. Would we still be as timid and afraid, with over a year of travel under our belts, as we were back then? We'd certainly come a long way since we first left home and learned that, despite exposure to seemingly endless grim news, people everywhere were good.

"Man we were newbies," said Brian. "I'm almost embarrassed to think about those first months on the road. We were so awkward..."

"I'm not sure that's really changed much," I said, remembering our recent night in the prayer room. We'd made so many mistakes and embarrassed ourselves, but we'd also stretched our boundaries, individually and together, and learned to trust the world and the people in it, including ourselves and each other.

For the next two hours we talked over the highs and lows of our time traveling. The moon made a slow crawl across the sky, and I looked out over the ocean and squinted at the stars. They were arranged in foreign constellations of which I had no attachment. The stars of my life back home, the stars I'd camped under as a teenager and wished upon as a child, were half a world away.

It is so important to travel, I thought, in order to see the world with fresh eyes. A friend of mine, after returning from a very long trip of her own, had told me that traveling had humbled her because it had shown her what a tiny piece of the earth she actually occupied. Traveling had humbled me too, a hundred times over, and continued to do so on a daily basis. Bolong and his turtle sanctuary humbled me. Sleeping in the prayer room humbled me. Even my dislike of Bali humbled me because it had shown me, once again, that life, and the degrees to which we lived it, was very big, and I was very small.

"We should get to bed," I said. "We've got to get up early to catch that boat."

Brian nodded. "But first, a toast." He raised his beer above his head and then clanged it against mine. "To this incredible life."

"To this incredible life of ours."

The following day we boarded boats, taxis, and airplanes— another long journey that eventually led us to Glenn and Michele.

VIETNAM

CHAPTER 18

BRIAN AND I STOOD AT THE INTERSECTION OF TWO BUSY roads, sweat beading down our necks, and watched the traffic in Ho Chi Minh City pulse. The weaving motorbikes reminded me of a colony of leaf-cutting ants we'd seen while hiking in Peru, individual specimens that moved in unison as if controlled by a solitary mind.

I could not get over the things the Vietnamese hauled on their motorbikes: hundreds of bunches of bananas, enough helium balloons to send a child lofting toward the clouds, livestock, entire generations of family. It was impressive and intimidating, since Brian and I would be joining them—not on motorbikes, thank God, but on bicycles.

The traffic light turned red, and a hundred spewing motorcycles puttered to a stop. We stepped into the crosswalk and sprinted across the street, cut across a tree-lined park, and pushed our way through the glass doors of a modern high-rise hotel. A blast of cold air blew my hair back as I stepped inside. Looking around at the sparkling lobby, my eyes landed on the marble desk where two men in suits stood at attention, ready to offer their services.

Quickly, I inventoried the people milling about, searching each face for the ones that I knew.

"Hey!" Brian yelled and pointed toward a bank of couches and overstuffed chairs. I swiveled my head in the direction of his gaze.

"Oh my God, *is that Michele?*"

Beside her Glenn popped up from a cushioned chair, a magazine folded in his hand. "Whoa," I said. "Look at Glenn!"

"You made it!" I screeched when we reached them, wrapping them in a hug. "You guys look amazing. Wow! I hardly recognized you."

Michele deflected my fawning. "You guys look great too." She stepped back to smile at me. "You look happy. Did you find the hotel okay?"

"Yes, it was easy." I shook my head, still hardly believing my eyes. "How was your flight? How do you feel? Are you ready for this trip?" When excited, I had a habit of becoming annoyingly overeager. I held up my hand. "Wait, don't answer that yet. Are you guys hungry?"

"I thought you'd never ask," said Glenn.

Down an alleyway lined with a rat's nest of electrical wires and neon lights that flashed like the Las Vegas Strip, the four of us dipped into a pho restaurant and settled at a wobbly plastic table that faced the street. Vendors walked by selling everything from illegally photocopied books and three-dollar sunglasses to plastic tubs of mixed fruit. They stopped at every outdoor table trying to sell their wares.

"So, how was your flight?" asked Brian.

"Oh, *very* enjoyable. So much legroom, such great food," joked Glenn, and began to recount the details. Sitting back in my chair, I stole another glimpse at Michele. She looked like a different person than the last time I'd seen her. Her blue eyes were the same, her fair skin and freckled face and blond hair the same as always, but everything else had transformed.

"I'm so glad to finally be here," Michele said when Glenn had finished his story. "This trip has been a long time coming."

"Have you been training?" I asked.

"Yes," said Glenn. "We've been biking and hiking and running."

"I can tell!" I felt myself blush, embarrassed to be putting so much emphasis on their physical appearance, yet unable to ignore how much they'd changed. The last time we'd seen Michele and Glenn had been at our going away party. In the year and a half since then Michele had lost one hundred thirty pounds, and Glenn was nearly eighty pounds lighter.

"We feel good," said Michele. "But we're still worried about those mountain passes!"

"You and me both. The only bike I've been on in the last two years is a stationary bike at a hotel gym back in Argentina. After riding it for forty-five minutes my butt hurt for a week."

Michele laughed. "I'm sure you guys will be fine."

"We'll power through. There's a support van, though, right? If we can't hack it?"

"Even better," chimed in Glenn. "There's an entire bus."

Later that evening we boarded that bus with our Vietnamese tour guides, Hao and Chien, and the seven other Americans with whom we would be spending the next two weeks.

Scooting down the aisle, I took a seat behind a man with graying hair and his very pretty wife. Brian sat down next to me. We'd introduced ourselves to them earlier, during our tour orientation in the lobby of Michele and Glenn's hotel, but I'd already forgotten their names. The man swiveled past me and reached for Brian's hand. "Hi," he said. "I'm Eddie and this is my wife Renee." Beside him, Renee smiled like a beauty queen. "We're from Louisiana. I'm a lawyer, and ol' Renee here works for me." He elbowed her in the ribs. "Don't ya, babe?"

Brian pumped his hand. "Nice to meet you."

"Where ya'll from?"

"Portland," I said. "Oregon."

Eddie flipped his eyes toward me, looking annoyed that I'd had the nerve to speak, and turned back toward Brian.

"Beautiful place," he said. "Whatcha all do up there?"

I slid my gaze toward Brian, curious to see how he'd handle this one. My eyes fell on his unkempt beard and ratty T-shirt emblazoned with the faded red image of Ganesh. Without thinking, I touched my own wild hair that had grown from its original pixie cut into a sort of winged '80s style. I'd stopped noticing our appearance a long time ago, but now I saw us through Eddie's eyes. *We look homeless*, I thought, before it occurred to me that actually we were. Eddie probably wondered how in the world we could afford such an expensive tour. Maybe he thought we were Silicon Valley start-up millionaires?

"Well," said Brian, "I'm not working right now. We're traveling full-time."

"Oh, *really?*" Eddie barked. "What are you, rich?"

I snorted and stared at Eddie's skeptical face. "No," replied Brian. "We saved our money and sold all of our stuff, and then we quit our jobs so that we could go traveling."

"Huh," Eddie said and furrowed his brow. "How unique." He turned back to his wife. "Did you hear that, honey? They quit their jobs so they could travel." His voice grew louder for emphasis. "Must be nice! But some of us have gotta work for a living."

My hand fell to Brian's knee and I squeezed. He looked at me out of the corner of his eye. Eddie had just nipped at my Achilles' heel, and Brian knew it. "Don't say a word," he hissed.

Eddie certainly wasn't the first person that had expressed his disapproval of our decision to travel. Before we left, my mom had begged me to buy a bigger house with our savings. Various others had questioned whether we'd inherited money or won the lottery. More than once I'd lamented to Brian about how backward I thought it was that our culture accepted that people spent lots of money on houses and new cars and buried themselves under mountains of debt but that saving up a modest pile of cash and then spending it on traveling could be considered irresponsible and selfish.

I knew how lucky we were. And after traveling to places where people struggled for basic human needs like shelter and clean water, education and safety and food for their families, things I'd never had to worry about, I felt it even more profoundly. I knew I was privileged beyond belief, simply because of the random luck of my birthplace. But so was Eddie. So was anyone who'd ever questioned our motives.

From across the aisle an older woman leaned forward in her seat and chimed in. "Well, I think what you are doing is wonderful. Pat and I took six months off when our kids were young and traveled all around Europe. We made so many wonderful memories."

The man, presumably Pat, shook his head in agreement. "And the best part," he said, "is that our kids are lifelong travelers now."

I smiled toward Pat. "I bet they are."

Eddie piped up. "Well, I for one couldn't do it. I'd miss my creature comforts too much."

Brian turned to face Eddie. "We missed those for a while, but we don't really miss them anymore. Honestly, we don't have a single regret."

"I believe you," said Pat from across the aisle. "Traveling is the best investment."

The following morning, ten minutes into our three hundred-mile bike ride, we approached a traffic circle plopped right into the convergence of four main roads in Da Lat, a largish city in Vietnam's Central Highlands region and the starting-off point of our bicycle tour. My mind flashed back to India. I hadn't thought

I'd be wistful for the protection that my busted down rickshaw provided, but now that I'd returned to chaotic Asian roads without even a doorless metal frame to protect me, Sunny suddenly felt like the pinnacle of automotive safety.

"Ah!" I screamed as I bicycled full-speed into the whirl of traffic and managed, somehow, to slip into an open space between the cars and motorcycles. I shot a quick glance toward Brian as he pedaled along beside me. He had a giant smile on his face. "This is stupid!" I yelled to him over the roar of the traffic, but the sound of my voice was swallowed up in the thrumming of all of those engines. I had not known it before traveling, but Brian's threshold for life-threatening activities was much higher than my own.

In front of us our tour guide, Hao, a twentysomething Vietnamese man with bulging quads, held up his arm to signal our exit from the traffic circle. Steering my bike toward the offshoot while sweating with anxiety, I popped out onto a much calmer two-lane highway. Taking deep breaths, I tried to quell my pounding heart as we followed Hao away from the city and onto deserted country roads. Beyond them, the Valley of Love stretched in green patches toward the horizon and the pine trees of Lang Bian Plateau stood as straight as arrows.

We followed the empty road in a long arch back to Da Lat and stopped for a late lunch at a local restaurant on the outskirts of the city. We took seats around a long plastic table at an openfaced restaurant run by an older woman that stirred and clanged big blackened pots in the back of her shop. A cat purred and circled our ankles. "Lunch will be ready soon," announced Hao. I sat back in my chair and tried to position my weight in a way that soothed my already aching butt.

The woman emerged and dropped steaming bowls of food in front of us. Hao looked at me, "Kim, yours is vegetarian." I glanced down at a mix of greens and tofu in a fragrant yellow broth.

Eddie looked up from his meal with a pinched face. "Is this gonna make me sick? How do I know this was made with clean water?"

Hao smiled and spoke in a tone that I imagined hostage negotiators used, straightforward but sympathetic, hiding their true feelings. "Don't worry Eddie. We will only eat at restaurants with the highest level of cleanliness."

"Hmph," grumbled Eddie as he glanced back toward the open kitchen.

Katherine, a high-maintenance tax attorney from Chicago, leaned across the table to look into my bowl. "What have you got?" I tilted the bowl in her direction. "That looks better than what I have. Hao!" she yelled. "I want what Kim's eating."

"Kim is vegetarian," said Hao. "I'm sorry, I did not know that you are also vegetarian. I have missed this on the paperwork."

"I'm not a vegetarian," said Katherine. "But I don't *want* the chicken. I want what Kim's eating."

I glanced around the table, embarrassed by Katherine's demands. The others were dipping their big plastic spoons into their bowls, avoiding Katherine's gaze.

Hao walked into the restaurant and came back with a vegetarian meal for Katherine. She took it without even a thank-you.

Beneath the table, I stomped Brian's foot. "Ouch!" he said. I threw my eyes toward Katherine. "I know, it's bad." He took a sip of his soup. "Just ignore her."

"That's going to be hard," I said through clenched teeth.

The next day we rode up Hon Giao Pass, the longest mountain pass in Vietnam, and flew down a twenty-mile hill on the other side. Ahead of me, I could see the silhouettes of Michele and Glenn, zooming faster than I dared to go. Brian was miles ahead of them, shooting with kamikaze speed toward flat ground below.

There were so many big things that I wanted to talk to Michele and Glenn about, but I'd begun to feel anxious that our highly-structured tour wasn't going to give us any time alone. Before our trip started I'd spent an entire day sifting through photos and putting together a PowerPoint presentation of yellow envelope recipients to show them. I had photos of the kids from La Bib, Veronica and her family, the rickshaw mechanic in Pune, and the rickshaw driver in Hampi. I had shots of the dogs we fed in India and the boys in Nepal who were collecting money for their school. I had a photo of the young monk who'd shown us his monastery, and one of the baby sea turtles at Bolong's sanctuary. I didn't have a picture of the waiter from Germany or the boy who'd slept in our rickshaw or of the mangy dogs I ran with from the rescue center, but I had their stories, and I intended to tell Michele and Glenn all about them if only I could find the time.

Lifting my eyes from the road, I stared at the surrounding mountains. In the distance a tall, skinny waterfall cascaded off the ridge of a foggy cliff, and clouds settled in the shadowed caverns between the tree-topped peaks. The mountains were beautiful and ominous against the low gray sky. A car passed closely on my left, and my attention snapped back to the road. Suddenly I felt very aware that I was made of bones and blood and hurtling down a mountain pass on two inflatable tires with nary a guard-rail to prevent a plunge toward death. Clenching the brakes, I slowed to a comfortable crawl.

At the bottom of the pass, the group had gathered around our parked bus. Snacks and drinks were piled in a cooler, and both a dog and a monkey were begging for bananas. Our bus driver handed me a bottle of water and offered to hold my helmet. "Oh, no thank you, I'll just hang it from my bike," I said, trying to shake the uncomfortable feeling of being catered to.

The road flattened as we cycled toward the coast. We rode past shrimp farms and rice fields. Farmers, bent at the waist beneath conical hats, squinted at us, expressionless, as we rode past. I was hyperaware that the bicycle I rode cost more than those farmers probably made in a year. What did they think of us, in our florescent spandex, snapping photos of them from the saddle without even bothering to slow down?

The dirt road we were on ran through a smattering of small villages with tiny tin-roofed houses lined square with the dusty curb. Children ran out to high five us and, sometimes, to throw rocks. When I raised a wobbly arm to slap hands with an elementary aged boy who stood on the brim of the road, he smacked me so hard I nearly lost control of my bike. Smaller children waved and shouted to us from the open windows of their concrete homes.

"What are they saying?" someone called to Hao.

"They are yelling *Hello Mr. Whitey!*"

The children smiled, the adults glared, and I could not tell if they liked or resented us. The differences between my life and theirs was stark, and I longed to stop my bike and sit down for coffee at a local shop, to put myself in a position where I might have a genuine interaction with one of the people I saw working the fields or staring from the doorways. But I was insulated in our caravan of tourists and felt, more than anything, like a voyeur. As a traveler, I'd only ever be passing through, but I wanted to slow down and stay still long enough for the country to make an imprint in my bones. As we cycled on, I knew I missed something that could only be learned by stopping.

That evening a colorful, rickety fishing boat took us to our accommodations on a spot of land called Whale Island. The breeze off of the water was cool but saturated with humidity. Waves crashed against the shoreline, Christmas songs played from the outdoor veranda's loudspeaker, and a fake pine tree sparkled with lights.

Brian and I unpacked our bags in our beautiful thatched roof bungalow and set out for a hike around the island, following a dirt path upwards and scrambling over rocks. When we arrived at an outcropping of boulders that overlooked the ocean, we sat down side by side and looked out at the water. Clouds had rolled in and dulled the sky, but a magnificent sunbeam broke through them and illuminated a patch of sea like a spotlight. Mountains rose up on the distant shore and a stiff wind blew around the leaves on the coconut trees.

I thought back to our lunch break earlier in the day, when I'd overheard one of the people on our tour talking about his plans to install a heated closet that would dry his bike gear when he came in from a ride in the rain. I'd looked around the table in shock, thinking it must be a joke, because I could not image that installing a heated closet to dry clothing was a good and practical idea. But no one else had seemed fazed by it. I wanted to scream, *there are people living in shacks without electricity and you want a heated closet to dry your BICYCLE GEAR?* Instead, I'd excused myself from the table and sat in the bathroom stall for such a long time that Brian eventually came to check on me.

At one time in the not-too-distant past I, too, would not have batted an eye at the idea of a heated closet for drying bicycle gear. But now it felt so ridiculously excessive to me. These days I was more comfortable at a teahouse in Nepal, sleeping in a simple room and eating simple meals, than I was in the upscale hotels we were staying at during our bicycle tour. And I felt more comfortable around other travelers, who asked not what I did for a living but where I had been and where I was going, than I did around people who were from my own country. During the course of our trip I'd learned to slip into new cultures, but my intolerance with a few of the members in our group made me afraid I was becoming uncomfortable with my own.

Back down at the bungalows, Michele and Glenn were

sipping fresh lime soda on the restaurant balcony. I'd still not found a chance to talk to them about how we'd used their yellow envelope money, and I hoped that this was my opportunity to bring it up. As I waited for an opening to broach the subject, Michele spoke up. "Hey," she said, "I've been thinking. We'd like to donate some money to a local school or two. I talked to Hao about it, and he said that he could pick up some school supplies on the mainland tomorrow before we take off. Do you guys want to donate too?"

I'd been hoping that we'd be able to give away yellow envelope money with Glenn and Michele. But because Brian and I had always given only when an opportunity presented itself, I figured we'd just wait and see if anything came up. It hadn't occurred to me to arrange something with Hao.

"Yeah," Brian said. "Definitely. That's a great idea."

"Because we are with a big group and on a tight schedule I figured that the odds of happening upon a situation befitting the yellow envelope might be slim. This way we can do something together."

"Speaking of," I said, "as soon as we can find some time I want to show you guys a little slideshow I put together of the people we've given your yellow envelope money to. My computer is back on the bus so we can't do it now, but I want to sit down and show it to you before our trip is over."

"That sounds wonderful," said Michele. "I can't wait to see it."

The next morning, we drove through rural villages linked by long stretches of rice fields. Livestock meandered slowly down the street as we weaved around old gray water buffalo. Plastic garbage lined the side of the road, as did pigs and monkeys and skinny dogs.

Our behemoth of a bus stopped in front of a two-room schoolhouse on an isolated road. Its tiled roof was chipped and eroding, and the sandy front yard was pitted by the indentation of child-sized footprints. An awning hung over a skinny porch that connected the two rooms of the school.

Hao stood at the front of the bus. "Excuse me everybody, I have an announcement! Michele and Glenn and Kim and Brian have made a donation to this school. I have bought school supplies with their donation, and now we will go into this school to give the children the supplies." He clapped his hands. "Okay! They are not expecting us, so I will go talk to the teacher first."

Hao turned to walk off the bus.

"Wait!" said Eddie. "What about us? Why weren't we asked to donate?"

The entire bus looked up at Hao. My cheeks burned pink with embarrassment. I hadn't considered how we'd explain the donation to the rest of our group or how they might react to it, and I definitely hadn't thought about asking anyone else to get involved. Sinking down in my seat, I waited for the moment to pass.

Hao did not skip a beat. "That is very nice of you, Eddie, but there's no need! This is already so much money. A little money buys a lot of school supplies here in Vietnam!"

He stepped off the bus and walked across the sandy yard to the schoolhouse. Everyone on the bus turned toward the four of us.

"What a good idea," said Pat's wife, Mary. I strained to hear Michele's response, curious if she would tell them about the yellow envelope.

"Thanks" was all she said.

Eddie grumbled to his wife. "I wish I would have known about it. I really would have liked to contribute."

For a moment I considered explaining to Eddie and the rest of the group the nature of Michele and Glenn's gift, in order to clear up any misunderstandings about why we'd decided to donate. But to complicate matters, the money I'd given to Hao had not come from Michele and Glenn but from Jaimie and Will, the couple who had unexpectedly emailed me back in Nepal and asked to contribute to the yellow envelope fund. The whole thing felt too convoluted to explain, so instead I stared out the window and waited for Hao to return.

Our arrival had drawn the attention of the villagers. Women and children who were not in school, though they probably should have been, wandered over and gathered in a crowd under the awning, watching Hao sort through the supplies.

Hao led us inside the first classroom and fourteen kinder-garteners stared up at us with dark, wide eyes. They looked so tiny behind their wooden desks and squirmed and giggled in their chairs at the gigantic, spandex-clad foreigners that had just interrupted their school day. We gathered in front of them, near the blackboard, unsure of what to do next. After Hao made an announcement, a little girl, her hair pulled back into a dark pony-tail, rose from her desk and sang us a song.

Hao had purchased colored clay, pencils, paper, pens, scissors, glue sticks, rulers, and a dozen other school supplies. I had assumed that we would give the supplies to the teacher and let him figure out what to do with them, but Hao told us to pass the supplies out to the children directly.

Some of our group began doling out the supplies, and a few others migrated to the back corner of the classroom. Feeling uncomfortable, I joined them there. Distributing the supplies this way felt like an awfully big production and something tugged at me on the inside like a snagged thread.

From my vantage, I watched as one of the men in our group named Brad snapped photos and dramatically handed out supplies, extending a pencil or a ruler to a child and then making sure he snapped a photo midtransaction. Then he'd pose with the kids by picking them up or sitting close to them at their desks. I felt myself recoil. They leaned away from him, their body language suggesting that they were uncomfortable, but he either didn't notice or didn't care.

Leave the kids alone! I wanted to scream, before rounding everyone up and corralling them back on the bus to leave the teacher to determine the best use of the supplies. Our presence felt invasive to me. It had been a mistake to make this donation.

Hao approached me and handed me a stack of notebooks. "Give them to the kids," he said, and nudged me encouragingly toward the center of the room. Reluctantly, I took the notebooks from his hand and walked from desk to desk, handing one to each child. They seemed amused, maybe confused, but they smiled and acted genuinely pleased with their new supplies. As I made my way around the classroom, I began to relax a little.

Outside of the schoolhouse a group of women and children huddled around Hao as he passed out the remaining supplies. As he got to the end of the pile they began to swarm him, grabbing for anything, and he had to scream and fight his way out from the mob.

We climbed back on the bus, and it lurched on toward our starting-off point for the day. The schoolhouse disappeared behind us in a cloud of dust kicked up by the wheels of our bus. The whole interaction with the kids in the classroom felt forced and contrived to me. Most of our group had been respectful, and most of the kids had seemed genuinely amused by our presence, but whatever Brad had done back there felt incredibly self-serving. And I didn't know what to think about the women and children that mobbed Hao. They'd probably needed the supplies more than the kids that were in school—it didn't feel fair. As I sat back in the seat and closed my eyes, I wished we had not come.

Later that evening, after we'd checked into our hotel room, Brian and I found Michele and Glenn in the bar. When I asked Michele what she thought about Brad interacting with the kids, I was surprised when she told me that she'd seen him in a totally different light. She said she thought Brad embraced life wholeheartedly and that visiting the school had been no exception. In fact, when she watched Brad taking pictures with the kids, she wished that she could fully jump into any situation and wring all of the joy out of it in the same way he could. Michele had watched Brad, and I had watched the kids, and we came away with two very different interpretations of the same experience. Was I allowing some of the difficult personalities and my own discomfort over being pampered to taint the way I experienced our ride through Vietnam? Michele saw the best in everyone, including me, and the least I could do to honor all she'd done for me was to do the same. From here on out, I told myself, I'd try to see our tour mates through Michele's eyes.

CHAPTER 19

WE BIKED ON THROUGH THE DENSE JUNGLE, PAST waterfalls and mountain peaks dripping in a mystical fog. Banana leaves reached out to us like ghostly arms as we cycled by. The whole world glowed intensely green.

We stopped for the night at another luxury hotel, everything prebooked and pristine for our arrival. Our room had a king-sized bed fluffed with overstuffed pillows and a showerhead as big as a dinner plate that dispensed a stream of piping hot water. Stripping off my stinking spandex, I let the water pound my shoulders and lower back. I had not felt so sore, or so pampered, in a very long time.

After showering and dressing, I joined the rest of our group in the lobby before dinner. Michele, Glenn, and Brian were sitting around a small table, and I took the open seat that faced out over the opulent foyer and toward the front desk where Katherine was engaged in a heated conversation with both Hao and the hotel manager.

"What's going on over there?" I asked.

"She's mad because the water pressure in her shower wasn't strong enough."

I couldn't help it—I rolled my eyes. Over the past few days, I'd heard Katherine complain about a fascinating array of topics: the food was too spicy or not spicy enough, the street was too dusty, our guide biked too fast.

"If all she wanted was good water pressure she should have just stayed home," I grumbled, remembering those I met in India and Nepal that had to haul water for miles and bathe from buckets.

"There's one in every group," Michele said, letting me know that our opinions about Katherine were the same.

The next morning, I flipped on the light, brushed my teeth, and stepped back into my skintight biking outfit. Sitting down on the bed, I dug through my day pack for a pen. When I found one I wrote "Thank you," on the little pad of paper on the bedside table and tucked a tip beneath the note.

It wasn't much, but I remembered the year that Brian and I graduated college and took placements as AmeriCorps VISTA volunteers working at an environmental nonprofit in the poorest county in Ohio. We received a meager monthly stipend but lived in poverty, just like the people we served.

My job was to drive around in a gigantic yellow box truck we called "the bird" and pick up donations, mostly furniture, and haul it all back to the nonprofit where we resold it to the community. No donation was turned away: claw foot bathtubs and hideaway beds were some of the most despised items we picked up because they were heavy and impossible to move. But Brian and I and the other volunteers moved them somehow anyway.

It was tiresome work, and at the end of an eight-hour work-day I'd made thirty-six dollars before taxes. Little expenses, like a copay at the doctor's office or a flat tire, were devastating.

One particularly bad day, it was the beginning of summer, humid, and I was working long hours over the weekend. I carried a donated mattress from the second-story bedroom in an apartment complex. I was tired and sweaty and pissed off to be working on a Saturday. The girl whose mattress I manhandled saw the AmeriCorps logo on my T-shirt and asked about it, so I explained that I was a volunteer. "I'm paid," I told her, "but just barely." I loaded her mattress into the back of the truck and slammed down the rolling door.

When I turned around she held two ten-dollar bills in her outstretched hand. "Thanks for your help," she said. "Will you share this with the other volunteer?"

Giving her a quick nod, I'd whispered, "Thank you," and shoved the bills into my back pocket. Then I'd climbed into the driver's seat and fixed my eyes on the road ahead, hoping that the other volunteer could not see my tears. It wasn't the money that had made me cry but the gesture.

My year in AmeriCorps had taught me that sometimes the monetary worth of a dollar was only a part of its overall value. Our yellow envelope donations were not changing the world, but I hoped that by doing something intentional and kind, no matter how small, they might change the *energy* that the recipient released into it. It'd been over a decade since that girl had given me that tip. I didn't remember her face, but I still remembered her kindness.

———

Over the next week we biked to the site of the Mỹ Lai Massacre, a quiet, solemn place, through Hội An with its paper lanterns and onto Hue's forbidden city and gilded tombs. We biked over a bridge shaped like a dragon, and we crested many mountain passes. We biked and biked, and I felt as I felt in India and in Nepal: the only real way to see a country was to see it slowly, on two feet or on three wheels or less.

One day, as we biked down a red dirt road outside of Quy Nhon near a rural village surrounded by emerald-green rice paddies, we passed a concrete building with tarps strung up in all directions. In the middle stretched an arched entryway decorated with bunches of fake yellow flowers and a sign in the shape of two conjoining hearts.

Though it was only 10:00 a.m., music pulsed from beneath the makeshift tent and down the road toward us. As we biked nearer, a cluster of immaculately clad women waved us over. Hao hit his brakes and dropped his bike. "Come on," he screamed over the thump of the music. "We will go to a Vietnamese wedding!"

The tent was stuffed with people. Old men sat around tables sipping beer, and a man in a suit crooned into a microphone on a stage at the front of the room. Strung above him hung a big vinyl banner with a larger-than-life sized photo of an impossibly young and grinning bride and groom that read HAPPY WEDDING.

We squeezed into the crowd, dressed in spandex, as usual, and a few in our group walked like wobbly toddlers in clip-on bicycle shoes. Our helmets were still strapped to our heads. Someone handed us beers as we were ushered toward the stage. "They want us to sing," Hao shouted above the noise.

"Sing *what?*" someone shouted back.

A chant of "Hotel California" rose from the crowd.

Hao distributed microphones. The speakers pumped out a steady beat of rhythmic background thumping. I looked out over the wedding reception at fifty smiling faces.

"How about 'Jingle Bells?'" Hao suggested.

We leaned into microphones and began to sing "Dashing through the snow..." The bride and groom stood in front of the stage, arms hooked around each other's waists, and smiled so wide their brains could have rolled out of their mouths. Behind them, the audience clapped and whooped as we bounced onstage.

In the middle of the third verse someone hooked their arm around mine and dragged me back outside again to take photos with the bride and groom. We stood on either side of them like a lycra-clad wedding party and gave the thumbs-up sign as the camera flashed. We were hopped-up from our performance and smiling like fools. Even Katherine appeared to be caught up in the moment. Hao took up a collection for the newlyweds, and I pushed all of the yellow envelope cash we had into the palm of his hand. We climbed back on our bicycles and waved good-bye.

On the second-to-last afternoon of our tour we biked deep into the countryside along dirt mounds that separated garden plots. We stopped for the night in Mai Châu, a rural village where the Thai people, a Vietnamese ethnic minority, lived. We followed Hao down dirt roads, past wooden houses built on stilts, until we came to our homestay for the night. Hao had done his best to warn us of the "rustic" sleeping conditions, and I dreamed up all manner of complaints from Katherine, but when we arrived she claimed her spot on the floor under a mosquito net and tucked her bag away without a peep.

When the sun sank we gathered at an outdoor table, a huge feast spread before us. We passed around bowls of rice, tofu, egg rolls, nuts, lettuce, sausage, and a number of other things, and fumbled with our chopsticks.

"Where's Eddie?" Katherine asked Renee.

"He's sick."

"That's too bad."

Renee looked up with a twinkle in her eye. "He'll manage."

Afterward, a local dance troupe arrived to lead us in a traditional Thai dance. The dance required just a bit of foot tapping and hopping, and I fumbled through it, still no better at dancing than I was in Ecuador but unencumbered by both my body and my thoughts in a new way, able to just let go.

As I stomped my steps into the dirt I knew that the dancing was a tourist production concocted for our sake, but it still felt beautiful and joyful, and I laughed, throwing my head back toward the moonless night as my body carried me around the yard. I hooked arms with one of the Thai dancers, and she giggled at me as I tried my best to copy the movements of her body. So much of Vietnam still felt out of reach to me, and I'd been feeling frustrated by that, fearing that I'd leave our tour knowing little more about the country than when I'd arrived. It bugged me because I'd become the sort of traveler that wanted to dig deeper into the places I visited. But as I kicked my feet into the dirt, arms intertwined with the dancer, it occurred to me that in that moment our lives were literally linked together. There were over seven billion people in the world, and we had found each other. The fact that I came face-to-face with her, or anyone, when there were so many more whom I would never know, was a miracle of odds. I'd been seeking a connection with the people of the world, including Brian, and myself, and though it did not always look like I expected it to look, I'd found it nonetheless.

That night I lay on the floor under a heavy blanket that smelled of musty earth and hay. A mosquito net hung above me like a veil, the other members of our group snored around me, and Brian's warm body rose and fell beside me in sweet, shallow breaths.

I'd gone traveling, seeking something that I could not quite define, but hopeful that I would know it when I found it. I *had* found it, though the definition of what *it* was still eluded me. On the outside, I still looked like me, except with shaggier hair and a few more wrinkles around the eyes. But internally, I was like Pangea after it split into the continents. The old parts of me were still there, but they'd cracked and drifted so far from their original location that the new map of my blood and breath was unrecognizable from the old one.

The next morning, we stood in a parking lot near the center of the village to give away the remainder of the yellow envelope gift. In addition to the leftover school supplies, Hao had also bought children's bikes and trikes, which seemed a fitting end to our bicycle tour. He had spread word with the locals that we had toys to give away, and a crowd of children and their parents had gathered near our bus.

We unloaded the child-sized bikes and tricycles and set them out for the children to play with. The first brave kids took the bikes for a spin before stepping aside to let the others ride. I could see that they were going to end up as communal toys, and I liked that so much better than the weird dynamic back at the school. In the bright morning sunshine, I stood and watched as a young mother loaded her chubby-cheeked daughter onto a toddler trike. The mother put the baby's feet on the pedals and rotated them. The bike lurched forward, and the baby shrieked with glee. I stood back and laughed with her.

I squinted across the parking lot and saw Michele and Glenn watching the little girl on the tricycle, laughing too. Around us, children were yelling and playing in the midmorning sunshine. Michele and Glenn had asked us to give away the yellow envelope money in ways that made us smile and made our hearts sing, and as we all stood there in the village, adults and children from different sides of the globe, I could hear the melody of joy as it wafted through the air among us.

We took the bus back to Hanoi for a final group dinner where we said our good-byes. Hao clanked his spoon against his water glass and stood up to say a bit about each of us. "Kim… She was a bit slow," he said. "But steady. Steady the whole way." I laughed and thought, *if he only knew.*

As we sat around the large dinner table and reminisced about the trip, I worried that our time with Michele and Glenn was running out. They were catching a flight home the following afternoon, and Brian and I had not yet told them what we'd done with their yellow envelope money.

As multiple conversations carried on around us, I caught Michele's eye across the table. "Hey, do you want to do an early lunch tomorrow before you take off for the airport?"

"Definitely," she said.

On the day of their departure we walked along the motorbike-packed streets to a restaurant in the Hanoi Old Quarter. I followed Brian as he ducked through an arched doorway to a secluded outdoor patio, a quiet refuge from the loud and busy city.

"Are you excited to get home?" I asked Glenn and Michele as I pulled out my chair and scooted toward the table.

"I'm ready to get back to work, see our dogs, and reestablish our routine," said Michele. "It's funny how being gone makes you appreciate home."

From my day pack I removed my laptop and looked up at them. "I want to show you guys the slide show I mentioned when we were on Whale Island." Sitting the computer on the table, I turned the screen toward them. "I know you guys said we weren't accountable to you, but we want to show you what we've done with the money that you gave us." When I hit the space bar, a picture of the children from La Bib appeared on the screen. It was a group shot; nine of the kids stood upright and smiling in front of Brian and me and the other volunteers. Behind us, painted on the wall in a purple cloud, were the rules of La Bib: *Don't use bad words, don't run, don't fight with the other children…* Brian began to tell Michele and Glenn about how we used the yellow envelope money to buy a memorial brick in their name.

While Brian spoke, I stared hard at the picture and studied our faces. We were grinning widely at the camera, and our clothes were not yet stained and puckered with holes. Brian's beard was cropped neatly near his chin, and my hair was still short and styled. We looked younger, fresher, happy. And I supposed we were. Because we were not yet aware of how we were about to crumble and, afterward, how we'd rebuild ourselves into new structures with joints that facilitated swaying, and more windows to let the light in.

When we'd clicked through the entire presentation I shut my laptop and sat back in my chair, folding my hands in my lap and fumbling with my wedding ring. "Brian and I don't really know how to say thank you. But we want you to know how much it means to us that you trusted us to give your money away. And we want you to know how much it means that you asked us on this trip. Everything you've done for us has meant more than you will probably ever know."

When I looked across the table at Michele I saw that her eyes were red, and she dabbed away tears. "I'm being honest when I say that it means even more to me that you guys are here. Someday I'll have to tell you about the kind of impact you've had on my life."

Back in the hotel lobby we hugged Michele and Glenn goodbye and watched as they climbed into the back of a taxi to start their long journey home. We'd become used to watching people leave while we stayed put on the other side of the globe. It didn't make me sad anymore though; it didn't make me feel lonely. Somewhere along the way my homesickness had dissipated. I pined only for the next country, the next adventure.

There was still so much I wished I'd said to Glenn and Michele. I wanted to ask Michele if she even recognized the woman that'd just biked hundreds of miles through Vietnam as the same woman who sat in the park at our going away party. I wanted to know what had motivated her to change and if she'd always known, somewhere deep down, one day, that change would come. And I had hoped to tell her how it had felt for us to give their gift away, how the yellow envelope had coaxed me into living in a way that I wouldn't have lived otherwise. I wanted to explain that at first I'd been worried I would feel like some pseudosuperhero looking for ways to save the world, swooping in when a situation called for it and fixing things with money. But it hadn't turned out like that at all. It was more like, when an opportunity to do something good or kind presented itself, I didn't have an excuse not to do it. I couldn't ignore it because I was too shy or too broke or in a rush or feeling grumpy. I had to do it. Not for me but for Glenn and Michele.

Out on the street their taxi merged into traffic, and Brian and I waved as it descended down the road. When it disappeared I turned to Brian and grabbed his hand. We were alone once again, our backpacks at our feet and our futures as malleable as they had been on the day our plane touched down in Ecuador.

⁓

And I thought that was the end of it. But a few weeks later I received an email from Michele.

Kim,

I want to express how your journey has had a profound impact on my life. I know I have told you in bits and pieces here and there, but I wanted to put it all in one place.

I've always been an active and adventurous sort. I played rugby and roller hockey in college. I've rafted raging rivers in Australia, hiked the Grand Canyon, got my nose pierced in Fiji and went scuba diving on the Great Barrier Reef. I spent several summers fighting wildfires in California and Nevada where I was one of the best on the crew with the chainsaw. I got my pilot's license before I was twenty and have jumped from a plane more than fifty times with a parachute I packed myself. You name it, I was up for it.

Nearly two years ago you and Brian said good-bye to your Portland friends at a going away party in a beautiful

Portland park and set out to begin your grand adventure. As I said my good-byes I was struck by two things nearly simultaneously: (1) Holy crap, they're actually doing it! (2) Huh, that could have been me.

Would have been me. I was overcome with the realization that the version of myself I described above totally would have done something like quit her job to travel the world. But that wasn't the version of me that was standing in that park that day. At that moment a big switch in my brain flipped, and I realized, quite to my astonishment, that I had somehow become a spectator in my own life.

I guess that is a natural progression really. We all grow up and move on. Falling in love, jobs, and mortgage payments become the focus instead of where to spend Spring Break. Don't get me wrong—my workaday world was great. I had an amazing partner, fabulous job, adorable pets, and good friends. I was living in a great city with spectacular coffee, beer, and food. What more could a person want? I certainly didn't think I wanted anything more.

But all the while I never realized that I had lost the spark in the core of my soul. I was no longer that adventure-seeker with a zest for life. It turns out she was, quite literally, buried. I have been overweight my entire life—was always the chubby girl in elementary and junior high. Described as "big-boned" by adults in an effort to be kind and as a great many other things by fellow kids in an effort to be not so kind. By the time I was a teen I was at least thirty pounds overweight, and in my twenties I was probably more than fifty pounds overweight. And so on, and so on, and so on...

I've really never been one to allow my weight to define me. The size of my pants didn't determine my worth, and it certainly wouldn't dictate what I could or couldn't do. If I wanted to jump out of planes, then by God I was going to jump out of planes! Even if it meant I'd have to get a custom-made jumpsuit because the ones at the jump school were too small.

But somewhere along the way my weight *did* start to define what I could and couldn't do. When you first met me I weighed over three hundred pounds. At that weight it was physically too hard to be an adventurer—I was literally carrying the weight of another adult around with me everywhere I went.

In early 2006, Glenn and I were making plans to take an "active vacation" through REI Adventure tours with Glenn's brother Chris. Chris, a well-seasoned traveler and adventurer told us to "pick a trip, any trip." So Glenn and I started scouring the REI catalog to make our selection.

Each trip was ranked on a scale from one to five based on level of difficulty. A level-one trip was the equivalent of sitting on a nice boat enjoying the scenery go by, and a level-five trip essentially meant you needed a doctor's waiver because you could die. We decided to focus on finding a level-two trip or *maybe* a level-three if it didn't promise to be too difficult.

That was when I first saw the trip of bicycling through Vietnam. I was so captivated by the descriptions and pictures. I couldn't imagine a trip I wanted to do more, but I knew my weight and fitness level wouldn't enable me to bike long distances over mountain passes. I found myself thinking, *bummer, too bad I'll never be able to see that*, as I continued flipping through the catalog looking for a less physically demanding trip. In the end we decided to get in better shape, lose some weight, and do a hiking trip of the islands of Greece. The trip was absolutely fantastic, but I always lamented not being able to do the biking in Vietnam.

Which brings me back to that lightbulb moment in the park at your going away party. I looked at you and saw living proof that just because something seems daunting, it's not impossible. Just because something you want is scary, it's still worth the risk of taking that first step…and then the next…and then the next.

I realized I had a choice to make. I could continue to be a spectator in my own life, all but snuffing out the internal flame that sought activity and adventure. Or, I could seek to uncover my former self and put her back together again.

Since you left Portland, Glenn and I have been working hard to be healthy and active each and every day. In many ways our journey toward health has been an adventure all on its own. It has opened up so many opportunities to see and do things that we had never imagined. And, most importantly, I finally got to do that bicycling trip through Vietnam!

To be able to share that experience with you and Brian meant the world to me. I was able to physically do a trip I thought impossible, see things I had only dreamed about, and best of all I got to share the experience with the person that was the catalyst for my transformation.

You continue to inspire me to this day. I often think of you during those moments of self-doubt when I wonder if I have it in me to keep going. Thinking of your courage and perseverance gives me the determination to keep taking that next step.

Glenn and I have a lifetime of adventures awaiting us! You were the catalyst that changed the trajectory of my life. You have helped me reconnect with that adventurous girl that lives inside of me. You gave me the courage to dig her out, dust her off, and put her back on her feet again. You have given me a precious gift for which I will forever be grateful.

Thank you.

Love,

Michele

I read Michele's letter once, quickly, and then again more slowly, letting the words sink in. The magic of everything, I realized, was that we would not have become who we became without each other.

MEXICO

Epilogue

ONE YEAR LATER

FROM THE SHADE BENEATH MY UMBRELLA, I SQUINTED toward the horizon at two tiny figures paddling past the breaking waves. Behind me, a row of palm trees divided the beach from town, and beyond them was our apartment, a one-room, light-filled thing built at the edge of the jungle. Brian and I settled there when the constant movement of travel began to lose its shine. And although we could not keep the ants out of the sugar or the hot water from turning cold, it had a particleboard desk for writing and a view of the ocean, and we were happy.

The warm breeze off of the water smelled of coconut sunscreen. I put my book down in the sand and closed my eyes, my second nap of the day. When I awoke, Brian and Wendy were beside me on their beach towels, drying their bodies in the sunshine.

"Hey," I said. "How was it out there?"

"Great." Wendy gathered her hair above her head and leaned forward to wring out the saltwater. "The waves were perfect for paddling. Not too strong but not too mellow either."

Brian shaded his eyes and squinted at me. "Are you staying hydrated?"

I held up my water bottle. "I've been sleeping in the shade, Brian, not running a marathon."

He shook his water bottle back at me. "Better to be safe than sorry. You're growing my baby in there."

Instinctively, my hand went to my belly, and I smiled. "Your baby is perfectly hydrated, I promise."

Just the previous week we'd climbed aboard a hot and bumpy bus that weaved along a windy road to Puerto Vallarta and watched as a hazy blob on the ultrasound screen kicked and flipped in my belly. "Strong heartbeat," the doctor said, as a *swoosh swoosh* sound filled the room.

"Oh my God," said Brian. I said nothing, too captivated by the black and white image, the tiny bundle of cells growing inside of me, for my mouth to form any words.

That evening, when we returned to our apartment, I'd stepped into the shower and cried so hard my shoulders shook. A simple truth had overwhelmed me: I had two hearts now.

"You up for a walk?" Wendy asked me.

"Yeah, actually," I said, standing to sweep the sand from my legs. "I feel good today."

We walked north, away from the restaurants and surfers, and toward the emptier end of the beach. To our left the waves pounded roughly against the shore, and pelicans dive-bombed the water hunting for fish.

"Sorry I've felt so crappy during your vacation," I said to Wendy. "I had no idea it'd be this bad." For the majority of her visit I'd been in bed, heaving into a trash can, and I was sad to be missing our time together.

"Don't worry about it. I came down here to relax, and that is exactly what I've been able to do."

I held my face up to the sun, grateful to be out and moving on such a beautiful day. "It's hard to believe that the last time I saw you was in India. So much has changed since then!"

Wendy laughed. "I know!"

We reached the end of the beach and turned back toward the crowds, talking of the developments in our lives. Wendy had a new job and a new boyfriend. I had a new perspective and a new life growing inside of me. We'd both crammed a lot of living into the year and a half since we'd last seen each other, and though we'd kept in touch, it was so much better to discuss it all in person.

Up ahead, an old woman walked toward us on the beach, barefoot, dressed in a white dress embroidered with bright flowers. Rainbow-colored beaded bracelets were displayed on her forearm. She gestured to them as we passed her and asked if we wanted to buy one.

"*No tengo dinero*," I told her and waved my arm at my swimsuit. "No place to put it."

"Ah," she said. "*Claro.*"

Wendy turned to me. "Speaking of *dinero*, I've been meaning to ask. Do you have any yellow envelope money left?"

I shook my head. "No, it's long gone." Like a movie, my brain flashed through everyone we'd given the yellow envelope money to. I would never know how the gift had impacted them, or if it even impacted them at all, but I did know that it had a profound impact on Brian and me. Like tendrils of a web, you cannot strum one thread without sending the others into vibration. The act of giving, and being *entrusted* to give, had shaken up our lives.

Wendy nodded. "I wonder how our rickshaw driver in Hampi is doing. What was his name?"

"Mahaj?"

"Yeah! Mahaj. I wonder if he's still driving a rickshaw?"

"I don't know. We should go back some day and see if we can find him. See if he remembers us." I patted my belly. "I'll bring the baby."

Wendy laughed. "Okay. Baby's first rickshaw ride!"

"Do you think we would have remembered Mahaj if I hadn't given him yellow envelope money?" I asked Wendy. It was a question I'd pondered a lot during our nearly three years on the road. While traveling, so many new people passed in and out of our lives every day. It would be impossible to remember them all. But when we gave away yellow envelope money it forced us to stop and pause, to act intentionally, and that made the interaction memorable.

Wendy said, "I don't know."

"The thing about the yellow envelope was, it made ordinary interactions more meaningful." I paused before continuing, unsure of how to explain the next part. "And it taught me how to give, not just give money, but to give of myself."

Wendy looked up at me, waiting for me to continue. I knew I wasn't explaining it right. "What I mean is, I learned how to set my own discomfort aside in order to do something for somebody else. Does that make sense?"

"Yeah, it helped you get out of your own way."

"Exactly…" My voice trailed off as I thought about it. More than anything, the yellow envelope money had taught me to be more mindful. And though it was gone now, it continued to make me pay attention to the many ways there were to do good in the world. Money was just one way to give. I could also give of my time and my energy. I could give compassion and respect and tenderness. Those gifts were renewable and they were free.

Wendy and I had reached our spot on the beach again. We sat down next to Brian beneath the umbrella and stared out at the rolling waves of the Pacific Ocean. These wide-open days were coming to an end, I knew. Soon we would head home.

Closing my eyes against the breeze, I tried to imprint the moment in my mind. Looking backward, I could see how these three years in the world had taken me exactly where I needed to go. I remembered the terror and uncertainty I felt before leaving Portland, and I was grateful I hadn't succumbed to my fears. In the end it had all been worth it—the hardest parts worth most of all.

⌒

The hot Mexican winter gave way to an unbearable Mexican spring. Brian and I puttered around our apartment and packed our backpacks in silence, thinking excitedly of the future. Taking a final glance at the place we'd called home for the past five months, I slung my backpack onto my back. Brian shot me a look, "You should not be lifting that."

"I've hefted this thing all around the world," I said. "You better believe I'm going to haul it on its final leg home."

The midmorning streets of our village were still shadowed by giant palm leaves. We walked down the quiet road and stopped to buy strawberries and two bananas from the back of a pickup truck. At the bus stop, a few dusty benches beneath a thatched palapa, we waited to begin our journey home. I reached toward Brian and squeezed his warm palm. Some unmistakably essential part of our lives was ending, but I felt certain that another essential part was beginning too.

We didn't know it yet, but it was a daughter we traveled home with. A baby girl who would arrive in this world on the first day of autumn, a red-haired, blue-eyed, wonder. And on the first night of her life, in the darkest and stillest hours before dawn, I would look into her newborn eyes and vow to teach her to love the world and, more importantly, to love herself enough to let the world love her in return.

We don't have the yellow envelope anymore. It ripped and

disintegrated along the way, and when we unpacked for the final time, I tossed it distractedly into the recycling bin. But we do still have the yellow bow that Michele tied around the envelope when she passed it across the table to us as we sat at the precipice between our old life and a new one. I keep it as a reminder of the powerful impact we have on one another, in ways that we see and in other ways we may never understand.

DEAR READERS,

It's your turn. Please use the yellow envelope at the back of the book as a vehicle to spread goodwill and kindness to family, friends, or strangers. Write a note to someone you love, buy a stranger a cup of coffee (and ask the barista to pass your envelope to the recipient), put a sticker or a knock-knock joke inside and give it to a child. The choice is yours, and the possibilities are endless. Just never doubt your ability to change the world—one kind gesture at a time.

Share your experience of giving or receiving on our Facebook page at www.facebook.com/yellowenvelopeproject.

Acknowledgments

I am deeply grateful to the many people who made this book possible.

It's probably clear by now that *The Yellow Envelope* would not exist without the kindness of Michele and Glenn Crim. Sometimes life gives you the people you never knew you needed, and that's what happened to me the day I showed up at their door. It is an honor to call them friends and to share their story of generosity.

Thanks to my agent, William Callahan, for believing in this book and giving an unknown writer a chance. Thanks, too, to my editor Shana Drehs and the team at Sourcebooks who gently guided it into the world.

I am profoundly grateful to my in-laws, Mike and Terry, who watched our beloved pups while we were away, and without whom this trip would not have been possible. Thank you also for always giving us a soft place to land each time we come home again.

My Mom and Dad encouraged my love of reading and are

avid readers themselves. Dad, thank you for being endlessly curious about the process of writing this book. Mom, thank you for the hundreds of hours you spent babysitting your granddaughter while I sat upstairs at my desk writing. I absolutely could not have done it without you.

To my little sisters, Amanda and Jessi, thank you for your love and support. In the cosmic sibling lottery, I definitely hit the jackpot.

Thank you to Wendy Gibson for your spot-on advice, boundless energy, roaring laugh and ability to run a painful amount of miles while talking the whole way. Jenny Lewis for your road-trip companionship, bottles of wine and perfect execution of text message emoji. Caitlin Fischer, Kelly Gliha, Jessy Martin, Jordan Mungin, and Kelly Ross Brown, who celebrate the big and small moments in life with me. Seriously, how did we get so lucky?

To the readers of my blog, many of whom have been cheering me on before I left Portland, I extend my heartfelt thanks. Your kind words and support continue to touch and inspire me.

I owe a thank you to the people we met on our travels, not just those mentioned in this book, but the hundreds of others that opened their homes and their hearts to us, or those who simply offered directions, a kind conversation, or a smile. It is because of you that I learned a great lesson: people everywhere are good.

Finally, the biggest thanks of all goes to my husband Brian, co-conspirator of dreams and Daddy extraordinaire. Thank you for your endless patience, support, and love. And to Juniper, who made my heart grow bigger than I ever thought possible. You make every day an adventure.